D1483746

DATE DUE

BRODART, CO.

Cat. No. 23-221-003

THE IDEAL EXECUTIVE

WHY YOU CANNOT BE ONE AND WHAT TO DO ABOUT IT

A New Paradigm for Management

by
Ichak Kalderon Adizes, Ph.D.
Director of Professional Services and CEO of
The Adizes Institute

Library of Congress Cataloging-in-Publication Data

Adizes, Ichak.
   The Ideal Executive: why you cannot be one and what to do
about it

© **2004 by Dr. Ichak Adizes.**
All rights reserved. No part of this book may be reproduced in any
form, by any means (including electronic, photocopying, recording
or otherwise) without permission of the author and the publisher.

Library of Congress Control Number: 2004092671

ISBN: 0-937120-02-2

Published by:
The Adizes Institute Publishing
2815 East Valley Road
Santa Barbara, CA, 93108,
805-565-2901
www.adizes.com

Printed in China

ACC Library Services
Austin, Texas

This book is dedicated to my teachers who introduced me to the field of management:

In the sequence of my exposure to the field:

Professor **Yehezkel Dror**, Department of Political Science, Hebrew University, Jerusalem

Professor **Kirby Warren**, Columbia University, Graduate School of Business

Professor **Bob Yavitz**, Columbia University, Graduate School of Business

and last but most importantly

Professor **William H. Newman**, Samuel Bronfman Professor of Management, Columbia University who chaired my doctoral work almost 40 years ago.

Acknowledgements

I want to thank Nan Goldberg who has diligently edited this book into a readable form and put up with my endless rewritings. Without her this book would not see the light of the day.

Zvonko Kuzmanovski labored on publishing this book and organized all that is needed for making it happen.

Martha Bright checked the spelling and did the copy editing.

Thank you all.

ABOUT THE AUTHOR

Dr. Ichak Adizes is one of the world's leading experts in improving the performance of businesses and governments by making fundamental changes without the chaos and destructive conflict that plague many change efforts. Over the past 35 years, Dr. Ichak Adizes has worked with some of the largest commercial organizations in the world and has consulted to many heads of state. The methodology that bears his name has helped organizations in a variety of countries to achieve results and gain leadership positions in industries ranging from banking to food services, and in organizations as different as churches and governments. He is the Founder and CEO of the Adizes Institute. His work has been featured in *Inc. Magazine, Fortune, The New York Times, The London Financial Times, Investor Relations Daily, Nation's Business* and *World Digest.*

Dr. Adizes is also a noted lecturer and author. He lectures in four languages and has spoken in over 40 countries. He was tenured faculty at UCLA Anderson School of Management for 30 years and was a visiting Faculty at Stanford University, Columbia University and both Hebrew and Tel Aviv Universities. Dr. Adizes is the author of seven books that have been translated into 22 languages. His *Corporate Lifecycles: How Organizations Grow and Die and What to Do about It* (1988) is a well-regarded classic in management theory that was selected as one of the 10 Best Business Books by Library Journal. A revised edition was published under the title *Managing Corporate Lifecycles* in 1999. The list of all his works is at the of this book.

ichak@adizes.com

Contents

Preface

WHY THIS BOOK?

Change is constant. The process has been going on since the beginning of time and will continue forever. The world is changing physically, socially, and economically. Change is here to stay.

And change creates problems. In fact, the greater the quantity and velocity of the changes, the greater the quantity and complexity of the problems we will have.

Why does change create problems? Because everything – *everything* – is a system, whether we are talking about a human being or the solar system. And every system is by definition composed of subsystems. When change occurs, the subsystems do not change synchronously. Some subsystems change faster than others. The result is disintegration, and problems are the manifestation of that disintegration. Any problem you might have – with your car, your marriage, at work – analyze it and you will find that something has fallen apart, and it has fallen apart because of change.

These manifestations of disintegration caused by change, which we call problems, require solutions. And whatever decisions organizational leaders make about how to deal with those problems will create new changes, and those changes will create new discontinuities and thus tomorrow's problems. The purpose of management, leadership, parenting, or governing – any form of organizational leadership – is to solve today's problems and get ready to deal with tomorrow's problems. And that means managing change.

How should it be done?

In one of my early books, *How to Solve the Mismanagement Crisis* (first published by Dow Jones Irwin in 1979 and subsequently reprinted several times by Adizes Institute), I introduced my theory of management: How to manage change, how to solve problems caused by change. The book, which presented a new approach to management, was translated into 22 languages and in several countries it became a bestseller. It is taught in nearly every school of social sciences at universities in Israel, Denmark, Sweden, and Yugoslavia, among other nations, and is still in print in the United States, despite being published almost 25 years ago.

As my knowledge of the subject increased with the experience of working with hundreds of companies in 48 countries, I expanded each chapter of that book into a book of its own. The chapter on corporate lifecycles became *Corporate Lifecycles: Why Organizations Grow and Die and What to Do About It* (Paramus, N.J.: Prentice Hall, 1989). A new and enlarged third edition of this book has been published in 2004 as a series of three books by Adizes Institute: Corporate Lifecycles: Volume 1: *HOW Organizations Grow Age and Die*; Volume 2: *WHY Organizations Grow Age and Die*, and Volume 3: *HOW to Manage Balanced Growth and Rejuvenate Organizations*.

The chapter on how to bring and keep an organization in its Prime condition of vitality became *The Pursuit of Prime* (Santa Monica: Knowledge Exchange, 1996, also reprinted by Adizes Institute), and the chapter on how to manage change grew into a book titled *Mastering Change* (Santa Barbara: Adizes Institute, 1992).

The parts of that introductory book that did not get expanded are being elaborated now in a set of three books, of which this is the first: *The Ideal Executive: Why You Cannot Be One and What to Do About It* (*A New Paradigm for Management*). In this book, I discuss why management education is barking up the wrong tree and why no one can be the perfect, textbook executive that management education is trying to develop.

The section on management and mismanagement styles – *not* collages of perfect traits that no one actually possesses, but the real styles of normal people – are covered in the second book, *Management and Mismanagement Styles*. In the third book of the new series I address the issue of how to deal with each management and mismanagement style: how to communicate, co-decide, implement, reward, manage change, etc.

It is not necessary to read the entire series in order to understand the principles discussed in these books; each book in the series can stand alone. That necessitates, however, that some concepts will be summarized or repeated from one book to another, in order to show the continuity of the logic: I cannot present point B unless the reader understands point A. In addition, because much has been learned during the past thirty years, a great deal of the information published in earlier books has been updated and corrected. Thus, for example, each book reviews the roles of management, and the ways in which those roles are incompatible. Even if you are already knowledgeable about those roles, I recommend that you reinforce your grasp of the material by reading the chapters that explain them.

THE BASIC PREMISE

A well-managed organization must be effective and efficient in the short and the long run, and the role of management is to make that happen.

In order to achieve a well-managed organization, I have found that four roles need to be performed, which I summarize as: (**P**)roducing the results for which the organization exists, which makes the organization effective; (**A**)dministering, for efficiency; (**E**)ntrepreneuring, for leading change; and (**I**)ntegrating the parts of the organization for long-term viability.

Think of the four roles as vitamins. For the health of an organization, these four "vitamins" are necessary, and together they are sufficient for the organization to be well managed. If one or more vitamins is deficient, a disease – mismanagement – will result, manifested by falling market share, lower profits, slow reaction to market changes and/or high turnover of staff, etc.

If one, two, or three roles are performed well and the others meet the minimum threshold of competence, a *managerial* style will be manifested. When (**I**)ntegration is among the roles a manager performs exceptionally well, a *leadership* style will emerge. (Why this seems to be true will become clear in this book.)

When one role is performed well, but the three others are performed below the necessary threshold of competence necessary for the task or not at all, a specific, predictable *mismanagement* style, depending on which roles are lacking, will result.

I have found that no one person can perform all four roles at the same time. A normal person can perform one or two roles at a time. Some, the rare ones, can perform three roles. A manager may be able to perform each of the four roles at various times and in the service of various goals, but no one can excel at all four roles *concurrently* in every situation.

Thus, my premise, which I develop in this book, is that the ideal leader, manager, or executive – ideal in the sense that he can fulfill by himself all the roles necessary for the long- and short-term effectiveness and efficiency of an organization – does not and cannot exist. And that is the problem with contemporary management literature: it presents what the executive *should* do, (because that is what the organization needs,) even though no one can do it. All the books and textbooks that try to teach us to be perfect managers, leaders, or executives are based on the erroneous assumption that such a goal is possible. This book explains why it is not. We are all barking up the wrong tree, spending millions of dollars to train and develop executives based on faulty logic.

Classic management theorists, including Howard Koontz, William H. Newman and even Peter Drucker, as well as the latest management gurus like Stephen Covey and Tom Peters, portray managers or executives as if they all have the same style and can be trained to manage the same way – ignoring the fact that different people organize, plan, and control differently. They present good management as a template. They appear to be focusing on what *should* happen. In reality, there are many styles of management and mismanagement. The permutations of various strengths and weaknesses are endless.

Focusing on what *is* happening instead of what *should* be happening leads inevitably to the discovery that people are individuals, with unique sets of strengths and weaknesses in their styles. In this book I offer an alternative approach to managing that is based on what people can have and expect from each other – realistically, in spite of their inherent weaknesses.

One more point on what is different about this book: In recent years there has been a surge in theories about leadership styles, and many books have addressed issues of leadership – but their focus has been mostly on behavioral patterns, from a psychological perspective. I am not a psychologist. My orientation is purely managerial. I am interested in how different people decide differently, communicate differently, staff and motivate differently – and how I can help them perform better for the organization. Thus, this book is not based on theoretical frameworks from psychology, or interviews, or analyses of controlled experiments. Instead, the material discussed here derives from my more than thirty years of clinical (consulting) work in the field, working with organizations in 48 countries that ranged in size from fifteen employees to one hundred thousand employees.

Organization of the Book

The book is divided into fourteen chapters, each of which poses a problem and asks a question, which the chapter proceeds to answer. Each solution, or answer, leads logically to a further question or problem, which is dealt with in the next chapter.

I deliberately chose to arrange the book in this adaptation of the Socratic method, because it both illustrates and mirrors the way life – including organizational life – works. Change causes problems, which require solutions, which when implemented cause further problems. It is a process, like the life of an individual – though unlike life, it does not necessarily end. If organizational change is approached in the manner I prescribe, organizations can go on growing and adapting to change indefinitely.

In Chapter 1, I discuss what the terms "managing" and "management" mean in the literature and why the management process is culture-bound and value-loaded – and thus not universal.

Chapter 2 presents a functionalist definition of management that is universal, value-free and is not culture-bound – by defining and explaining the four basic roles of management. In Chapter 3, I show how and why those roles are incompatible and thus why the ideal executive does not and cannot exist. Chapter 4 describes five extreme archetypes of mismanagement styles, using the roles described in Chapter 2 as a code.

Since the ideal executive does not exist, are all organizations doomed to be mismanaged? In Chapter 5, I introduce a new paradigm for successful management: Complementary teams composed of mixed managerial styles. Chapter 6 deals with the inevitability of miscommunication and thus conflict among team-members whose priorities, speed, process, and focus can be wildly different because their styles differ. To prevent this natural conflict from becoming destructive, in Chapter 7 I discuss the necessity for a culture of mutual trust and respect (MT&R), in which *con*structive rather than *de*structive conflict can thrive.

How does one build that kind of culture? Chapter 8 focuses on designing a corporate structure that nurtures mutual trust and respect, where "good fences make good neighbors." Chapter 9 describes how to match individual managerial styles to tasks in a correctly designed organizational structure.

But even having all the right people in the right jobs in the correctly structured organization will not guarantee an atmosphere that fosters mutual trust and respect. In Chapters 10 and 11, I introduce the topic of how the different styles must learn to communicate and deal with each other: Both one on one (Chapter 10) and in meetings where multiple styles must interact (Chapter 11). The problem of communicating with those whose styles differ from yours is vast enough to require a book of its own; these two chapters are only an introduction to the topic.

In Chapter 12, I return to the role of leaders, who are needed to design the right structure, foster the right process, etc. Ideally, under the new paradigm of complementary team membership, leadership traits is what best executives should exhibit.

Finally, Chapters 13 and 14 focus on training and developing managers, executives and leaders, both within the organization and as a revised mission of our managerial schools, so that this new paradigm shift can become a reality. In Chapter 13, I describe the evolution of management schools and training. I evaluate the current trends and conclude that, by starting with the wrong paradigm and using flawed assumptions to dictate the core curriculum, the management schools have flunked their biggest test. Chapter 14 presents some considerations for those who design and do training: What is the real purpose of managerial training? What skills are organizations hungry for? Can those skills be taught or can they only be acquired through experience?

STYLE OF PRESENTATION

Throughout this book I have most often used the masculine gender, because I found it cumbersome to switch back and forth and inaccurate to assign one gender to any specific managerial style. My insights apply equally to female managers. When, occasionally, I use the female gender to refer to a managerial style, again I intend my comments to refer to both genders equally.

Because my theories apply not only to business at all levels but also to statecraft, to marriage and parenting – in fact, to any relationship that must deal with change – readers may find the typology helpful in understanding their non-professional relationships. However, since I have written this book mainly for managers, I tried to minimize personal examples and anecdotes.

Some jokes and cartoons have been included, specifically to illustrate that as people go through their daily lives; these same issues present themselves again and again in different forms.

METHODOLOGY AND SOURCE OF DATA

This book summarizes for the reader my insights based on thirty years of work in the field of organizational transformation ("consulting"). Since my work as an organizational transformationist (therapist, consultant or what I like to call myself the most is organizational symbergist®) and lecturer frequently takes me around the globe, I have been able to compare notes and share my observations with executives around the world.

I have treated companies in forty-eight countries that range from $1 million to $15 billion in sales or $120 billion in assets, and employ anywhere from fifteen to hundreds of thousands of people. They are involved in numerous technologies, including aircraft, insurance, banking, the performing arts, museums and government agencies, in both the profit and not-for-profit sectors. I have also used my insights about leadership style to counsel several heads of state.

I've found that my insights on managerial styles are valid for all the countries in which I've lectured, including cultures as different from each other as those of China, Japan, Sweden, Mexico, Greece, Israel, and the United States. Managerial styles and behavior are independent of culture – although social culture, I have noted, tends to reinforce managerial styles.

APPLICABILITY

My approach to management is value-free and applies to all cultures, technologies, and industries with any purpose, whether the organization is profit-oriented or not-for-profit. It applies to organizations of any size: Small self-contained units such as a family, mezzo-level organizations like businesses of any size, or macro systems like nations; in fact, I have organized the cabinets of three Prime Ministers using this methodology. In other words, this theory provides tools that can be universally applied to diagnose management, mismanagement, and leadership styles, predict behavior and recommend how to develop, train, and staff organizations, as well as how to communicate and reward staff, allowing organizations to achieve their goals with the least amount of wasted energy.

A Request

I have learned from everyone who cared to share their thoughts with me. If any reader wishes to communicate agreement, disagreement, experience, or anecdotes, jokes or cartoons that illustrate the content of this or any other of my books, I would appreciate the feedback. Please write to me at the Adizes Institute, 2815 East Valley Road, Santa Barbara, CA 93108 – or better yet, send an e-mail to: Ichak@adizes. com.

Thank you.

Ichak Kalderon Adizes
Santa Barbara, California. 2003

NOTES

1. Frost, Robert: "The Mending Wall," from the poetry collection *North of Boston* (New York: Henry Holt, 1915).

Chapter 1

Barking Up the Wrong Tree

PROBLEM: Despite the proliferation of management schools, the inflation of incentives and the flood of management books and consultants, the goal of finding or training the "ideal manager" remains as elusive as the unicorn.

A CORPORATE FAIRY TALE
(THE OUTDATED PARADIGM)

According to the classic managements textbooks and best-selling guides, the ideal manager is knowledgeable, achievement-oriented, detail-oriented, systematic, and efficiency-oriented; organized, a logical and linear thinker; charismatic, visionary, a risk-taker, and change-oriented; and sensitive to people and their needs.

He can integrate all the necessary people to successfully achieve goals. He knows how to build a team while making himself dispensable. He judges himself by how well his *group* performs; by how well, together and individually, the group members achieve their goals, and by how well he facilitates the achievement of those goals.

He listens carefully, not only to what is being said but also to what is *not* being said. He understands the need to change, but introduces change cautiously and selectively. He is able to identify leadership potential among his staff and is not afraid to hire and promote bright, challenging subordinates. He is self-confident enough to respect people whose styles are different from his own.

He doesn't complain when things go wrong, but offers constructive criticism instead. His subordinates are not afraid to report failures; they know that he will be reasonable and supportive. He encourages creativity and looks for consensus in decision-making. He is charismatic, capable of motivating others to work hard to achieve the goals of the organization. He can delegate. He trains his subordinates systematically. He resolves conflicts diplomatically, respecting people's expectations and ambitions and appealing to their social consciences. He shares information instead of monopolizing it and using it to gain power.

He is driven by a strong code of values. He is analytical and action-oriented; sensitive without being overly emotional. He seeks results, but never by sacrificing the process. He systematically develops markets, production facilities, finances and human resources for the organization.

His organization is a well-integrated entity with defined goals, whose members fully accept and cooperate with one another. No dysfunctional behavior on the part of his subordinates is easily observable.

The problem is: Where on earth do you find this animal?

With the exception of ourselves, of course, there aren't too many of those managers around.

"Who is wise? He that learns from everyone.
Who is powerful? He that governs his passions.
Who is rich? He that is content.
Who is that?
Nobody."

BENJAMIN FRANKLIN

Joking aside, the reason you cannot find this ideal manager is because he is perfect, and the perfect manager is as mythical as the unicorn. That's why I call this theoretical person "the textbook manager" – because he or she exists only in textbooks.

Expecting to find perfection is a characteristic of adolescence; we should have passed that stage by the time we reach adulthood. That is why I am bewildered by textbooks and schools that keep trying to produce something that cannot be produced. No wonder many executives are frustrated with their MBA-trained managers. No wonder, also, that management consultants are losing credibility and that management trainers are paid poorly.

What is "Management" ?

The *New York Times* once wrote an article about me in which it called me "the corporate exorcist"[1]: I go from company to company trying to exorcise management from believing they can do that which they cannot.

What is it they cannot do?

They cannot find, or even train, the ideal manager, executive or leader.

Why not?

Well, before we can say why not, let's define our terms. What do we mean by the words: "To manage," "manager," "management," "mismanagement," and "leader"?

I remember the day a door-to-door salesman tried to sell me the latest edition of the Encyclopedia Britannica. "What do you do, sir?" he asked. "I teach management," I replied. "Well," he said, "let's see what the encyclopedia has to say about the subject."

With increasing uneasiness on his part and bewilderment on mine, we soon discovered that there was no entry for "management" in the encyclopedia. There was management science, which involves mathematical models for decision-making. There was organizational behavior, which is the sociology of organizations. But plain simple management – what millions of people around the world do day in and day out – wasn't there.

So, what is "management" as it is taught and practiced today?

1. **It denotes hierarchy**. When people use the word "management," what they usually mean is a group of people whose role is to

manage. Each individual in this group is called a "manager." "Management" refers to a certain rank in an organization; in the United States it generally refers to the middle and lower upper ranks – one level above supervisors and one level below executives.

2. **It is unidirectional.** A search through the Funk & Wagnalls, Oxford Illustrated, Random House, and Webster's Third New International dictionaries found synonyms for "manage" including: "Accomplish," "achieve," "administer," "alter by manipulation," "be in charge," "break in," "bring about," "coerce," "communicate," "conduct," "connive," "contrive," "control," "coordinate," "cooperate," "cope with," "decide," "develop," "direct," "do," "dominate," "educate," "effect," "evaluate," "execute," "gain one's end with flattery," "govern," "guide," "handle," "husband," "implement," "influence," "inspect," "inspire," "integrate," "judge," "keep in a desired state or mood by persuasion," "lead," "listen," "make and keep submissive," "make happen," "make tractable," "manipulate," "mold," "monitor," "motivate," "operate," "order," "organize," "plan," "react," "regulate," "render subservient," "render submissive by delicate treatment," "restrain," "review," "rule," "run," "steer carefully," "succeed in one's aim," "supervise," "take care of," "take charge," "teach, "train," "treat with care," "utilize," and "wield (a weapon)."

Is there a common denominator shared by all these synonyms? Yes: They are all a one-way process. The managing person is telling the managed person what to do. In this context, "motivating" makes the assumption that the motivator has already decided what should be done; motivating is about getting someone else to do it willingly.

"Leadership: The art of getting someone else to
do something you want done because he
wants to do it."

DWIGHT D. EISENHOWER

There was a cartoon in the New Yorker some time ago that illustrated this point nicely: A mother who is a psychologist is trying to convince her son to take out the trash. Wearily, the boy says, "OK, OK! I'll take out the trash, but *pleeeease*, Mom, *don't* try to motivate me." Even a child perceives motivation as a kind of manipulation.

In motivating, the focus is not on the *what* and *why* but on the *how*. The manager is the head of the department, and the subordinate (note the literal meaning: Sub-ordinary) is at best the right-hand man. And what does the right hand do? Unless you're left-handed, the right hand does exactly what the head tells it to do.

3. It is elitist. In Hebrew, the word for subordinate is *kafuf*, which literally means "bent at the hips" – like someone who bows before you out of respect or fear.

Managers, on the other hand, have superior vision; that is the source of the word "supervision." Military insignia illustrate this principle: A first lieutenant's badge has one branch to denote his rank; a lieutenant has two branches, a captain has three. As we ascend in the military hierarchy, we are climbing the tree. A major has a leaf, signifying the top of the tree. And a general, with the highest supervisory authority of all, is way above the treetops, with a star.

So you can see that the managerial process, as it is described and taught, is not a value-free process. It is not only a science and an art, but also an expression of sociopolitical values.

4. It is individualistic. Try the following exercise. Call all your top management into a room. Ask each one of them to write down the company's top five problems. The rules are that, first, no names be mentioned; and second, that they not use the word "because" — no explanations for the problem are necessary.

Just ask them to note on a piece of paper, which they do not have to show anyone, the top five most critical, significant problems, undesired results, or processes that the company has.

All of these problems must be *controllable* by the people in the room; and it is not acceptable to define a problem as something "they" are not doing. Focus on what "we" are not doing. In other words, instead of saying: "Competition is increasing," they should write: "We are not meeting competition head on".

Now ask them: How many of these problems did the company have last year? Don't look at or allow them to share what they've written. Just ask them: How many of the problems on your list did you also have last year? The answer is usually: One hundred percent.

How about two years ago?

Most of them, right?

How about three years ago?

Again, most of them!

Now, if this is true, then how many of these same problems are you likely to have three years from now?

Most! Right?

Why, though?

Because look at your list of problems again. How many of them can any individual in the room solve by *himself?*

None!! Right? If they could have, they already would have.

Now ask them: How many of these problems would disappear if I gave you a magic pill that would permit you, as a team, to agree on the solution?

All of them, right? If you followed my instructions correctly and only wrote down problems that are controllable by the people in the room, then it is true by definition that a solution is possible if only the people in the room would agree to it.

So what is the problem?

The problem is that we usually have one executive or manager chasing ten problems, rather than ten managers chasing one problem at a time.

"The problem is not what you have on your list. What you have are manifestations. The problem is YOU!!!" I say. "You do not know how to work together. That is the problem!!!!"

The business world, in other words, is trapped by misguided principles of individualistic management that personify the whole process in a single individual who should excel at planning and organizing and motivating and communicating and building a team and making him - or herself dispensable.

In reality, however, such a manager does not exist and why it can not exist and what to do about it is the purpose of writing this book. *The managerial process is far too complicated for one person to perform*

A similar bias can be seen in economic theory, which sums up the processes and dynamics of any organization in two words: "The firm." "The firm" will do this, "the firm" will do that – all depending on the conditions that prevail in the market. But left out of the equation is how this "firm's decisions are made; thus the economic theory that results from these assumptions tells us only how the decision-making process *should* work – not how it does work. (More about this later.)

Likewise, to the best of my knowledge, the questions of *who* is involved in management and *how* they actually make decisions together – versus how they *should* make them together – has not been addressed. Management theory, like economic theory, personalizes the entire process as if practiced by a single entity. This error leads to a misperception that ultimately hampers our efforts to manage successfully.

That is why, when I use the words "manager" or "management," what you should be visualizing is not a *person* but a *process*, which by nature encompasses people who may not officially be identified as managers by rank or title.

5. It is industry based. The classic management textbooks teach that managers plan, decide, lead, organize, control, and motivate an organization. However, there are organizations in which management is *not supposed* to perform some of those functions. Some years ago I studied the management of performing arts organizations – opera, dance, theater, orchestras – and I became aware that artists cannot be managed in the same way as, let us say, one manages workers in industry. Administrative directors need artistic directors to lead the organization. They practically co-manage. Decisions cannot be made by either of them alone. "We are the two wings of the Austro-Hungarian eagle," the administrative director of the New York City Opera told me in the 1970s about his relationship with the artistic director. "Without both of us, this opera will not fly."[2]

I noted the same phenomenon in the health and educational systems. Here, again, the administrators do not perform all the functions of management: For example, they do not decide policy matters, since the physicians in health delivery institutions and educators in educational institutions have a major say on those subjects.[3] In high-tech companies, an engineer who knows the technology or may even have significantly contributed to inventing it is indispensable to managing the company. But his financial know-how and business acumen are usually limited. For successful management, he needs someone to make the business decisions with him.

Why does our definition of management exclude so many important organizational models? Because management theory was developed based almost exclusively on industrial experiences. Fayol was a mining engineer. Urwick was a military officer. Koontz took his insights from the airline industry. Taylor was an industrial engineer. Drucker's early experiences, from which he derived his ideas on management, were in the automotive and publishing industries. Even recent gurus such as Tom Peters and Steven Covey bring experience from the for-profit and industrial spheres to their books.

6. It is socio-political. The managerial process as understood in the West is not universally accepted or practiced. In some countries around the world, the managerial process the way we teach it in our Western textbooks is actually prohibited by law. In Yugoslavia, for instance, during the Communist era of self-management, managers were constitutionally prohibited from making decisions the way we do – in other words, *for* the organization. Rather, the manager's role was to suggest to and convince the workers, who had the ultimate authority for determining salaries, production quotas, investments, etc.

The self-management system, which adapted democratic principles as they had been conceived for nations and then applied them to industrial organizations, was called industrial democracy. In industrial democracy, the managers belonged to the executive branch. Their role was to recommend and implement decisions that were made by the legislative branch, or the workers council.[4]

In some other countries, management is socially discouraged. During the heyday of the Israeli kibbutzim, for instance, management was deliberately rotated every two or three years, so that nobody became what in the United States is called a professional manager: A person whose profession it is to *decide for* other people what they are to do.[5]

7. It is culturally bound. In certain languages, such as Swedish, French, Serbian and Croatian, the word "manage" does not even have a literal translation. In those languages, words like "direct," "lead," or "administer" are often used instead. When people in those countries want to say "manage" the way we mean it in the United States, they usually use the English word.

In Spanish, the word *manejar* – the literal translation for "to manage" – means "to handle" and is used only when referring to horses or cars. When they want to say "manage" in the American sense of the word, they use the words "direct" or "administer."

I suggest that there is a confusion in the field, which stems from our difficulty in defining the process and what it is supposed to do, and is manifested in our vocabulary – or lack of one.

Management is not a group of people in the hierarchy of the organization. It is not a rank. It is a *process*, by which organizational goals are identified and continuously re-identified and eventually achieved. *Whoever* is involved in this process and *wherever* he is in the organizational chart – whether he is called an executive, administrator, consultant, leader, manager, or worker – is involved in the managerial process and by this definition is a manager. (I want to emphasize the word "worker" in the previous sentence, because although workers are not customarily considered part of management, they can and often must perform *managerial roles* if a company is going to be effective and efficient in the short and long run.)

Usually we look at the managerial role as one of managing PEOPLE. If no one reports to you, you are not management. (Do you see the elitism, the hierarchy here?) As should be clear from the above paragraph I define management as the process of defining and accomplishing tasks and whoever is involved in this process is part of the managerial team even if no people report to him or her. While no one REPORTS to them they still have to interrelate with others to accomplish the common task. They will not be telling but they must be selling their ideas and perspectives on the task. Instead of controlling that the reporting structure affords (maybe?) they have to motivate and communicate. Thus it is not the reporting relationships that makes one a manager. It is interrelating for a common cause that makes them part of the process and thus, of the management team.

THE FALLACY

There is a big confusion in the field on what management is granted. But one thing we *do* know is what *mis*management is and it is a subject of books, articles and gossip at cocktail parties

But how successful have we been? In spite of the thousands of books written, and the millions if not billions of dollars spent on training managers and consulting services, we have not yet produced a viable, consistent theory and practice of management that is robust, repeatable, universal and holistic. In order to fix mismanagement we need to correctly define it.

A proof of this failure is our inability not only to define the process adequately, but even to name it. We are continually creating new words to label new processes that we hope will achieve the desired results.

The word that was originally used to describe the process was "administration." That is why business schools used to be and some still are called Graduate Schools of Business Administration, and those that are in the profession of managing and have the diploma to prove that they have been professionally trained are Masters of Business Administration and the first journal in the field was the *Administrative Science Quarterly*. But since administrators failed to produce the desired results, the word "administrator" is now used mostly as a synonym for "bureaucrat."

So a new word came into use: "Management." Educational institutions became Graduate Schools of Management instead of Administration. But when the desired outcomes were still not achieved, the word "management" came to denote only the middle level of the hierarchy – and the need for a new word emerged.

That word was "executive"; thus we began to hear the terms "executive training," "executive action" and "Chief Executive Officer." When even this did not work, the word "leadership" evolved to replace "executive," and this is where we are today (2004).

Although there are plenty of books that will tell you how leadership is different from administration, which is different from executive action, which is itself different from management[6], I suggest that this new fad will not work either. In fact, I would not be surprised if in the next few years yet another new word is coined to define the process, while the word "leadership" is redefined to mean some piece of the managerial process or hierarchy – exactly what happened to the words "administration" and "management."

The root problem is that the paradigm has remained the same; it is the same woman in a new dress. The paradigm that has not changed is that the entire managerial process is always personified in a single individual, whether we call him administrator, manager, executive, leader, tsar or sultan, who should do this and should do that. This is a manifestation of the American culture of individualism.[7]

The paradigm of the "lone leader"– all-wise and all-powerful – has never worked – and as the rate of change keeps accelerating, increasing the level of uncertainty that needs to be dealt with, and as businesses become global instead of local, a paradigm shift is now more necessary than ever.

WHAT IS NEEDED THEN?

So, then, how *should* we define "managing," if in some countries management is prohibited, in others it's socially discouraged, in some organizations it is shared with those who are not even considered to be managers – and in some countries the word doesn't even exist?

What is needed, first, is to recognize reality, and second, to deal with it – which involves finding a definition of the process that is value free, universal, applies to any industry – both for- or not-for-profit – and that works in the marketplace; in other words, produces the desired behavior and results.

As a faculty member at UCLA, and while teaching at Stanford, the Columbia University Executive Programs, and Tel Aviv and Hebrew Universities, I have observed that management theory and texts deal with what *should* happen, while organizational development (OD), Organizational Behavior, people focus on how things *are* – on the dynamics of the system. OD is more descriptive/analytical, while the management theory and the strategy group is more analytical/*pre*scriptive. The Org Beh group is phenomenological in its approach while the management theory group (which practically disappeared over the years in most universities that teach MBAs) are structuralists as a school of thought. And there is no love lost between the two groups of thought. But the reality is that both approaches are necessary for good management. The question is how does one integrate the behavioral thinking with the prescriptive structuralist thinking.

A workable, robust system of management must be descriptive analytical and prescriptive and be based on an honest reflection of reality. And that is what I am trying to do in this series of three books, starting with this one.

Please note that this first book in the series is only an introduction, which defines and analyzes what we are doing wrong and what we should be doing differently. The second through the third books in the series will address *how* to develop good managers based on this paradigm shift.

Even these three books could be considered as an introduction. At the Adizes Institute, we offer many courses, manuals, workshops and exercises aimed at deepening one's knowledge and capability to develop and practice good management, using the new paradigm of working in complementary teams to co-lead organizations.

NOTES

1. Fowler, Elizabeth M.: "The Team Approved at the Top," *The New York Times* (Business section, Sept. 16, 1977).

2. Adizes, Ichak: *Essays on the Management of Performing Arts*; Santa Barbara, CA.: Adizes Institute Publications. The manuscript, which is not yet published, is available by request from the Adizes Institute.

3. Adizes, Ichak and Zukin, J.: "Health Planning for Developing Nations," *HCM Review*/Winter 1977, pp., 19-28.

4. Adizes, Ichak, and Elizabeth Mann Borgese: *Self-Management: New Dimensions to Democracy* (Santa Barbara, CA: Center for the Study of Democratic Institutions and ABC-CLIO, 1975), pp. 30-31.

5. Ibid., Chapter 6.

6. See, for example, Kotter, John P., *Force for Change: How Leadership Differs from Management* (New York: Free Press, 1990).

7. Ross, Joel E., and Michael J. Kami, *Corporate Management in Crisis: Why the Mighty Fall* (Englewood Cliffs, N.J.: Prentice-Hall, 1973). Other authors who oppose one-rule man include: Leavitt, Harold J.: Managerial Psychology (Chicago: University of Chicago Press, 1964), pp. 297-99; and Drucker, Peter F.: *The Effective Executive*, first edition (New York:: Harper & Row, 1967).

Chapter 2

The Functionalist View

PROBLEM: How, then, do we define management as a value-free and universal process?

THE TASKS OF MANAGEMENT

Let us try to understand the role of management by the function it performs: Why do we need it? The function should be value-free, without any sociopolitical or cultural biases. Whether we speak of managing, parenting, or governing – whether we are managing ourselves, a family, a business, a non-profit organization, or a society – it should be one and the same process conceptually. The only difference is the size and nature of the unit being managed.

Let us start with a basic hypothesis: The purpose of the managerial process is to make an organization effective and efficient in the short and long run – nothing more, nothing less. If we can achieve effectiveness and efficiency, in the short run and in the long run, that will be sufficient to maintain a healthy and successful organization, whether it is a marriage, a government, a multinational corporation or a candy store.

How an organization measures its success is secondary: If the organization is a for-profit company, it will measure success by profits. If it is a political party in power, success might be measured by whether its candidates are elected or re-elected. If it is a research institution, the honors and prizes won by its scientists might be its measure of success.

THE ORIGINS OF THE THEORY

What makes an organization effective and efficient in the short and long run?

Some 40 years ago, I discovered that there are four roles that are essential to make an organization effective and efficient in both the short and long run. Each role is necessary and the four together are *sufficient* for good management. By "necessary" I mean that if any one role is not performed, a certain pattern of mismanagement can be identified.

I made this discovery while preparing my doctoral dissertation on the Yugoslav system of self-management.[1]

The Yugoslavs' system was alien to Western minds and experience. Nobody owned capital. Owning capital was like owning air; the whole society had access to it. The Yugoslavs called it "social ownership."

Capital was the society's heritage. It could not be owned, nor could it be depleted. Thus, organizational profits before depreciation had to be at least equal depreciation. Instead of salaries, people received allowances based on a system similar to surplus sharing among the partners of a law firm. Employees elected representatives to a workers' council, and the council interviewed candidates for the job of managing director. Each of the candidates presented a business plan – very much like a political candidate's platform in a democratic country. The managing director served a four-year term, but could be impeached if he acted illegally: Acting without the authorization of the workers' council, for example.

Yugoslavs applied political democracy to both their industrial and non-industrial organizations; the system was called industrial democracy or the self-management system. Workers' councils functioned as its legislative branch, deciding everything from salaries to budgets to investments. Its executive branch, headed by the managing director, was management, which made recommendations to the workers' councils and implemented whatever plan the workers chose.

But the system had an enormous weakness: It discouraged – often even destroyed – the (E)ntrepreneurial spirit. In fact, for all practical purposes, (E)ntrepreneurship was illegal. The goal was to create a "new human being," whose motivations, according to Karl Marx, would be very different from the exclusively materialistic motivations of "old humans."[2] The system mandated group (E)ntrepreneurship or bust. And bust it went. Because (E)ntrepreneurs are by nature individualistic, few were willing to serve as managing directors under circumstances that limited their freedom to take risks and make decisions independently. [3]

Observing organizational behavior in Yugoslavia, I was able to make certain connections, like Dr. Linde, the British physician in the mid-18th century who found himself aboard a ship with no available sources of vitamin C and recognized the connection between that deficiency and scurvy, a common disease among sailors. I discovered that if a certain role of management – say, Entrepreneurship – is suppressed, organizations will develop certain predictable managerial "diseases." Over the course of thirty years I studied the relationship between each role and specific types of organizational behavior. I analyzed which role combinations would result in which managerial style, and how a deficiency in any particular role would lead to a predictable mismanagement style. This insight led naturally to a diagnostic and therapeutic methodology that I tested successfully at hundreds of organizations worldwide.

THE (PAEI) CODE

What are those roles and how should they be managed together? They are (P)roducing, (A)dministrating, (E)ntrepreneuring, and (I)ntegrating; or (PAEI). Let me begin by giving a brief definition of each.

The first role that management must perform in any organization is to (**P**)roduce results, making the organization effective in the short run. Why are people coming to you? Why do they need you? What is the service they want? The (P)roducer's job is to satisfy this need. It can be measured by how many people come back to obtain your competitive products or services.

The second role, to (**A**)dminister, sees to it that the organizational processes are systematized: That the company does the right things in the right sequence with the right intensity. It is the role of (**A**)dministration to ensure efficiency in the short run.

Next, we need a visionary who can foresee the direction the organization is going to take, someone who can naturally pro-act in an environment of constant change and thus guarantee the company's effectiveness over the long run. This is the role of the (**E**)ntrepreneur, which combines creativity with the willingness to take risks. If the organization performs this role well, it will have the services and/or products that its future clients will want and seek.

Finally, management must (**I**)ntegrate, which means to build a climate and a system of values that will motivate the individuals in the organization to work together so that no one is indispensable, ensuring that the organization will survive efficiently in the long run.

A healthy organization is one that is effective and efficient in the short and the long run.

In problem-solving, each role focuses on a different imperative:

INPUT	THROUGHPUT	OUTPUT	
The Roles	**Make the organization**	**To be**	**In the**
(**P**)roduce results	Functional	effective	short run
(**A**)dminister	Systematized	efficient	short run
(**E**)ntrepreneur	Proactive	effective	long run
(**I**)ntegrate	Organic	efficient	long run

(P): What should be done?
(A): How should it be done?
(E): By when/why should it be done?
(I):   Who should do it?

If all four of these questions are not answered before a decision is finalized, then that decision will be only "half baked."

If you both (**P**)roduce the expected results and (**A**)dminister well, you'll be effective and efficient in the short run. But you will be profitable for the short run only. (Why this is so will be discussed later in this book.) If you (**E**)ntrepreneur and (**I**)ntegrate only, you'll be effective and efficient in the long run, but you will suffer in the short run. For a company to be profitable in the short and long run, it must perform all four roles well. In a not-for-profit business – for example, a government agency – then by capably performing the four roles you will achieve service, political survival, or whatever goal you are looking for.

Even parents have to perform these roles, because a family is an organization and thus a system that requires all four roles to be performed. In the traditional family, the husband performs the (**E**) and (**P**) roles, building a career and bringing home the bacon. The wife is the (**A**) and the (**I**), transforming a house into a home and a group of adults and children into a family.

By contrast, look at what we call the modern, extended, two-career family. What could happen if the roles aren't carefully divided and shared? Two (**P**)/(**E**)s – and a family that needs a maid to do the (**A**) housework and a family therapist to do the (**I**) work.

In any organization, in any technology, in any culture, of any size, these four roles are necessary and together they are sufficient for good management. Any time one or more of these roles is not being performed, there will be a predictable, repetitive pattern of mismanagement – all over the world, regardless of culture, regardless of technology, regardless of the size of the organization or the purpose of the organization.

MANAGEMENT AND MISMANAGEMENT STYLES

These four roles can codify many phenomena. When applied to managerial styles, the codification is a kind of shorthand for predicting a managerial "style," determined by how well and in what combination the four roles are performed. If the combination is known, the style is predictable.

Most managers excel at one or two roles, are comfortable with them and tend to rely heavily on them in their behavior. Although no single person can excel at all four roles, good managers *must* have at least a modicum of ability in each.

It is these dominant roles and the deficient ones that I use to characterize a basic management style. For example, a manager may excel at (**P**)roducing while being merely competent at the other roles. I would "code" that manager's style, then, as a (**Paei**) – the upper-case "**P**" designating excellence and the lower-case "**a**," "**e**," and "**i**" designating competence.

Another manager may excel at organizing – a (**pAei**); while a third – (**paEi**) – may be good at sensing future trends, and a fourth – (**paeI**) – at motivating. A manager codified for the basic archetype style is in most situations a (**P**)roducer, an (**A**)dministrator, an (**E**)ntrepreneur, or an (**I**)ntegrator.

Any permutation of the combined performance of these four (**PAEI**) roles, if each role varied from 1 to 100, yields a management style, and there are innumerable permutations – as many as there are people on earth: (**PA--**) for the slave driver, (**paEI**) for the Statesman etc. (see volume 2 in this series: *Management/Mismanagement Styles* op. cit.)

A "leader" is one who excels at two or more roles, one of which must be (**I**)ntegration, while also meeting the threshold needs of the other roles and there are many leadership styles too like the Small League Coach (**PaeI**), etc. Whether a leadership style is functional will depend on the task on hand.

When one or more of the (**PAEI**) roles is not being performed at all (signified by a dash in the code), a corresponding mismanagement style emerges: A (**P---**) is a mismanager whom I call a Lone Ranger; an (**-A--**) is a Bureaucrat; an (**--E-**) is an Arsonist, and an (**---I**) a SuperFollower. (For a description of these styles, read Chapter 4 of this book. For a more detailed discussion, read the second book in this series, *Management/Mismanagement Styles* op. cit.)

The (**PAEI**) code can also be applied beyond codifying behavior or style. For example, the (**PAEI**) roles develop and decay in a predictable sequence in the lifecycle of any organization. Because not all roles are present and fully developed from start-up, and because over time some roles become more pronounced and other roles less pronounced, a typical pattern of problems will be created, which can be foreseen and prevented.

Knowing which roles will be missing or weak at any point in time allows us to predict which problems the organization is going to have and what it needs to do to accelerate its development or slow its decay. It tells us which roles will be needed in the next stage of the lifecycle, and thus which leadership styles will be most effective. There is a reason why certain leadership styles are preferred at one stage in the lifecycle of an organization and rejected in another. [4]

In other words, once you understand the pattern, you practically have a crystal ball in your hands: The current problems indicate where your organization is in its lifecycle, and based on that you can predict your next generation of problems. You have a tool to identify what is normal and what is abnormal at each stage of the lifecycle. It's analogous to the lifecycle of human beings: We expect a baby to cry a lot and wet itself, but if a 45-year-old person is doing that, we know we have a problem – unless he is a venture capitalist. (I once asked a VC who invested in dot.com companies: "How do you sleep at night?" "Like a baby," he answered. When I expressed surprise, he explained: "Sleep for two hours, cry the rest of the night!") For how the (**PAEI**) roles grow and change over the life cycle of an organization and thus how to predict your future problems today and what to do about it, please see the three volumes of *Corporate Lifecycles: Volume 1: How Organizations Grow, Age, and Die;* Volume 2: *Why Organizations Grow, Age, and Die* and Volume 3: *How to Manage Balanced Growth and Rejuvenate Organizations* (Published by Adizes Institute 2004, Third expanded edition of *Corporate Lifecycles* first published by Prentice Hall, 1999).

Over the years I have perfected tools that develop and nurture all four roles, enabling organizations to manage in periods of rapid and turbulent change while avoiding the dysfunctional and destructive managerial "diseases" that usually come with the territory. For example, if an organization is losing market share, that means it is being ineffective in the short-term, or lacks the (**P**) role. Once you know how to develop (**P**), you can cure the problem.

For thirty years, I have used these (**PAEI**) tools, among other tools that are covered in my other books, in my consulting work in companies around the globe, as have my associates, who are trained and certified in this methodology, and we have solved problems in companies worldwide. It is a tested methodology for analyzing and solving problems and predicting behavior, for leading sustainable, accelerated growth or organizational rejuvenation without destructive conflict. I have coached one company to grow from $12 million to $1.5 billion in sales, and another to grow from $150 million to $4 billion in sales — without diluting ownership.[5]

Let's talk about the four roles in detail and the four basic managerial styles that correspond to those roles.

A Raison D'Etre

The first and most important role that management must perform in any organization is to (**P**)roduce the desired results for which the company or unit exists.

What does this mean? Every organization has its *raison d'etre*; it is not put together just to be put together. Some sociologists claim that the purpose of organizations is to survive. To me, that's not normal;

that's a pathological phenomenon, like cancer. An organization must have a larger mission than survival.

So what is the purpose of a given organization's existence? Let's use an analogy:

Five friends get together on a Friday night and have some beers. As they are drinking, someone suggests they go on a hike to the nearby lake the next morning. The rest of the group enthusiastically agrees.

The next day, the five friends follow a mountain path that leads to the lake. It's a very narrow path so they must walk single file. They have been walking on the path for hours. They're singing, whistling, joking, and laughing.

This group can be described as an organization; in other words, it has common goals that continually change and progress: The first goal was to get together Friday night. The second was to have some beers. And the latest is to hike to the lake. A social scientist or psychologist would have a field day studying this primary group: Their interactions, their style, their leadership, how they communicate. But there is no management in this group – *until* this group of five people comes across a big rock that's blocking the path and that none of them *individually* can lift.

Organizational management is born when a task evolves that cannot be performed by one person alone. That task, once defined, will drive the behavior – the interactions and the interdependencies – of the group. To lift that rock, they need to plan and organize and control and delegate; in other words, make decisions. They might decide to move the rock, or they might decide to camp out right there instead of trying to reach the lake, or they may go back home and have a barbecue.

Can an organization exist without management? In my consulting role, I have come across such organizations. But they are rather stressed places, where people continuously argue about why they are together or what their common goal is. There are interdependencies, but they are not managed; those interdependencies just happen organically. There are people who get paid as managers – but the organization is not being managed; it is like a plane flying without a pilot, and how it flies depends on the winds and the weather.

There can be no management without a task that requires inter-dependency, whether it is in the immediate term, the intermediate term (in which case it is called an "objective"), the long term (which is called a "goal") or when it is more spiritual and continuous in nature (a "mission"). But no matter which word you use, there must always be a telos (the Greek word meaning "a purpose") that cannot be achieved by one person alone.

This, to me, is the first major difference between social scientists and management practitioners. We have "a rock" to move. It's not enough to talk about interactions and communications: *Why* does this organization exist? *Why* are we communicating? *What for?* Sometimes, reading books on social psychology, you start to wonder: *All of this interaction, but what is the rock that they are moving?*

I have seen organizations whose managers remind me of a group of hikers, sitting next to the rock and complaining that they cannot get to the lake. *But no one is lifting a finger to move the rock.*

So, what is the rock of a business organization? Why does a business organization exist? What result is it supposed to give you?

The typical answer, particularly from students of economics and those who distrust big business, is: "Profit!!!!!"

But guess what? Profit is not the answer.

We probably all know organizations that are extremely profitable and yet are going bankrupt – not *in spite of* but *because of*. In other words, constantly thinking about profit instead of about what the client needs is as futile as saying, "The purpose of my existence is to be happy." If, every morning, you wake up and ask yourself, "Am I happy?" you will soon become quite miserable.

Playing tennis is another analogy. If you want to win, you don't look at the scoreboard all the time; you watch the ball. If you hit the ball effectively, efficiently and repetitively, you will win. In other words: I know you want to go to the lake (profit), but for now, you need to focus on moving the rock.

And what is the rock? Instead of profit, you must concentrate on this: Who needs this organization? Who will cry if you die? Who needs you? What for? And these are not the stakeholders. Stakeholders are those you have to take into account and hold at bay or treat them right and satisfy their needs so that you can fulfill the purpose of your existence which is to satisfy your clients needs. Because unless you produce that for which your clients come to you, you are not going to be effective and if you do not fulfil your effectiveness efficiently, you're not going to be profitable. For me, profit is a *result* of good management, not the purpose of it. If you perform all four roles, profit will occur in the short and long run.

Profit in a competitive market economy is how an organization adds value.

Let me explain. When people buy a product or a service in a competitive market, they are telling you, literally in dollars and cents, how much it is worth to them to satisfy a particular need.

But to (**P**)roduce that desired service or product, the company has to spend money. So when the company's costs to satisfy a need are lower than the price the client is willing to pay and has a choice where to spend it, there is profit which can be seen also as a value added, because the company has (**P**)roduced that service or product for less than its perceived value to the client.

Thus, if a company (**P**)'s and (**A**)'s effectively and efficiently, it will be profitable and add value to the society – *in the short run.*(*Note that I repetitively said that this is true only in a competitive environment where the clients have a choice*)

So what, then, is the purpose for which your organization exists? What must your organization (**P**)roduce?

The answer is: Client satisfaction. That is the (**P**) function of every organization. The (**A**) function is to make it profitable.

Please note that I did not say *customer* satisfaction. Customers are the private case of the sales department; they are *external.* But every manager has clients, which are either external or internal. If your accounting department does not satisfy the needs of its client for information – the operations people or the marketing department, for example – there is a problem, isn't there? Clients are all those people whose needs the organization was established to satisfy.

And how do you measure satisfaction? By repetitive sales! Are they coming back? Would they come back if they had a choice?

Marketing people use research to find out what their customers (clients) need, how they need it, when and at what price, etc. The same applies to any manager of production, accounting, or safety. First, find out who your clients are, then find out what they need, and then go and do what needs to be done and do it efficiently.

This applies to a marriage, too. Who is the client of each spouse? If your spouse is continually coming home late or not at all, there must be a reason. If the kids, who are also clients of the entity called "family," leave and rarely come back, there must be a reason.

Your organization is effective in the short run if it provides for the present needs for which it exists – verified by the fact that your clients are coming back even if they could get the same or similar services elsewhere.

THE (P)RODUCER – (Paei) STYLE

Let's describe the style of a manager who excels in (P)roviding for the needs of the clients, thus (P)roducing the expected results while also meeting the threshold needs of (A)dministration, (E)ntrepreneurship, and (I)ntegration. This manager, whose code is (**Paei**), I call a (P)roducer, or (P) type.

As a manager, in order to (P)roduce, you must possess two qualities. The first quality is you must know what your clients need and why they are coming to you. What is your particular niche in the marketplace? Second – very important – you must know something about the technology of how to provide that for which they come to you.

Input	Throughput	Output
The roles	Make the organization	In the
(P)rovides for client needs	Functional; thus effective	short run

Thus, it's not true to say, "To manage is to manage is to manage is to manage – you can manage anything if you are a professional manager." That is dangerously over-simplified, unless we add three more words: *After some time*. And what do you do during that time? You try to learn the peculiarities of the organization that you are managing. Because there are no two "rocks" alike in the world.

Any time you move from one branch to another in a bank – the same bank! – "the rock" is going to be different. The clients have particular needs – they might need parking or drive-through banking, which your previous workplace did not have. Even if you move from one department to another in the same organization, "the rock" is going to be different. So what does a good manager do before he starts doing anything else? He learns "the rock." He learns what it is that his particular clients come to him for. Organizations are like men and women – everybody is different. You cannot treat them all alike. You have to know the particularities of what you are trying to manage, so that you can (**P**)roduce results, or (**P**)rovide for the expected needs.

But that's not enough. Some people, despite being very knowledgeable, do not (**P**)roduce results. They can give you a beautiful report, they know the technology, their judgment is correct – but they lack what psychologists call "achievement motivation" – the urge to get in there and do it! Don't just talk about it – do it! This is the desire to see the finalization of a task, like a salesman who won't stop selling until he has a signature on the dotted line. They won't let go until the need of the client is satisfied or the task is done and completed.

For me, then, a manager, a (**P**)roducer of results, must be a knowledgeable achiever.

RUNNING THE RAILROAD

Is (**P**)roducing results sufficient? No. What happens when the manager is an excellent (**P**)roducer of results: A knowledgeable achiever?

This person is so good, productive, diligent, reliable, that we reward him with a promotion.

But now, he is no longer merely a (P)roducer; he has to work with five or six or more other people, he must coordinate and delegate and control and oversee. Instead of (P)roducing by himself, he must make the *system* (P)roduce results. And that is a different task altogether. That's why we need another role: To (A)dminister.

The (A) role is indispensable for good management. It is the role of (A)dministration to pay attention to details, to systematize the (P)roduction process so that a wheel does not have to be reinvented each time a wheel is needed, and to ensure that staff follows those systems and routines. (A)dministration ensures that the organization does what it was intended to do – efficiently. It moves the organization up the learning curve so it can capitalize on its memory and experience. It analyzes successes and programs them so that they can be repeated.

If you (P)roduce results, your organization will be effective. If you also (A)dminister, your organization will be efficient. If you (P) and (A), the organization will be both effective and efficient in the short run. And if it is effective and efficient in the short run, it will be profitable in the short run, if that is how you measure success.

Input	Throughput	Output
The roles	Make the organization	In the
(P)rovides for client needs	Functional; thus effective	short run
(A)dminister	Systematized; thus efficient	short run

If an individual is (P)roductive but lacks (A), he will be very disorganized. He will work hard – harder than necessary – but not intelligently. He will waste a lot of time reinventing the wheel.

The same applies to organizations. There are organizations that satisfy their clients' needs but lack an organized (A)dministration. They have no system. Their management of the supply chain is atrocious; their salary administration is a patchwork of individual agreements; their recruitment processes and policies are haphazard. This company will be effective but inefficient. It will have growing sales with declining profits.

An American analogy for management is "running the railroad." How do we run a railroad? First of all, we need the railroad engineer to (**P**)roduce results: That's transportation. The engineer takes the train from station A to station B. Then we need someone to manage the engineers, making sure they get the train from station A to station B correctly and on time. The latter role, in companies, is called Operations. That is the (**P**) function of the railroad organization, which should be managed by a person with a strong (**P**) style.

If the railroad engineer does a bad job or if Operations does not perform, then the organization is going to be mismanaged and ineffective. The trains will not run; the need for transportation will not be satisfied.

But to run a *profitable* railroad organization, we also need supplies and money, collection and payment, and universally communicated timetables to get the right train to the right town at the designated time. Budgets must be adhered to, costs must be controlled, systems developed, and their implementation supervised. All this is the role of (**A**)dministration, which should be managed by a person whose style is compatible with the needs of this role.

THE (A)DMINISTRATOR - (pAei) STYLE

This person has the capability and natural inclination to pay attention to detail, especially details of implementation. He is methodical and likes his environment to be well thought-out and organized. He thinks in a linear fashion.

When you have a business idea – especially a crazy one or one you are afraid *might* be crazy – you go to this manager to help cool your enthusiasm. She will think things through for you. She will ask you questions you hadn't thought of. She will see all the pitfalls you didn't consider. Give her a business plan to read and she will tear it apart.

And you will be grateful! It costs less and hurts less in the long run if problems are anticipated; either you can find ways to solve them before they become crises, or you can reject the plan as unworkable.

A good Administrator, or (**A**) type, can foresee the problems inherent in an idea. People have told me, about such executives, "He can find a hair in an egg while it is still in its shell," and "He can smell a rat a mile away." In psychological terms, the (**A**) role is best served by a person with a need to control; while the (P) role requires a person with the need to achieve.

If you trust him, then if your idea passes his scrutiny, you know you can do it. And *should* do it. And if it does not pass his scrutiny and you decide to do it anyway, at least you know ahead of time what risks you are taking.

A good (**A**)dministrator always knows what is going on. He cannot sleep if he doesn't know what is going on. He keeps track of the details. He is well organized and concerned with follow-up and implementation. He has an excellent memory (or is fortified by systems, which means he does not have to rely only on his memory), and he works to see that the system operates as it was designed to operate.

The (**A**)dministrator is good at worrying, but he worries *appropriately*. He worries about precision, about integrity of information. He worries that the organization will lose its memory, its database, or its intellectual property.

A good (**A**)dministrator is indispensable to a growing organization. A young organization usually grows too fast and in too many directions, and can easily trip and fall on its face (i.e., go bankrupt) without even realizing that it's been bankrupt for quite a while.

The good (**A**)dministrator protects your back. He keeps the gateway to the castle closed so that the enemy – chaos – cannot enter.

What he does *not* do is (**P**)roduce that for which the organization exists.

If you look up the word "administration" in a thesaurus, you will find that its synonym is "to serve." (**A**)dministration serves those who (**P**)roduce; i.e., meet the needs of their clients. One (**A**)dministers *for* someone, *for* something. In public service organizations, government (**A**)dministers for the society, and the people who work in such organizations are called public (**A**)dministrators, or public servants. The need they (**P**)rovide for – their (**P**) – is (**A**)dministration; if the job is to be done efficiently, however, they must also (**P**)rovide (**A**).[6]

A lawyer who has a (**pAei**) style is the one you want to write up your contract. But do not ask him to be your trial lawyer. He will lose in court. He can write an agreement that is faultless, but if you have to sue, you're much better off finding a creative, (**paEi**) lawyer who can interpret night as day and turn a liability into an asset.

The same is true for accountants. I need two: One to advise me on my taxes – the (**paEi**) type – and the other to *file* my taxes – the (**pAei**) type. If the (**E**) *files* the taxes, I might find myself in trouble for creative accounting. If the (**A**) *plans* my taxes, I will probably pay more than necessary.

Let us turn now to the (**E**)ntrepreneuring role.

SEEING THROUGH THE FOG

Are (**P**)roducing and (**A**)dministrating enough? No. Every manager should be able to (**A**)dminister. But is the reverse also true? Is every (**A**)dministrator a manager? No. Beyond (**A**)dministering, an organization must also be capable of planning what work to do next, deciding what direction it should take as it acts to address change. This is the role of (**E**)ntrepreneuring.

The (**E**) role analyzes changes in the environment as they affect the organization. Whereas (**A**) involves systemizing and implementing plans that have already been determined, (**E**) must generate a plan of action for what the organization should start doing now because planning is not what you are going to do tomorrow. It is what you should be doing *today* in light of what you expect tomorrow to be.

A metaphor I find useful for the (**E**) role is "the ability to see through the fog." The creative person will look into the fog and see pieces of information appearing and disappearing, and all at once something clicks. He sees a big ear, then a big trunk, then one big leg, and he concludes: "Aha! There is an elephant there."

The non-creative person waits until the fog lifts, until the sun is shining and it's totally clear. Then he will go and touch the elephant, and even smell the elephant. And *still* he is not quite convinced: "OK, *maybe* it's an elephant!" This person has not added any information or created anything, while the creative person, using his imagination, has filled in the blanks in the information fog.

Returning to the railroad analogy I used above, it is the (E) role to determine which stations to close and which new stations to open; whether to add or subtract the number of cars on each line; and to decide how often the train should stop at each station. It is the (E), in other words, who will guide the organization as it deals with changing realities.

(E)ntrepreneurship is not confined to the business world. In addition to business (E)ntrepreneurs, who try to exploit the monetary opportunities of the market, there are social (E)ntrepreneurs, who initiate cultural and political change, and educational and artistic (E)ntrepreneurs, who satisfy aesthetic needs and generate new ones. All are of tremendous value to society.

Since change is inevitable and constant, the (E)ntrepreneurial role is also essential to good management. It makes the organization effective in the long run. If there is no one to perform the (E)ntrepreneurial role in an organization, that organization will eventually lag behind its more creative and proactive competitors.

THE CREATIVE CONTRIBUTOR – (paEi)

In my book *How to Solve the Mismanagement Crisis*,[7] in which I first presented the (**PAEI**) model, I identified the person who performs the (**E**) role, whose code is (**paEi**), as an "(**E**)ntrepreneur." That book was written almost 30 years ago. Since then, in studying these codes in greater depth, I have changed my mind.

A (**paEi**) is not quite an (**E**)ntrepreneur. To be an (**E**)ntrepreneur, who creates organizations and develops them, one must be strong in the (**P**) role as well. A focus on (**E**) alone is not enough.

A person who focuses mostly on (**E**), whose (**P**) orientation is adequate but not strong – (**p**) – I now call a Creative Contributor. This is the manager who has plenty of ideas – some good, some bad. But he has lots of them, sometimes non-stop. He is like the kid in school whose hand goes up even before he hears the end of the question. He is the person in a meeting who does the most talking. Whatever solution is proposed, he has another option.

This manager adds lots of energy to meetings. He is not merely focused on what the discussion is about and what the goal is. He is not without some sensitivity to what others are saying, and he is capable of paying attention to details. But without a strong (**P**) focus, he is not the person to say: "Let *me* lead, let *me* do it."

Without a strong (**P**), he will be constantly moving from one idea to the next, without finishing anything. He will not be capable of building an organization.

THE (E)NTREPRENEUR – (PaEi)

To be (**E**)ntrepreneurial, a manager must have two major characteristics. He must first of all be creative, able to visualize new directions and devise strategies for adapting the organization to a perpetually changing environment. He must have a feel for the organization's strengths and weaknesses, and the imagination and courage to identify strategies in response to such changes.[8]

And yet being creative is not sufficient. Some people are very creative but are not (**E**)ntrepreneurs.

Faculty members at business schools often fit this profile. Why? Because they are *only* creative. They may even be prolific in their creativity, as measured by the number of articles they publish. And the focus of their creativity may even be (**E**)ntrepreneurship, or how to make money. Nevertheless, if they do not have the second characteristic I believe is necessary for an (**E**)ntrepreneur – the willingness to *proact*, to walk *into* the fog, to take risks, to follow a vision – they cannot be (**E**)ntrepreneurs. They will not succeed at making money even if they wrote the book on how to do it.

It is risky to follow a dream in the fog. There may be dangerous pitfalls; and when you finally get to your destination, you may find that where you are is not where you wanted to be. So an (**E**)ntrepreneur not only has a vision; he is also willing and able to risk what he has in order to get what he wants.

Both qualities, creativity and the willingness to take risks, are necessary for (**E**)nrepreneurship. If a manager is willing to take risks but lacks creativity, he might be more at ease in a Las Vegas casino than in the corporate world. If he is creative but unable to take risks, he may end up as a staff person, a consultant, or a business professor – someone who can identify a course of action but does not undertake it himself.

The (**E**)ntrepreneur knows what he wants and why he wants it. He is creative – but in the service of a goal. He has an idea, a purpose, and he can translate that idea into reachable and achievable outcomes. His creativity is focused on how to make that outcome a reality. He is a no-nonsense person, creative and focused. Ideas without results annoy him, and results that are not born out of big ideas are a waste of time.

The focus of the (**E**) role is on what needs to be done next. What are the emerging needs; who are the next generation of clients that the organization will have to satisfy? Thus, the (E) role, if fulfilled, makes the organization effective in the long run.

Input	Throughput	Output
The roles	Make the organization	In the
(**P**)rovides for client needs	Functional; thus effective	short run
(**A**)dminister	Systematized; thus efficient	short run
(E)ntrepreneur	proactive; thus effective	long run

GETTING RELIGION

In the analogy of the five friends who went hiking to a lake, their friendship and sense of belonging expressed itself in a need to do something together. First, that need was satisfied by drinking beer; then by hiking to a lake; then by working together either to lift the rock or to come up with another plan.

The process of identifying a new way to satisfy that ultimate purpose – going on a hike rather than drinking beer – was (**E**)ntrepreneuring, the (**E**) role. The organizing of the hike – where to meet, what time, who would bring the picnic basket – belonged to the (**A**) role, or (**A**)dministering. The actual act of drinking beer, hiking to the lake, or removing the rock from the path – the act of doing whatever satisfied the purpose of the interrelationship at that moment – was (**P**)roducing, the (**P**) role.

But what is the common denominator in all these activities? Why are these people drinking beer together, going on a hike together, lifting the rock together, in the first place?

Physiological studies show that humans need to interrelate. What is the worst punishment in a prison? Solitary confinement. Come to think of it, imprisonment in itself is a partial isolation and thus a punishment. The role of developing and nurturing the need to affiliate is what makes an organization viable and thus effective in the long run.

What would happen if your organization were managed by an executive who was an outstanding (**P**), (**A**), and (**E**)? This person is a knowledgeable, achievement-oriented, task-oriented, effective, no-nonsense (**P**)roducer, as well as an outstanding (**A**)dministrator running a tight ship: Everything is systematic and well organized, correctly done at the right time. In other words, the organization is effective and efficient.

In addition, this executive is an outstanding (**E**)ntrepreneur, constantly adapting and improving the organization so that it is really moving and adjusting to the changing environment.

Now, what happens to the organization when this manager dies?

The organization also dies.

Why? Because the (**P**), (**A**), and (**E**) roles are necessary, but they are not sufficient if the organization is to be effective and efficient *in the long run*.

Organizations should be managed so that they can survive for thousands of years. Look at the Catholic Church, for example. It has existed for two thousand years and it could go for another two thousand. Why? Because it has established a set of values that each individual in the organization identifies with.

To do that, you must have (**I**)ntegration.

(**I**)ntegration means uniting people to develop agreement and build group support for ideas and their implementation.[9] If the role of (**I**)ntegration is performed well, people will learn to work as a team instead of as individuals, able to compensate for any task that happens to be missing or deficient.

(**I**)ntegration builds a climate, a system of ethics and behavior, that encourages everyone to work together so that no one is indispensable. To (**I**)ntegrate means to change the consciousness of the organization from mechanistic to organic.

What does this mean? To be mechanistic is to care only for your own interests while I care only for mine. Look at a chair. If one of the legs breaks, do the other legs care about it? No, that's the broken leg's problem.

If the four legs were internally interdependent – i.e., organic – then if one leg broke, the other three could realign themselves into a tripod shape to maintain the chair's functionality. But there is no internal interdependency, no organic relationship among the parts of the chair. Thus, when its functionality is damaged, it is dependent on external intervention for repair.

Something similar happens in mechanistically oriented organizations. Let's say there is a problem with sales. The company is going broke. The (**P**)roduction department says, "That's not my problem.

That's a sales problem." In reality, however, there may be something (**P**)roduction could do differently that would save the company.

In comparison look at your hand. If one finger breaks, your whole body feels it. There is empathy. And not only that: When one finger breaks, the other four fingers on that hand will try to compensate for the loss. That is organic consciousness. There is interdependency, there is cooperation; it's synergetic instead of being individualistic, independent, and frequently adversarial.

"Yes, but in the case of a hand, the fingers all share the same head," a cynic might argue. Not always. What if the finger that broke belongs to your four-year-old son? It's not *your* finger. So why are *you* in pain and unable to focus? Because it belongs to someone you love, and his pain is your pain.

So (**I**)ntegration does not have to be physical. It can be emotional and/or spiritual. It is driven by a sense of belonging and affiliation.

When your kids are fighting, you don't always solve their problems for them, do you? Why not? Because you are trying to promote just that sense of interdependency and affiliation. You might say, "Hey, you're family; you're supposed to be helping each other. I'm not going to be here forever. You must solve your own problems."

Let's say you and your family are packing up the car for an outing, and you find your son sitting in the car and waiting. "Why aren't you helping?" you ask him.

"My stuff is already in," he responds.

"Get your rear end moving and help the family!!" you'd probably shout. "You are not alone here. Your job is done when the *whole family's* job is done." Right?

A family is more than a group of people; a hand is more than five fingers. There is a sense of interdependence fostered by common values and vision, among other variables. (**I**)ntegration involves creating and nurturing a culture of mutual trust and respect and thus cooperation; it involves the leader making himself dispensable so that the group can continue to function if anything happens to him – or any other individual member.

Look at a sports team. If you put together a team of stars, each from a different team, who have never played or trained together, and play them against an above-average team that's been playing together for a long time, who would probably win the *first* game? It's likely that the above-average team would win. Why? Because the star team has not yet developed its team consciousness; its members cannot yet predict: "If he does that, I can back him up by doing this." That sense of cooperating to reach a common goal is what we mean by teamwork.

(**I**)ntegration turns individual (**E**)ntrepreneurship into group (**E**)ntrepreneurship. If a manager does not (**I**)ntegrate, does not nourish group (**E**)ntrepreneurship, then in extreme cases the group will be unable to initiate action or determine goals in his absence. Thus, (**I**)ntegration is a necessary component of good management. Companies that rely on any one individual for continuous success in their operations inevitably will face a crisis if that individual leaves or dies. Even organizations that have been managed by a (**PAE–**) – the dash in the code signifying that the (**I**) role is missing or deficient – will find themselves in trouble if that manager leaves before a team feeling – an *esprit de corps* around an effective course of action – has been developed.

Since an organization's life span should be longer than the life of any individual, effective long-range continuity depends on building a team of people who understand, trust, and respect each other, and who complement each other's abilities. (**I**)ntegration creates that effect.

When there is no (**I**)ntegration taking place, no one is focused primarily on the company's long-range, holistic interests. Instead, everybody is looking out for himself, often at the company's expense. The stockholders are trying to milk the company. Management is trying to get maximum rewards for itself, with stock options, golden parachutes, and endless fringe benefits. Labor is campaigning for the best salaries and job security. Among all of these competing interests, it's possible to arrive at a working consensus in which everyone is getting his interests satisfied while the company is actually going bankrupt. That is what is said about certain developing countries: "Rich people, poor country."

When I find a situation like this in the organizations I coach, I often dramatize the dilemma by bringing an empty chair to the table. I place the company name on the front of the chair and ask, "If someone were sitting in that chair, what would he say? What does this *company* want?" When I let the participants play out that scenario, I hear voices that have previously been silent. In this exercise, I am playing the (**I**)ntegrating role.

So, although (**P**) *appears* to be the purpose of our existence – to satisfy our clients' needs – it is in fact only the immediate, short-term purpose. What is our continuous endless purpose? To satisfy our need to interrelate.

I repeat: Interrelating is the ultimate purpose of our existence. We are social animals. We need each other, period. We even keep dogs or cats sometime for no other reason than because we need to be needed, to interrelate. In the United States, dogs are trained to visit patients in hospitals; some studies have shown that a dog's attention and affection can speed up the healing process.

There is nothing in this world that doesn't exist to serve something else by functionally interrelating to it. If it serves only itself, then it is a cancer and serves death.

The pen I write with is useless if it does not leave a mark on paper. Breathing has no meaning unless the oxygen feeds my body. Nothing in itself is functional; everything is functional *in relation* to something else. The ultimate reason any system exists is (**I**)ntegration, the (**I**) role. Indeed, managers with the ability to perform that role have the potential to go beyond good management and become leaders.

The Integrator – (pae**I**) Style

There are two types of (**I**)ntegration – passive and active – and three directions: Upward, lateral, and downward.

A passive (**I**)ntegrator will (**I**)ntegrate himself into a group of people. An active (**I**)ntegrator can (**I**)ntegrate a group of people among themselves. Because in management, (**I**)ntegration must be active, we will concern ourselves here only with active (**I**)ntegration.

Upward (**I**)ntegration is the ability to (**I**)ntegrate people who are higher in status, authority, rank, and so on. Lateral (**I**)ntegration is the ability to develop peers into a cohesive group. Downward (**I**)ntegration provides leadership by establishing cohesion among subordinates.

A very effective lateral (**I**)ntegrator may function poorly as a downward (**I**)ntegrator, tending to be arrogant with subordinates. In fact, it is unusual for a person to be an excellent (**I**)ntegrator in all directions.[10]

Let's talk about the characteristics that a good (**I**)ntegrator brings to the organization.

Perhaps surprisingly, the (**I**)ntegrator is the most creative of all the management types, since he must make decisions from a more diffused and less structured database. (**I**)ntegrating is even less programmable than (**E**)ntrepreneuring, because (**E**)ntrepreneuring does not necessarily deal with people, whereas (**I**)ntegrating involves uniting individuals with diverse interests and strengths behind a group decision.

In (**I**)ntegrating (**E**)ntrepreneurs, one has the additional burden of forging their individual creativities into a cohesive unity, to develop group risk-taking out of individual risk-taking, to fuse an *individual* sense of responsibility into a *group* sense of responsibility.

The (**I**)ntegrator clarifies issues by finding the common threads of deep – not just superficial – agreement, and by assimilating contrasting values, assumptions, and expectations.

A successful (**I**)ntegrator also must make himself dispensable. His subordinates must be trained to be capable of replacing him. Ideally, in a cohesive group almost any member should be able to lead. To take a military example, if any soldier in a squad can take the squad leader's place and be accepted when the leader is killed, this demonstrates that the leader was a good (**I**)ntegrator. If the squad scatters when the leader is killed, then the (**I**)ntegration of the unit was insufficient, although the leader may have been a competent commander in other respects.

The (**I**)ntegrator is sensitive to others (i.e., empathetic), and he is capable of deductive thinking (i.e., able to infer what people really want to say from what they *do* say). He has few ego problems of his own, which enables him to hear and respond to other people's expectations, problems, and needs rather than his own.

The late Juscelino Kubitschek, former president of Brazil and founder of Brasilia, was such a leader. When asked whether he was for or against a certain political program, he replied: "I am neither for nor against it: I am above it."

The (I) Role in Leadership

The (**I**)ntegrator is unique in that he not only provides for future organizational continuity, he also enables the organization to function smoothly in the present. His role is essential for success, both in the short run *and* in the long run. Finally, his is the one role that *must* be present in order for leadership to occur.

Input	Throughput	Output
The roles	Make the organization	In the
(**P**)rovides for client needs	Functional; thus effective	short run
(**A**)dminister	Systematized; thus efficient	short run
(**E**)ntrepreneur	proactive; thus effective	long run
(**I**)ntegrate	organic; efficient	long run

You can be a good manager even without (**I**). Managers can be strong in two or even three roles – (**PAei**), (**PaEi**), (**pAEi**), (**PAEi**) – but unless one of them is (**I**)ntegrating, they will not be leaders. For leadership to occur, the (**I**) role must enhance whatever other roles a manager excels at performing. (See Chapter 11 for a more detailed description of leadership.)

Summing up the Functionalist View

Before we continue, let me summarize the points I have made so far:

"Management" is defined as the process that makes organizations become and remain effective and efficient, now and in the future. These, I suggest, are the goals of every organization, regardless of how it measures its success, regardless of technology, size, and culture.

The organization will achieve these goals if four roles are performed well: (**P**)roviding for the clients' expected needs, (**A**)dministering, (**E**)ntrepreneuring, and (**I**)ntegrating – or (**PAEI**). In other words, the organization must be results-oriented (**P**); it must be flexible and adapt well to change (**E**); but that flexibility must be controllable and generate predictable results (**A**). Finally, its system must be self-adaptive (**I**), so that no outside corrective action is called for.

The role of management, then, is to perform those four roles – because they do not happen by themselves. Thus, "to manage" means to perform any or all of those four roles, regardless of an individual's title or position in the hierarchy – or whether he is even on the payroll.

Now that we have defined "management" and know what we are looking for, we should be well on our way toward finding the ideal manager, right?

Wrong. But we are closer to finding out why the ideal manager does not and cannot exist.

NOTES

1. Adizes, Ichak, and Elisabeth Mann Borgese: *Self-Management: New Dimensions to Democracy; Alternatives for a New Society* (Santa Barbara, Calif.: Clio Books, 1975).

2. Djilas, Milovan: *The New Class: An Analysis of the Communist System* (New York: Frederick A. Praeger, 1957).

3. Adizes, Ichak: *Industrial Democracy Yugoslav Style: The Effect of Decentralization on Organizational Behavior* (New York: Free Press, 1971; reprinted by Adizes Institute, 1977).

4. For more details, see: Adizes, Ichak: *Managing Corporate Lifecycles* (Paramus, N.J.: Prentice Hall Press, 1999).

5. See www.adizes.com for testimonials about the Adizes Institute.

6. In government, the **(P)** and **(A)** functions are the same. In other words, the **(A)** actually **(P)**roduces what the organization exists for. Take a government agency that issues licenses or monitors the health and safety of food service establishments. Its **(P)** function is to **(A)**. Of course, this organization will have its traditional **(A)** roles too: To organize, systematize, and monitor the system.

7. Adizes, Ichak: *How to Solve the Mismanagement Crisis* (Santa Monica, Calif.: Adizes Institute, Inc., 1979).

8. For a definition of **(E)**ntrepreneurship, see Schumpeter, Joseph: *Business Cycles* (New York: McGraw Hill, 1939), pp. 102-9; and Drucker, Peter F.: *Management: Tasks, Responsibilities, Practices* (New York: Harper & Row, 1973), Chapter 10.

9. On the role of **(I)**ntegration, see Lawrence, P.R., and J. W. Lorsch, "New Managerial Job: The **(I)**ntegrator," *Harvard Business Review*, 45 (November 1967), pp. 142-51.

10. The **(I)** component, as has been pointed out, is essential to good management at all levels, because the manager must work through others to achieve organizational goals. Where management has succeeded in **(I)**ntegrating the individual members of an organization into a group, we may expect greater identification with the organization, more job satisfaction, and better performance. The importance of interpersonal relationships for the success of organizations has been repeatedly demonstrated in the literature. Chris Argyris found that the worker's skill and pride in his work were directly related to his on-the-job friendships. See Argyris, "The Fusion of an Individual with the Organization," *American Sociological Review*, 19 (1954), pp. 145–67; and "Personality vs. Organization," *Organizational Dynamics*, 3 (1974) no. 2, pp. 2–17.

    A similar association between level of competence and degree of **(I)**ntegration with the organization was reported by Peter M. Blau in a study of law enforcement agents. See Blau, "Patterns of Interaction among a Group of Officials in a Government Agency," *Human Relations*, 7 (1954), pp. 337-48.

Chapter 3

What Causes Mismanagement?

> PROBLEM: Now that we've defined management, why can't we find the ideal manager?

The Myth of the Perfect Manager

We have established that there are four roles of management; each of them is necessary and together they are sufficient for good management. If you (**P**)roduce results – i.e., satisfy the needs of your clients for which your organization exists – and you (**A**)dminister, you'll have an effective and efficient organization in the short run; if you (**E**)ntrepreneur and (**I**)ntegrate, your organization will be effective and efficient in the long run. If you do all four, the organization will be profitable – if that is how you measure your success – both in the short and the long run. If you're not in the for-profit business, then you will achieve whatever short- and long-term results you're looking for: Service, political survival, whatever.

So far, so good.

Now the bad news.

It's not so simple.

While one manager may excel at planning (**E** for **P**), another may excel in organizing (**A** for **P**), a third in motivating (**I** for **E** or **P**), and so on. But never do you find a manager who excels at all four roles – in other words, a perfect (**PAEI**) manager. He or she doesn't exist.

Why not? This question reminds me of a joke:

A preacher, in his sermon one day, said, "There is no such thing as a perfect man. I can prove it to you. Anyone who has ever known a perfect man, please stand up."

Nobody stood up.

"Anyone who has ever known a perfect woman, please stand up," the preacher said.

One demure little woman stood up.

"Did you really know an absolutely perfect woman?" the preacher asked, amazed.

"I didn't know her personally," the old woman replied, "but I have heard a great deal about her. She was my husband's late first wife."

If someone is "perfect," she must be dead. And the truth is, she was never perfect. We have simply forgotten all her deficiencies.

In one of his books, the guru Osho writes that he concluded that people believed he was dead.

"Why?" he was asked.

"Because they are only saying good things about me!"

THE IMPOSSIBLE DREAM

In other words, one big reason that the perfect, all-encompassing (**PAEI**) manager does not exist is that nothing is ever perfect when it is subject to *change* – or, to put it more bluntly, is alive. Nothing is perfect because nothing is static. There is a lifecycle to everything. One does not parent a baby the same way one would parent a 40-year-old son, obviously. Treating a baby as if it were an adult would physically endanger him; babying a 40-year-old would psychologically destroy him. The parenting style has to change as our children change; life does not allow us to stay in one place. We change, either for the better or for the worse. And we do not necessarily change perfectly to reflect the needs that we must respond to.

There is no perfect parent, no perfect leader, and for that matter no perfect flower. Something may be perfect for the moment or, to paraphrase Andy Warhol, at some point in our lives we might each achieve our fifteen minutes of perfection. But conditions change, and the functional synchronization of what we do with what must be done cannot remain perfect forever.[1] It may seem contradictory to say that everyone is a good leader and no one is a good leader, but it actually makes sense in the following context: Everyone is a good leader (in some situations), and no one is a good leader (forever, under all conditions).

"The closest to perfection a person ever comes is when he fills out a job application form."

STANLEY J. RANDALL

Peter Drucker has recognized the complexity of the managerial task.

"A peculiar characteristic of top management is that it requires a diversity of capabilities and, above all, temperaments," he writes. [2] I will add, in italics, my interpretations of the roles he points out.

"It requires the capacity to analyze, to think, to weigh alternatives (*A*), and to harmonize dissent (*I*). But it also requires the capacity for quick and decisive action (*P*), for boldness and for intuitive courage (*E*). It requires being at home with abstract ideas and concepts (*E*), calculations and figures (*A*). It also requires perception of people, human awareness, empathy, and an altogether lively interest and respect for people (*I*). Some tasks demand that a man work... alone (*P*). Others are tasks of representation and ceremonial outside tasks, that require enjoyment of crowds and protocol (such as the task of a politician) (*EI*)."

"The top management tasks," Drucker continues, "require at least four different kinds of human being." Drucker identifies them as "the thought man" (*A*), "the action man" (*P*), "the people man" (*I*), and "the front man" (*E*). These are, of course, analogous to the styles of the (*PAEI*) model.

Although Drucker was referring only to top management, I believe that all management positions within an organization require all four roles, although the balance of the roles shifts as you move through an organization. Top management in America, for example, must exercise a lot of the (**E**) role. But the (**I**) role, in American companies, is often consigned to the Human Resources department, where it is neglected, because HR managers are inundated with (**A**)dministrative tasks and record-keeping that not only keeps them too busy to concentrate on (**I**)ntegrating, but also undermine their credibility as (**I**)ntegrators.

Meanwhile, (**P**)roduction is delegated all the way down to the workers or the people on the line, the (**P**)-eons. They are not asked for their opinions – no (**E**) – and if they try to (**I**)ntegrate they might be seen as threatening management's authority by trying to unionize.

Yet, at any level, managers must perform all four roles simultaneously and with the same degree of perfection. This makes the textbook manager a necessity – and an impossibility – at all managerial levels. For example, a foreperson needs to be knowledgeable (**P**); to have administrative capabilities (**A**); to be flexible, adaptive, and innovative (**E**); and to relate well to people (**I**). But how many forepersons actually have all of these qualifications? According to Drucker, "Those four temperaments are almost never found in the same person."[3]

Four Roles in Eternal Conflict

Why not? Because – and here is the second reason why no manager can be perfect – the managerial roles undermine each others performance at a point in time.

Although Drucker concluded that more than one style is necessary to manage any organization, he did not go beyond that thought to analyze how the different styles might interact. And that is the gap I am trying to fill here.

Let us look more closely at the incompatibility of roles.

We all know managers who are brilliant at conceptualizing plans and ideas but not very good at monitoring the details of implementation; or who are sensitive, empathic, and good at (**I**)ntegration, but just can't seem to make hard decisions.

The explanation is simple: The four roles are not mutually exclusive, but they are incompatible in the short run and thus mutually inhibitive: In other words, the ability to excel at one of the (**PAEI**) roles is likely to impede one's ability to perform another.

"Everybody is ignorant, only on
different subjects."

WILL ROGERS

For example, (**P**)roducing and (**E**)ntrepreneuring are incompatible. (**P**) and (**E**) are in conflict because (**P**) requires short-term feedback, whereas (**E**) takes time to develop and looks to the long term for feedback.

How many times have you said, "I'm working so hard, I have no time to think." In other words, moving the rock, or satisfying present demands, is so overwhelming that you have no time to think about future opportunities. But while you've been sweating, pushing that rock out of your path, someone else may have built a big highway close by. So (**P**) actually endangers (**E**), because if you work very hard, day and night, focusing on short-run results, it is difficult if not impossible to also stay aware of the changes that are coming your way. Your mind is like a camera. You can either focus on the close-up view, rendering the long view out of focus, or the opposite.

I have met many (**E**)ntrepreneurs who were lucky enough to be fired from their former jobs, where they were busy (**P**)-ing. If they had stayed put, they would never have started anything new.

Conversely, (**E**) threatens (**P**): (**E**)ntrepreneuring means change, and that threatens the (**P**) role. People in (**P**)roduction are forever complaining to the engineering department, "If you guys don't stop changing things, we'll never get anything done!" At some point, you have to freeze the planning so you can proceed with the doing.

(P) and (A) Incompatibility

Any combination of the four roles is incompatible, not just (P) and (E). Let's look at another combination: (P) and (A).

When you play doubles in tennis, and a ball is coming at high speed directly to the center of the court, do you wait until you're sure where it's going to land before deciding who is responsible for hitting it back? Obviously not. Do you make a line in the middle with some whitewash so you and your partner know exactly who is responsible for what area? I don't think so. You divide the court among yourselves, more or less. And when the ball hits the middle of the court, in the "gray area" of responsibility, then you both move for the ball. That is effective, because one of you will hit the ball, but it is not very efficient.

In the efficient scenario, no one moves until the ball has landed – although by that time it's too late for anyone to return it. That, of course, is ineffective.

Effectiveness (P) and efficiency (A) are incompatible goals.

When you want to be very effective, you have difficulty being efficient. That's why start-up companies, which are constantly putting out fires and dealing with unanticipated problems, are disorganized and inefficient. They accept the fact that organization and order – (A) – will have to wait.

The opposite is also true: If you are very efficient, you end up less effective. In other words, when you have too much (A), you end up with reduced (P). That is the case with bureaucracies, in which every detail is planned and no variable is left uncontrolled.

Ironically, the more control you have, the less control you *feel* you have – because the more control you have, the more granularity you have and the more deviations you can identify that need to be controlled. So what happens? As the granularity of control increases, the system becomes increasingly inflexible – thus non-responsive to the changing needs of its clients.

To use another tennis analogy: It is as if a player stands in one place, practicing and practicing until his hand and body movements are perfect, and then tells his opponent, "Send the ball *here*" – to the spot he practiced in, where he can be the most efficient. In reality, he can only hit the balls that come directly to his racquet. He is just going through the motions, hoping that when he swings, the ball will be there to be returned.

That is what I call being precisely wrong rather than being approximately right. And that is how bureaucracies work. Everything is planned and controlled to the minutest detail. No variable is left unattended. The fact that the ball – the client's changing needs – is over *there* now instead of over *here* does not preoccupy anyone. They just go through the motions as planned for maximum efficiency and control. They are efficient to the extreme, making them inflexible and thus, eventually, extremely ineffective.

To be approximately right, to be effective, you must go to where the ball is, even if it means your body is not moving most efficiently.

This dichotomy of form vs. function, effectiveness vs. efficiency, could be observed as the Berlin Wall came down and the Communist system started to thaw. That system experienced tremendous difficult in its transition to a market economy, because in order to be more market-driven and -oriented – in other words more effective – they had to learn to be less efficient, with less regulation, less government planning and supervision. But when I lectured at the Academy of Science in Russia and tried to explain this concept, it was like selling pork to Hassidic Jews. The whole Communist system was based on (**A**); switching to a (**P**) orientation needed more than learning new principles of accounting; it needed a huge cultural change.

This (**P**)/(**A**) incompatibility is in essence a struggle between form and function, and there are plenty of examples of that in life. For example, I used to wonder why women buy so many shoes. My wife explained it to me. She said a woman wants a sexy shoe. So she buys shoes that look good, but then they are not very comfortable; who would feel comfortable walking in high heels? So the next time, she buys comfortable shoes, but guess what? They don't look sexy. Thus, those rooms full of shoes are the result of an endless and useless search for the perfect shoe in which form and function are in perfect balance, the impossible-to-find shoe that is both sexy and comfortable.

You may have noticed the same problem with teapots: The shape is very attractive, but the tea spills all over the table. In that case, form got a higher priority than function.

When something is created in which from and function, effectiveness and efficiency are in perfect balance, that creation is put in a museum; it is that rare.

(A)DMINISTRATION VS. (I)NTEGRATION INCOMPATIBILITY

Like (**A**), (**I**) is concerned with form. Each is concerned with an accepted set of rules that both drives and puts boundaries on behavior.

(**I**) represents organic form, whereas (**A**) represents mechanistic form. By mechanistic, I mean that (**A**) is externally driven: (**A**) establishes parameters, and you must accept these parameters as they are given to you, whether you agree with them or not. If you break the rules, or deviate from them, you understand that there will be a penalty.

(**I**) also sets parameters, but (**I**)'s parameters are internally driven. Thus, an (**I**) can be even more constraining than an (**A**). Why? Because when you are both rule-maker and rule enforcer, cheating is impossible. You cannot deviate, even in the darkness where no one can see you – because you are watching *you*. And you cannot escape from yourself.

Here is an example: A man says to a married woman, "Why don't we make love?"

She says, "No, I cannot."

He says, "Why not? Your husband will never know."

She says, "Yes, but *I* will know."

That's (I). "Why not?" Because "I will know. Nobody else has to know. *I* will know that I did something I shouldn't have done." It's internal, in contrast to (**A**), which is external: "If I break these rules, I may be caught and punished; they will stone me to death or send me to Siberia."

If you accept a code of external rules and make it your own – in other words, if you internalize it – that is (**AI**). If you are a dedicated Communist – you believe in Communism and are willing to die for it – then you have internalized the external rules of Communism. That can be an overpowering combination that makes you extremely inflexible. It is not strange at all, then, that many Russians committed suicide when Stalin was denounced and exposed as a criminal. It destroyed many people's internal belief system.

Does this similarity of function mean that (**A**) and (**I**) are actually compatible?

Not at all.

(**A**) undermines (**I**) because the organization will rely on external, legalistic mechanistic rules to control interdependencies and relationships, and thus rely less on internal and cultural values. Why does (**A**) replace (**I**) so easily? Because it is easier to legislate a rule than to develop a value. To make a new law might take a few months. To develop a new code of ethics might take a lifetime. Furthermore, some (**A**) rules might be in conflict with some (**I**) values. Thus, (**A**) will always tend to increase as a regulatory mechanism – which in turn will make (**I**) less necessary and poorly reinforced. The more (**A**) you have, the less (**I**) you will have. All those (**A**) mechanistic rules and policies devour any effort to remain organically interdependent.

In the beginning years of a new religion, for example, the founding group of believers don't have a lot of (**A**). What they have is a commitment to God and a shared value system, which enables them to decide among themselves about what is the right thing to do. They have lots of (**I**).

Later on, as the religion becomes successful and expands, the group loses its tight (**I**)ntegration and by necessity becomes more and more rule-driven. Eventually, the tail begins to wag the dog: The (**A**) rules start to dominate. Instead of (**I**)ntegration serving as the "glue" that unites the community through consistency of beliefs, the organization emphasizes rituals and rules, (**A**), and the religion becomes more and more rigid. It becomes an *organized religion*, and its believers conform to the rules of conduct rather than the spirit of the content. (**A**) destroys (**I**).

Here is another example of (**A**) undermining (**I**): Which country has the most lawyers per capita? The United States. (**A**) is very high and growing; our court system is overloaded. We are constantly seeking external-to-ourselves interventions to solve our interdependency problems. (**A**) is penetrating deeper and deeper into our social fabric – dictating how we should raise our children, how to address our spouses, where and how we can and cannot smoke, eat, talk....

At your local bookstore, the largest and fastest-growing section is very likely the "self-help" aisle, where you can find "rules" for doing everything from finding a life partner, to planning a party, to resolving an argument or making friends. It is lots of rules for everything. (**A**) galore. How about (**I**)? It is flourishing too. Endless courses on intimacy, love, relationships, communication, self growth, self actualization. Look at many bumper stickers on American cars. "LOVE" is probably the most repeated word: "I love New York." " I love my dog." "Jesus loves you" etc. Why this preoccupation with love? Because love is the ultimate integration and it is in high demand because it is threatened by change. The more change the more alienation which seems the overwhelming result of modern life. Furthermore, the bigger the city, the more lonely people feel, because the less (**I**) there is.

So both the need for (**A**) and (**I**) are growing because of change. But the more you rely on (A) rules to solve whatever interrelationship you have the less you will rely on your internal guide, your internal voice. (**A**) is easier to follow. It is mechanical. (**I**) is more difficult and it is natural that when confronted with choice, easy or difficult, the easy approach wins.

Now let's look at the reverse: How does (**I**) undermine (**A**)?

Actually, the word "undermine" is inaccurate in this context; rather, (**I**) retards the development of (**A**), because the more (**I**) you have, the less (**A**) you need. In a tribal community, the tribe relies on its internally developed values to make decisions and resolve conflicts. They do not need external intervention, like police or the courts, to solve problems. They have a very strong value system that tells them what's right and what's wrong; thus, they don't need anybody else to tell them what to do. So the more **(I)** there is, the less need for **(A)**.

I want to point out that this **(I)**/**(A)** incompatibility is unlike any of the other combinations of roles. Incompatibility can be positive or negative. When **(A)** pushes **(I)** out, the two roles are being incompatible in a destructive way. But when **(I)** retards the growth of **(A)**, they are being incompatible in a *positive* way.

This is in opposition to all of the other pairings. As we have seen, when **(E)** undermines **(P)** or **(P)** undermines **(E)**, it's undesirable. When **(P)** undermines **(A)** or **(A)** undermines **(P)**, it's undesirable. We shall also see that when **(I)** undermines **(P)** or **(P)** undermines **(I)**, it's undesirable. And so on. But when **(I)** undermines **(A)**, it's *desirable*. Why that is true, I don't know.

Now, I have found in my work that when my theories come together correctly, there is a balance to them, an elegance, as in mathematics. Any time something is off balance in my work, I know there is a fallacy in the argument. Sometimes it takes me years to find what the fallacy is and how to correct it. The above is one of them.

This **(I)**/**(A)** anomaly demonstrates a lack of elegance, which means to me that there is something missing, something not quite accurate about my theory. But it is a problem for which I do not have a solution. This is the best I can do today. I prefer to point it out to my readers rather than ignore it or gloss over it. Perhaps one of the readers will be able to help solve it. What I do know already is that for **(I)** a threshold of **(A)** is necessary of **(I)** can not grow. But for **(A)** there is no threshold of **(I)** necessary.

What is going on and why? Go figure it out, I do not know.

(P) Threatens (I); (I) Endangers (P)

Have you ever attended a course or workshop where you were taught how to be a better **(I)**ntegrator: How to relate better to people and be a good communicator and a sensitive human being? Then you returned to work, and soon there was a crisis, and time pressure, and you had to have a meeting in which you had to (**P**), then and there. There was no time to convince, explain, or motivate. What happened to your team orientation and ability to listen patiently?

When there is time pressure to (**P**)roduce results, it is normal to become rather dictatorial and assign a lower priority to (**I**)ntegration and the needs of some stakeholders. The (**P**) squeezes the (**I**) out.

No matter how many times you may have gone to a meeting promising yourself that *this* time you'll be patient and understanding and people-oriented, situations inevitably arise in which decisions have to be made *now*! And what are you thinking, as you sit fidgeting in a meeting and checking your watch for the fifteenth time? "*The hell with people's expectations to be heard fully! We have a railroad to run here!*" Right?

By the same token, (**I**) undermines (**P**) by applying parameters, very much the way that (**A**) does.

How does applying (**I**) parameters undermine (**P**)? I'll give you an example, again from religion: If the very religious Jews, dressed in black, don't have much to eat and there is no work and no food, and you ask them, "What are you going to do?" what do they say? "God will help." "God will provide." Period. They have total confidence. This is true of very religious Muslims and Christians too.

Now, if you are not religious, you are not going to sit around waiting for God to provide, are you? You're going to go and find work or food or both. You're going to (**P**).

So people with a large amount of faith, or (**I**), will stay within the parameters of their value system, and this interferes with their ability to (**P**). Even if it is a matter of life and death, they will not violate any rules. What if the exigencies of a situation require them to break a rule? Still, they will not do it. Why? Because it violates their internalized rules.

THE STRUGGLE BETWEEN (E) AND (I)

Why are (**E**) and (**I**) in conflict? Because (**E**) want to change, to create, to make a difference; whereas (**I**) wants harmony, agreement, (**I**)ntegration. What (**I**) tries to put together or keep together, (**E**) wants to take apart.

When Martin Luther tried to reform the Catholic church in the 16th century, the church reacted by undermining him at every step. The church hierarchy saw Luther's innovations as a threat to Catholicism.

Here's another, rather complicated example of how (**I**) undermines (**E**): Which country once had the fewest lawyers per capita? Japan. In Japan, until just a few years ago, there was a great deal of loyalty and interdependence in business because their (**I**) was high. Corporations offered lifetime employment and a family environment. They took care of each other; they were guided more by their culture than by their legal institutions. Their need for (A) – strict rules and policies – was low.

However, in recent years Japan has changed: Its (**A**) has grown and its (**I**) has declined.

Why has this happened? Because the four roles were never in balance in Japan, and that created an unstable situation.

The Japanese have not, historically, been individualistic innovators. Japanese education system has always been weak in (**E**). They teach to know and to remember not to disagree and stand out as an individual. Their (**E**)ntrepreneuring stems from group interactions – essentially getting to (**E**) through (**I**).

Why is their (**E**) low? Because their (**I**) is so enormous, and (**I**) threatens (**E**). When I work in any other country in the world, when the group agrees on a subject, we clap our hands and shout, "*Yes!*" When I work in Japan, I reverse my rules: When somebody in the room says, "I have a different opinion," *that's* when we clap hands and shout "*Yes!*" Why? Because the Japanese rarely disagree with each other. They are always watching to see where the consensus is, and that's where they want to go.

Remember my analogy in the preface, of the four roles as vitamins? In order to get benefit from taking lots of vitamin (**A**), you also have to take lots of vitamin (**E**). If there is no more (**E**), the benefit stops. A shortage of one will limit the effectiveness of the others even if the others are in excess. And that is because the roles like vitamins are interdependent. If one component is missing from your diet, the other components can not make you healthier unless you get more of the missing component.

When did Japan lose its competitive advantage? When the rate of change, worldwide, began to accelerate, and decision-making needed to be faster. With too much (**I**) and too little (**E**), Japan could not adapt and speed up. At the same time as interdependencies increased (governments with corporations; banks with governments, etc.), their (**A**) increased. In Japan, because (**I**) is high, (**E**) is low and (**A**) increased, (**P**) eventually had to decline.

When Japan hit the skids, what did they do? In order to increase (**P**)roduction, the Japanese had to sacrifice a lot of their (**I**) and replace it with more (**A**). Why? When (**P**)roduction declines, or the economy is in trouble, management often chooses to reduce (**I**)ntegration methods of managing interdependencies in favor of more systematization, or (**A**). The manifestation of that is that Japanese businesses no longer make a lifetime commitment to people; the family atmosphere is gone; people can actually be fired. What is left is an enormous (**A**) bureaucracy that is further eroding Japanese (**P**) and (**I**) and will not allow (**E**) to grow.

As a result, Japan is in a very difficult decline, for which there is no short-term solution. Without any homegrown (**E**), they are being forced to bring in corporate officers from abroad in order to grow. (For example, the head of Nissan is from Brazil, and he is hailed as a hero. The Japanese auto industry sees this experiment as a model to follow.)

What does Japan need? It needs to change its educational system in order to support and increase its (**E**); in other words, it should start teaching people how to *learn* rather than how to *know*. It must begin to prize deviant thinking, out-of-the-box thinking, and reward individualism instead of rewarding (**A**). And the country must learn to do this without losing its own cultural competitive advantage – (**I**).

If that is impossible, then the Japanese need to open their gates and stimulate immigration by other nationalities with a lot of (**E**) – the Greeks, the Jews, or the Indians – which Japan, a particularly closed society, finds undesirable.

THE CONFLICT BETWEEN (E) AND (A)

Finally, how are (**E**)ntrepreneurship and (**A**)dministration incompatible? This one is easy to see. (**E**)s are radical, whereas (**A**)s are conservative. (**A**)s want control in order to maximize efficiency, and they try to get it by minimizing deviations; whereas (**E**)s *live* to create deviations – by introducing change, which is in fact necessary for long-term effectiveness. Thus, (**E**) threatens (**A**) because too much change hinders systematization, routine, and order.

And of course the opposite is also true: (**A**) endangers (**E**). As you freeze new ideas for the sake of efficiency, your ability to be proactive and effective in the long run will become limited. Policies, rules, and institutionalized behavior inhibit change.

Let's take the example of Communist Russia. (**A**) was so dominant that anybody who was an (**E**)ntrepreneur was called a spekulant, or speculator, which definitely had a negative connotation: It meant somebody who would undermine the centrally planned economy of Russia. Hardly anybody dared to be an (**E**)ntrepreneur in Communist Russia, which carried the danger of being sent to prison. My own father, who owned a mom-and-pop store, was thrown in jail in Yugoslavia for not following the Communist ideology of public ownership of property. By trying to innovate outside of the rules, he became an "enemy of the people."

The Impossible Dream

Now, let's go back to our Chapter 1, to the summary of what a manager should do, and classify each task in (**PAEI**) terms. It should become clear that what is expected from ideal managers, executives, leaders, is to be (**PAEI**)s and since the roles are incompatible, at a point in time, that can not happen, or it will be extremely rare to happen.

The ideal manager is knowledgeable and achievement-oriented, (**P**); detail-oriented, (**A**); systematic and efficiency-oriented, (**A**); organized, a logical and linear thinker, (**A**); charismatic, visionary, a risk-taker, and change-oriented, (**E**); and sensitive to people and their needs, (**I**).

He can integrate all the necessary people to successfully achieve goals, (**I**). He knows how to build a team while making himself dispensable, (I). He judges himself by how well his group performs; by how well, together and individually, the group members achieve their goals, and by how well he facilitates the achievement of those goals, (**IP**).

He listens carefully, not only to what is being said but also to what is *not* being said, (**I**). He understands the need to change, (**E**), but introduces change cautiously and selectively, (**A**). He is able to identify leadership potential among his staff and is not afraid to hire and promote bright, challenging subordinates, (**I**).

He doesn't complain when things go wrong, but offers constructive criticism instead, (**I**). His subordinates are not afraid to report failures; they know that he will be reasonable and supportive, (**I**). He encourages creativity, (**E**), and looks for support, (**I**), in decision-making. He is charismatic, (**E**), capable of motivating others to work hard to achieve the goals of the organization, (**IP**). He can delegate. (To delegate, one transfers the (**P**) role to someone else.) He trains his subordinates systematically, (**A**). He resolves conflicts diplomatically, respecting people's expectations and ambitions and appealing to their social consciences, (**I**). He shares information instead of monopolizing it and using it to gain power, (**I**).

He is driven by a strong code of values, (**I**). He is analytical and action-oriented, (**P**); sensitive without being overly emotional, (**I**). He seeks results, (**P**), but never by sacrificing the process, (**A**). He systematically develops markets, production facilities, finances, and human resources for the organization, (**E**).

What else does management involve? According to the dictionary definitions we examined earlier, "to manage" means to: Operate, (**PA**); organize, (**A**) or (**pAei**); rule, (**A**) or (**pAei**); control, (**A**) or (**pAei**); achieve goals (**Paei**); and lead, which could be any of these three combinations: (**PaeI**), (**pAeI**), or (**paEI**). (See Chapter 11 for more detail on the qualities of leadership.)

Finally, he must be able to plan. This requires having specific results in mind, (**P**); having a vision for the future, (**E**); paying attention to the details of implementation, (**A**); and gathering support from those who will perform implementation, (**I**). Thus, this one task alone requires all four roles.

He must be able to control, (**A**) – but here, again, the control must be in the service of facilitating a result, (**P**), without losing flexibility, (**E**); and it must be generally supported by the people to be effective, (**I**).

When you add it all together, what do you get? A (**PAEI**) – and that is too much to ask for. That is why neither you nor I nor any of the gurus who teach and preach management can actually be the ideal managers they claim they can create.

What should we do, then? Does this mean that every company and organization, by definition, will be mismanaged?

Now that we have defined management, and why the idea executive does not an can not exist and described the styles of normal managers with strengths and weaknesses, we should proceed to describe mismanagement styles that should be avoided, and than we will bc ready to prescribe what good management is and how it works.

NOTES

1. For more details, see Adizes, Ichak: *Corporate Lifecycles* Volumes 1, 2, 3 third and enlarged edition published by Adizes Institute 2004, first edition (Paramus, N.J.: Prentice Hall Press, 1999).

2. Drucker, Peter F.: *Management: Tasks, Responsibilities*, Practices (New York: Harper & Row, 1973), p. 616.

3. Ibid., p. 616.

Chapter 4

Mismanagement Styles

PROBLEM: How do we define mismanagement, and what are its manifestations?

CONFRONTING THE INEVITABLE

As a result of the compatibility issues I described in the previous
chapter, all managers have strengths and weaknesses in their ability
to perform the four key roles. In any person with a managerial task, a
(**PAEI**) role can be completely missing, squeezed out, threatened into
extinction, or never fully developed.

If the (**PAEI**) roles are necessary and together they are sufficient
for good management, then any time any of the four roles is not being performed, what will happen? Mismanagement – a predictable,
repetitive pattern of mismanagement.

In order to simplify comparisons between managerial and mismanagerial behavior, I have chosen to profile five exaggerated archetypes of mismanagement. Why? The difference between normal and
abnormal people is only one of degree. So by studying abnormal
people, whose behavior is so acute that it's readily visible, you learn
to understand what is normal.

Thus, instead of seeing what happens when one role is missing,
I will ask what happens when *one* role is performed and *three* are
missing.

These archetypes – the Lone Ranger, (**P**---); the Bureaucrat.
(-**A**--); the Arsonist, (--**E**-); the SuperFollower, (---**I**); and the Dead-

wood, (----) – represent mismanagers who exhibit none or only one of the four essential elements of management – (**P**)roducing, (**A**)dministrating, (**E**)ntrepreneuring, and (**I**)ntegrating – while failing to meet the threshold needs of the other elements.

Learning to recognize these patterns can be a significant tool in treating the "disease" of mismanagement. It can also help you to analyze the normal and abnormal problems that organizations have over time; guide you in resolving conflict in your organization; and evaluate whether your team is working well together.

The following pages give a short description of each style. For a much more detailed description and analysis, read the second book in this series, *Management/Mismanagement Styles* op.cit.

For prescriptions for how to deal with each style and how to compensate for your own managerial weaknesses, read book 3 in this series.

The Lone Ranger (P---)

What happens when an organization has a manager who is a knowledgeable achiever, a doer, an outstanding (**P**) but no capability to (**A**), (**E**) or (**I**), who functions like the ideal railroad engineer? You show him the track, tell him what stations to go to, give him the train, and off he goes, full speed ahead – through walls if necessary. He is such a good doer, such a good achiever, so diligent, that naturally you promote him to a higher level of management.

That's when the problem arises: He's not an (**A**), not an (**E**), not an (**I**). I don't know why. It's irrelevant. I am only marginally interested in the *why* of behavior. I am mostly interested in *what* that behavior is and *what* to do about it. The fact is that he can't (**A**)dministrate: Organize, coordinate, delegate, follow up, supervise, and control. He's not an (**E**)ntrepreneur: He doesn't come up with new ideas; he's not creative, he dislikes taking risks. And he's not an (**I**)ntegrator: He is not sensitive to interpersonal relations; he doesn't worry about group dynamics or individuals' feelings. He does not relate well to people.

He does not build a team or develop the capabilities of others around him – he is too busy (**P**)roducing.

In the United States he is called The Lone Ranger. In Mexico and in Scandinavia he's called the Lonely Wolf. Every country has a name that reflects the style that might be different but the behavior of that style is identical.

Once he identifies a task, the Lone Ranger is a good soldier. And he will get the job done. That's his advantage: He's loyal, dedicated, and a compulsive doer – but because he overdoes one aspect or role of management to the exclusion of the other roles, he can become a liability.

What are the characteristics that typify a Lone Ranger?

The Lone Ranger focuses on the *what*, not the *how*, not the *who*, not even the *why*. "What do we need to do now? Come on, guys, let's go to it. Let's not waste any more time." He doesn't really care whether he is doing the right thing as long as he is doing *something*.

Does he work hard? Yes, very hard. Too hard. When does he come to work? First one in. When does he leave work? Last one out.

In fact, the Lone Ranger measures his success and his value to the organization by how hard he works. When you ask him, "How are you doing?" his typical answer might be, "I've been working till midnight lately." And "lately," in his case, might be his entire working life!

How is his desk: Clean? Never. It's piled to the ceiling with papers, and somehow, although he's always working hard, he's always behind, always complaining that the day is too short. "The new week has already started, and I haven't even finished last week's work!"

Yet how would he feel if he came to work and found his desk clean and nothing to do? He would panic. Why? Because he's worried when he's not worried. He needs to be constantly doing something.

Over the years, I've discovered that the Lone Ranger is an addict, just like an alcoholic. He is a workaholic.

One of the characteristics of an alcoholic is that he's never far away from a bottle. Similarly, the Lone Ranger is never far away from work. It's 11 o'clock at night; what is he carrying home with him? A briefcase full of work – in case he can't sleep, at least he can do some work.

To a workaholic, going on vacation is a punishment. It's like saying to an alcoholic, "You must go to a dry island for two weeks." That's *scary*. So what will he pack for his vacation? A trunk full of work, like an alcoholic who hides a bottle in his suitcase.

If you say to an alcoholic, "I have a bottle of the best booze there is; what should I do with it?" he's going to say, "Give it to *me*." Similarly, if you go to a Lone Ranger and say, "I have a problem; what should I do with it?" he's going to say, "Put it on my desk." In fact, the more difficult the problem is, the more likely he is to say it.

Those tons of overdue paperwork and projects on the Lone Ranger's desk aren't work. They are all bottles. Bottles, bottles, bottles. Only when he's sure he cannot do a job by himself – only *then* will he delegate. But by then, of course, the problem is already a crisis.

The (**P---**) is like a kid: "Let's go! What's next?" He has only a short-term attention span; he moves quickly from one thing to another, and if it doesn't work out he loses interest and goes on to the next thing. When a new problem is brought to his attention, he drops whatever he was doing and plunges indiscriminately into the new task. In fact, he is always rushing from task to task, from crisis to crisis. The more running around he does, the "better" he thinks he is working.

The Lone Ranger takes things literally: "Yes" means yes, and "no" is no, even if that's not what other people really mean. Lone Rangers do not understand nuances. For them, everything is simple. Everything is literal. Give them a "yes" or a "no"; just don't give them a "maybe."

Lone Rangers hate to deal with uncertainty, with alternatives, with ambiguity. They see everything as either black or white; (**P---**)s are exceedingly uncomfortable with gray. They can't take the pain of sitting in a meeting, thinking things through. They cannot accept that it might take three days to solve a major problem. They want things simple and they want them *now*. Going full speed ahead makes the (**P---**) feel good – even though he might be speeding directly into an abyss.

The (**P---**) prefers doing the job himself to directing others. Let's take a (**P---**) architect as an example. He is such a good architect that eventually he heads his own firm and hires other architects and draftsmen to work for him. But when he comes to work, where do you think he drifts? Does he drift to the accounting department? No! He drifts to the design department. He watches his employees work for a little while; then he says, "OK, let me show you how to do it." And he sits down at the drafting table himself and starts designing.

Why does the Lone Ranger prefer to do everything himself? One reason is that he wants to make sure things are done properly. "If you want to be sure something is done right, you'd better do it yourself," is one of his typical expressions.

Also, he hates being idle; it makes him feel like a parasite. The Lone Ranger measures himself by how hard he works – so if he were to delegate, what would be left for him to do? He needs to be indispensable, to have problems waiting in line for him. He is always rushed, and he likes it that way.

"And just how long have people accused you of being a 'take charge' type?"

The (**P---**) only delegates when it's too late or almost too late. He delegates today what should have been done two weeks ago. That's why he is always in a crisis. His subordinates are hanging around, waiting, coming in late, doing very little. Then all at once there's an emergency: Everybody's running here and there, firefighting. That's why another nickname for the Lone Ranger is the Firefighter.

Lone Ranger types are like bulldogs; they get their teeth around the other dog's neck and lock their jaws and don't let go. They are compulsive about getting the job done unless there is a bigger or graver crisis that needs to be addressed. For them, more is better. They confuse quantity with quality.

And this is also how they treat others. If they want to make something happen, they do not touch, they hit. A (**P---**) will come down on others in a dictatorial style, telling them what to do and when he wants them to do it – "You do it right *now!*" He overdoes it.

By the same token, if you want to convince a (**P**) to change direction, hinting will not work. You'd better hit him with everything you have. A (**P**) will hear you only when you are deafeningly loud.

Managing, to the Lone Ranger, means managing the task, getting the job done. To him, other people are merely tools for serving that goal. As a result, the Lone Ranger is politically naive. He doesn't realize that people's judgments might be colored by their own needs and desires. He can make political blunders that lead you to seriously question his intelligence.

The ultimate do-it-yourselfer, the Lone Ranger hates meetings with a passion. If he is required to come to a meeting, he will come reluctantly.

The same principle applies to the Lone Ranger's own staff meetings: He will avoid them as long as he possible can. "There's too much work to do; I have no time for meetings." If you force him to hold meetings, he'll probably initiate a conversation, one-to-one, very likely standing in the hallway on his way to somewhere else, and he'll call that a meeting. Because he's addicted to e-mail and voice mail, he truly believes that leaving messages or short instructions are sufficient for fostering teamwork, and are certainly a fine alternative to those time-consuming meetings.

The Lone Ranger's subordinates are the same everywhere, though their nicknames vary from one country to another. In the television series "The Lone Ranger," the subordinate was called Tonto. In the United States, they are called gofers. In Mexico, they are called *inginiero ibeme*, which means, "Go bring me something." In Israel, they are called errand boys.

Since the Lone Ranger cannot do everything himself, he uses his subordinates as "expediters" who assist him with errands and short-term assignments but have no permanent, long-term responsibilities. These people spend most of their time waiting to be summoned to deal with the next crisis – for which they generally have no experience or training. These gofers and errand boys are not always low-level managers. In many companies, top vice presidents are gofers for a Lone Ranger. I once worked in a developing nation with a Prime Minister whose style was predominately (**P**). He had cabinet ministers waiting in the corridors, never knowing when they might be summoned in.

When do these gofers come to work? Late. When do they leave? Early. What do they do in the meantime? They wait.

Does the Lone Ranger delegate to his subordinates? No. When you ask him, "Why don't you delegate?" he responds, "They can't do it. They're not ready. They're not prepared."

"How long have they worked for you?"

"25 years."

"So why don't you train them?"

"I have no time to train them."

"Why don't you have time to train them?"

"Because I have no one to delegate to."

Because everything has to go through him, the Lone Ranger inevitably becomes a bottleneck. Since he has limited time, not everything gets done and things get lost on his desk.

The (**P---**) sees no value in the systematic *ex catedra* classroom training of subordinates. He prefers the apprenticeship approach: Subordinates learn how to perform a task by watching him do it himself. "In this business there aren't any secrets; just get the job done," he insists. "If someone is willing to work hard, he should have no problem getting the job done."

The Lone Ranger has a very limited, short-term perspective; he sees only the nearest horizon. Thus he is typically an improviser – "All right, let's get going! Does it work? Done! *Finito*! Go! Next!" He won't take the time to pay attention to the larger questions: What is ultimately needed? What are the details that are necessary to make it work? His view of time is that it should be used to solve the immediate problems of the organization. He has no concern for "ten years down the pike," and is always promising to plan later, "after I finish clearing my desk." But of course that never happens.

The organization that a Lone Ranger manages cannot grow, since he is not growing. He is inflexible and simple-minded. He can easily burn out and become obsolete. When he leaves a company, he leaves untrained people behind.

THE BUREAUCRAT (-A--)

What happens if a manager is exclusively (**A**)-oriented? Zero (**P**), zero (**E**), zero (**I**). An (-**A**--).

What is the (-**A**--) interested in? While the Lone Ranger – the (**P**---) – is exclusively interested in *what*, the (-**A**--) is only interested in *how*. That's why I call him a Bureaucrat: "Never mind what we do; it's *how* we do it that counts."

Bureaucrats tend to rise in their organizations by following the rules, often to the point of excess. A Bureaucrat may be the easiest to spot of the four mismanagement types. Certainly he is one of the easiest to satirize.

In literature, there's a great example of a Bureaucrat. Captain Queeg, in Herman Wouk's novel *The Caine Mutiny*, has risen through the ranks of the Navy, not because he was especially competent at leading a crew or running a ship, but because he followed the rules. He says so himself:

> *"Now, I'm a book man, as anyone who knows me will*
> *tell you. … When in doubt, remember we do things on this*
> *ship by the book. You go by the book and you'll get no argument*
> *from me. You deviate from the book and you better have a half*
> *dozen damn good reasons – and you'll still get a hell of an*
> *argument from me."* [1]

What are the characteristics that typify an (-**A**--) type, or Bureaucrat?

The Bureaucrat spends an excessive amount of time worrying about (**A**)dministrative details. He prefers to do things right rather than do the right things. In other words, he would rather be precisely wrong than approximately right.

Here's a joke that will illustrate this point: I was flying over Brazil some years ago. Sitting next to me was a leading accountant from a leading accounting firm, a big (**Λ**). We were looking through the window, and we saw the Amazon River. He said, "Dr. Adizes, did you know that this river is a billion years and seven months old?"

"How did you get a billion years and seven months old?" I asked, amazed.

"Well, seven months ago someone told me it was a billion years old."

Bureaucrats pay attention to the form, to the number to the very last digit – at the expense of the total picture. The Bureaucrat may be focused on the wrong market, the wrong product – the wrong direction! – but his reports always look very good because the numbers are calculated to the third decimal.

If you ask a Bureaucrat to give you a report analyzing whether your company should try to penetrate the New York market, he'll say, "Sure," and disappear for a while. He'll accumulate data and analyze it ad infinitum. But by the time he comes back with his recommendation, that market may already have been claimed by your competitor.

Why? Because the Bureaucrat prefers not to take risks. He does not want to be embarrassed by making the wrong decision. He wants everything safe and organized. He's precisely wrong. He's running a very well-controlled disaster: The company is going broke, but on time.

"The motion has been made and seconded that we obey the law."

When does he come to work? On time. When does he leave work? On time. How is his desk? Clean, all in neat piles.

He wants everything to be perfect and under control, and he is capable of spending an inordinate amount of time and money on a marginal control that is really not worth it. Such demanding perfectionism can suffocate a company.

While the Lone Ranger focuses exclusively on function, assuming the form will follow, the Bureaucrat behaves as if he believes that form produces function. Now, sometimes that is true; military leaders assume that the form produces the function, that if you polish your shoes and shave exactly as required and hold your head exactly as required and march exactly as required, when the time comes and they tell you to go and attack and sacrifice your life, you will run and do exactly as instructed. So the form will produce the function.

But here is the danger: Sometimes the form is so inflexible that it will *not* produce the function. That's why partisans and guerrilla forces invariably defeat organized establishment armies: They rely more on (**I**) than on (**A**) in asking people to put their lives on the line.

The Bureaucrat has an organizational chart readily accessible – if it is not on paper it is in his head. He has no trouble finding any of the organization's rules or procedures at a moment's notice. He manages by means of directives, usually in writing. Even when violations are necessary to produce the right results, he won't tolerate his subordinates' breaking the rules.

The (**-A--**)'s free time is spent looking for new transgressions against the system. When he finds one, he designs a new form, a new report, or a new policy that will prevent the transgression from being repeated.

Like the Lone Ranger, the Bureaucrat is very literal-minded. An (**-A--**) needs to see something for himself in order to believe it. Unlike an (**E**)ntrepreneur, who can look at shapes through the fog and discern an elephant, an (**-A--**) will not infer anything. A big ear and a big leg and a big back do not add up to an elephant, until the fog rises. Even then, he'll want to touch it and smell it before he's totally convinced.

"I'm sorry, dear, but you knew I was a bureucrat when you married me."

Bureaucrats are also prone to what I call "manualitis": Everything is documented, processes are monotonously described step by step, and the written word begins to dominate the organization's behavior.

People who are managed by an (-**A**--) spend an enormous amount of time reading memos and writing memos and filing memos and responding to memos. This cuts down efficiency tremendously.

A Bureaucrat knows the cost of everything but the value of nothing, for the following reason: The cost is for sure, the value is maybe. He will tell you, "We cannot do this, it's too expensive." But the truth is that very often the cost of *not* doing may be higher than the cost of doing. I'll give you an American expression that exemplifies this principle: "If you think education is expensive, think of the alternative."

But an (-**A**--) will prefer not to take the risk or spend the money. He will waste precious time gathering more information and more details and more justifications and more studies and more analyses – all to minimize risk. But time costs money, and meanwhile the opportunity will slip away.

The Bureaucrat can subvert the goals of the organization through his insistence on observing the letter of the law, even when departures from it are essential. His primary and often exclusive commitment is to the implementation of a plan, regardless of its wisdom or even its ethics.

At his 1961 trial in Jerusalem for implementing the genocide of European Jewry, Adolf Eichmann's defense was a morbid and extreme example of this type of behavior. Eichmann described his role in the Third Reich as having been "an administrator of trains." The fact that at one end of the railway line were the victims and their homes, and at the other end were the extermination camps, did not preoccupy him.

Bureaucrats frequently have difficulty revisiting a decision during the implementation phase. "We decided," he'll say. "We spent a lot of time on this decision. We spent a lot of money on it. We are not going to open this chapter again!" Unfortunately, the world often changes even faster than you can implement a plan to adapt to the changes. A typical Bureaucrat resists such change.

While the Lone Ranger evaluates himself by how hard he works and by the results he achieves, the Bureaucrat evaluates himself by how well he *controls* the system and by his success in eliminating deviations and minimizing uncertainty. Because of this, he tends to be a crowning example of Parkinson's law.[2] He gets increasing numbers of subordinates to implement the same task, trying to control every detail, without achieving any apparent increase in productivity.

Bureaucrats are linear thinkers: A, B, C, D, E, F, G. They do not understand that sometimes G relates to H and H relates to A and A relates to J and J relates to B. They get very upset when they perceive a discussion as getting out of order. Discussions do need to be open to lots of different options, but an (-**A**--) can't see that.

The Bureaucrat hires people like himself – people who do as they are told and will not take the initiative. They do not ask questions that challenge the status quo; they avoid rocking the boat.

I call the Bureaucrat's subordinates yes-yes men, or office clerks. But although they have a clerk mentality, they are not necessarily clerks. They could be vice presidents earning $100,000 a year or more. Regardless, they have to come on time, leave on time, and do everything by the book.

There's even a joke about this kind of subordinate: A new person arrives in Hell and is sent to a bureaucratic department in Hell to work. When he gets there he finds that all the other workers are standing in fecal matter up to their lips. Horrified, he asks, "How do you work here?"

"Just don't make waves!" is the reply.

Why? Because the Bureaucrat's subordinates know that if a problem is revealed, the Bureaucrat is going to have to find out who did it, why, how, where, and when. In a word, there is going to be a witch-hunt.

Does the Bureaucrat hold staff meetings? You bet your life: Every Monday and Friday from 9 to 12. Secretaries take minutes; the last meeting's conclusions are discussed and verified as to their implementation. There is order, and along with it there is boredom with the myriad details that the Bureaucrat insists on covering.

Does he have an agenda? Absolutely. In detail. Does the agenda deal with important subjects? Not necessarily. The company might be losing market share, even going bankrupt, but the Bureaucrat will be droning on about the need to fill out the necessary forms in duplicate and on time.

The Bureaucrat loves training. He wishes he could program everybody and make every process a routine.

Change, to a Bureaucrat, is a threat of major proportions. His ingenuity in finding reasons to discourage new projects makes him an obstructionist. The organization has to achieve its goals in spite of him, and those in the organization who are committed to getting things done will quickly learn to bypass him in trying to implement change.

What is an (-A--)'s typical answer when a subordinate asks for permission to do something different? "No." Before you even finish the sentence: "No." Here is a typical Bureaucrat on the phone (this is a Russian joke): "No. No. No. Yes. No. No. No."

"What was that one 'yes' about?" you ask.

"He asked me if I heard him clearly."

Under the Bureaucrat, strategic planning is at best an exercise in forecasting, and quite often it simply analyzes the past and projects it into the future.

So what is next year's budget or goal? "What we are sure we can achieve. How about some sure number above the one we reached last year?" is the Bureaucrat's typical approach.

By the time an (-**A**--) is eliminated from an organization, that organization may have become so mired in regulations and rules that it will have difficulty adapting to long overdue changes, either internally or externally or both.

THE ARSONIST (--**E**-)

What happens if the (**E**)ntrepreneurial role is performed exclusively, and the other three roles are not? This manager's efforts would consist entirely of innovating, just charging at any target that appears on his organizational horizon.

This is the type of mismanager I am most familiar with, because I usually work with CEO's and company founders, who are strong in the (**E**) role. I call him the Arsonist.

What are the characteristics that typify an Arsonist?

What we do is not important. *How* we do it is not important either. The Arsonist is concerned with *why not*. Change. Ideas.

When does the Arsonist come to work? Who knows? When does he leave work? Who knows? When do his subordinates come to work? Before him; by the time he comes to work they'd better be there. When do they leave work? Right after him. I've seen vice presidents working for this type of mismanager – it's seven, eight, nine o'clock at night; there's nothing to do, but they can't leave, because if they leave what might happen? The boss might call a meeting: "Drop everything you're doing. Everybody to the meeting room, right now."

Do his meetings have an agenda? If they do, nobody knows what it is. And if there is an agenda he violates it anyway, moving from subject to subject at will. Nevertheless, he expects people to be prepared for the meeting.

Luckily for them, who does all the talking in these meetings? He does.

Meanwhile, what do his subordinates do? There is a joke that illustrates their behavior. It is an ethnic joke but I don't think it's in bad taste. I hope I am not offending anyone.

Italians are known as great lovers and for their music and food – but not for their military accomplishments. The smallest book ever written is titled *Italian Military Accomplishments*. Now, the joke:

It is the First World War. The Italian soldiers are in the trenches, ready to attack. Out of the trenches emerges the captain – in a beautiful blue uniform with red sashes, all the decorations, golden epaulets, hats and feathers. He looks dashing. He pulls out his sword and shouts: "*Avaaaaaaaantiiiiii!*"

What do the soldiers do? They clap hands and shout: "*Bravooooooo!*" But nobody gets out of the trenches.

Why? Because an Arsonist doesn't say, "Attack in *this* direction!" He says, "Attack in *this* direction, *that* direction, that *other* direction, and that *fourth* direction." All simultaneously.

Who usually gets out of the trenches and attacks? Only the people who are new to the organization. Those with some experience know there is no use in getting out of the trenches and attacking. Very soon, the (--**E**-) will change direction or decide on a new strategy.

So what can the soldiers do? They stay in the trenches and shout "*Bravooooooo!*" And when they're asked, "Are you attacking?" their typical answer is "We're working on it."

Here is another analogy: Picture an organization as an axle. There is a big wheel at one end (in English, "a big wheel" even has a corporate meaning) and a small wheel at the other end. When the big wheel makes one revolution, the small wheel must turn many times. If the big wheel is an Arsonist, he will frequently change direction while the smaller wheels are still in motion. Eventually the gears of the smaller wheels are stripped and the axle breaks down. The big wheel is left spinning alone.

But the (--**E**-) does not realize that he himself is responsible for the breakdown. Instead, he thinks, "Somebody must be undermining my efforts." He becomes paranoid and looks for someone to blame.

Still, the Arsonist is usually very likable, because he is stimulating, enterprising, and full of energy. Working for him can be exciting – until you figure out that no matter what you do the Arsonist will find fault with it, because his priorities are continually changing; before you've completed one project, he wants to know why you haven't made any progress on a new one.

The Arsonist likes chaos: He loves to witness the furor that his initiatives cause. He seeks maximum short-run impact, and he obtains it by generating crises.

Under such managers, projects are always being completed under pressure. The staff is forced to work overtime and crucial details remain in a state of flux right up to the last minute.

Details are the Arsonist's Achilles heel. The (--**E**-) tends to ignore details; he works with a big brush on a wide canvas, as if he were looking down from 40,000 feet at a topographical map. For an (--**E**-), a million is somewhere between 700,000 and a million and a half – while for an (-**A**--), 999,999 is not the same as a million. You can see why (**E**)s and (**A**)s don't communicate well.

Picture the (--**E**-) as an eagle, flying thousands of feet over the mountains and seeing the big picture but not the small details. From up there everything looks simple; with one movement of its wings it can fly from one boulder to another. The eagle cannot comprehend that down on the ground, in order to make the move from one location to the other, you have to go up and down mountains and canyons.

Arsonists act out of emotion and nervous energy; very often it's negative energy. They have a huge need to build something new, which often means destroying what's already in place. In order to "own" their idea, they feel they have to start from scratch or change what is there even if it is more than adequate already.

Because they create on the run, Arsonists often contradict themselves: The mouth is talking, the mind is working, but there isn't necessarily a connection. An (--**E**-) often says, "It's too late to disagree with me; I've already changed my mind." He starts with one angle, and changes to another angle and then a third angle, and eventually you can't follow what he's saying.

Yet not being understood upsets and offends Arsonists, and they can react with unbelievable hostility when their argument is challenged or even when inconsistencies are pointed out.

An Arsonist habitually works on the "why don't we?" principle: "Why don't we do this?" "Why don't we do that?" But what is a mere question for an (--**E**-) is assumed to be a decision by his subordinates, especially the (**P**)s. Sometimes the (**P**) subordinates believe the boss has made a decision, so they begin to implement it and then they get penalized for acting without authorization. Then, the next time the (--**E**-) thinks out loud, his subordinates don't act, thinking that this, too, is just an idea. The Arsonist then becomes upset – this time because the staff *didn't* implement his instructions. Subordinates feel they can never satisfy him, no matter what they do or don't do.

Of the four types, the (--**E**-) is the worst listener. Why? Because he's full of ideas and it's so easy to trigger more. Anything you say might trigger a chain of thought in him, and while he's developing the little seed you planted, he's so busy listening to himself that he doesn't hear what else you are saying.

In conversation, the Arsonist is emotional and expressive. He uses words like "never," "always," "impossible." He exaggerates in order to really push his ideas through.

In a company managed by an Arsonist, Monday mornings are dangerous, because over the weekend the Arsonist has had time to think; and guess what? New directions, new priorities, new goals, new objectives.

Ironically, however, not much happens in a company run by an Arsonist, because he doesn't like to finalize anything; even in mid-change he might change things again in yet another, "better" direction. Every idea leads to another idea. He does not understand that by adding an idea, he's diminishing the value of other ideas because there's a limit to how much one person or one company can handle.

Nor does he measure the cost of his plans against their value. The opposite of the Bureaucrat, the (--**E**-) "knows the value of everything, but the cost of nothing." An (--**E**-) is always talking about the brilliant innovations he's going to make. But how much will they cost? "These are details," he'll shrug. That is why an Arsonist can build a big company and lose it overnight.

The Arsonist cares about the process, the novelty – not necessarily the results. He is interested in the why not, whereas the Lone Ranger is interested in the what and the Bureaucrat in the how. The Arsonist typically will develop fantastic ideas and then expect others to figure out how to implement them. If he is pressed for specifics, he gets annoyed.

Arsonists do not play well with others. If you give an (--**E**-) an idea, he immediately says, "No, I don't agree with you," but then next week he will give you back the same idea, rephrased, as if he'd thought of it himself. That makes people very upset.

Arsonists are often seen as narcissistic, self-centered trouble-makers. They always act like they know best. They are constantly giving advice and can hardly stand to take it. But the truth is, they need a tremendous amount of approval and applause.

It takes a very strong person to work with an Arsonist, and yet (--**E**-)s tend to surround themselves with weak people. Why? Because an (--**E**-) has to win every argument, and a weak subordinate will never challenge him.

If the Lone Ranger's subordinates are gofers and the Bureaucrat's subordinates are yes-yes men, the typical subordinates of the Arsonist are claques. Claques (it's a French word; in Mexico they are called *palleros*) are the hired hands in opera houses who are paid to start clapping when a singer ends an aria, to encourage the rest of the audience to clap as well.

Claques are paid to agree with the Arsonist's ideas, at least in public. The result is that the Arsonist invariably receives tumultuous applause, but it isn't real.

The Arsonist's subordinates learn not to reject his plans outright, because he will interpret a rejection of his ideas as a rejection of himself. Thus, the subordinates are forced to accept tasks that they already know are impractical. They come up with creative excuses instead, trying to appear cooperative without actually cooperating.

The Arsonist's typical complaint about his staff is, "Nobody understands me." No one is following his priorities; he feels he's surrounded by idiots. The following unattributed aphorism was probably first said by an Arsonist: "It is difficult to soar like an eagle when you surrounded by turkeys."

"Treat people as equals and the first thing you know they believe they are."

Sometimes the Arsonist will go through successive stages of firing and then bring in someone new. For a little while, he thinks this new kid on the block is a genius: "Look at him! Look how good he is!" He walks on water – for a while. Six months later, the Arsonist has become convinced that this man does not understand his genius either – and he's gone.

Still, (--**E**-)s dislike firing people personally.. They prefer to get a hatchet man to do the firing or, more often, they'll make your life so miserable that you'll eventually resign. They demean you, put you down, criticize you in public, humiliate you. They force you to resign and then accuse you of disloyalty. But they personally don't usually fire.

For the Arsonist, planning does not mean committing the organization to a course of action. Planning means making long lists of ephemeral goals. Whereas the Lone Ranger rarely takes the time to plan at all, and the Bureaucrat derives next year's budget by adding some percentage to last year's results, the Arsonist may not even have a budget, and if he does it is usually unrealistic.

The Arsonist is so preoccupied with opportunities that he sees few if any threats. He can endanger an organization by recklessly trying to exploit too many opportunities at once and spreading himself and his organization too thin.

One might expect to find creativity throughout an organization managed by an Arsonist, but in fact the opposite is usually true. An organization managed by an Arsonist is not a creative, flexible structure but a slave ship. The Arsonist sets the course, changes direction, ignores the suffering of his subordinates, and takes all the credit for successes.

Because he is bored by details, the Arsonist's attitude and preferences are to decentralize. But it's equally important for him to maintain control of the decision-making process. The result is a catch-22 for his subordinates. They are *expected* to decide – as long as their decisions coincide with the decision *he* would have made. But they don't know what he would have decided, because he keeps changing his mind. For his subordinates, that decision is a moving target, and the result is paralysis.

Like the Bureaucrat, who is so focused on efficiency that he over-does the controls and creates an inefficient bureaucracy; and, like the Lone Ranger, who wants so much to be effective that he does it all by himself, thus creating an ineffective organization; the Arsonist is so exclusively focused on causing change that he creates paralysis.

When the (--**E**-) leaves, the organization is a shambles and its people are exhausted. They're desperate for peace and quiet, for stability. As a result, they usually ask for, and eventually get stuck with, a Bureaucrat.

THE SUPERFOLLOWER (---I)

How would a manager function if he were deficient in the areas of (**P**)roducing, (**A**)dministrating, and (**E**)ntrepreneuring and were only capable of (**I**)ntegrating?

What is he mostly concerned about? He's interested in *who*. He doesn't care *what* we agree about, nor *how* we agree about it, nor *why* we agree. The important thing is: "*Do* we agree?" I call him the SuperFollower.

What are the characteristics that typify a SuperFollower?

He's not a leader. He's the one who asks, "Where would you like to go? Let me lead you there."

An (---**I**) accommodates endlessly. He wants everything to run smoothly. He tries to find out what plan will be acceptable to the largest number of powerful people. In other words, he does not really lead – he follows. That's why I call him a SuperFollower.

The SuperFollower is like a fish monitoring the undercurrent, always seeking the right tide to join. He's a politician, always listening to what is going on, trying to sense the undercurrent.

What is the difference between a politician and a statesman? The statesman worries about the next generation, while the politician worries about the next election. The SuperFollower is not concerned about the future as much as he worries about present support for his political standing. "Do we agree?" is his motto. He might be running a very happy disaster. He negotiates an *appearance* of agreement rather than resolving the deep-seated issues that cause conflict.

The SuperFollower welcomes any training – *if* it improves his ability to understand human nature or contributes to the appearance of unity. He rejects any solution that creates heat, even if it's necessary for the company's success.

If the SuperFollower has free time, he spends it socializing, listening to complaints or agreements and then amplifying and accentuating them with his support.

It's difficult to get a SuperFollower to commit to a point of view. In Mexico, they call this type of manager "the soapy fish," because you just can't catch him. He always has some way to slip away; he always wiggles out of your hands. His typical complaint is: "You really didn't understand what I really wanted to say …" "What I really meant to say is …" You can't corner him. That's how he remains in power for a long time: He figures out which side is winning and adapts himself to that side.

The SuperFollower doesn't tell you what he thinks; he asks you what you think. He's noncommittal. He might say something like, "I have an idea, but I'm not so sure I agree with it," or "I suggest we declare dividends, but I don't feel too strongly about it." He is launching trial balloons to see where everyone else stands before he makes any commitment; he wants to see which way the wind is blowing. This makes him a perfect weathervane: If you want to know which changes will most likely be accepted and which will not, watch him.

The SuperFollower tends to avoid making decisions as long as he can. He has no ideas of his own that he would like to implement – no (**E**); no tangible results that he wants to achieve – no (**P**). Unlike an (**A**), he is indifferent to any particular system, as long as agreement is achieved or is *seen* to be achieved.

Because he lacks strong convictions, his mind can be changed quickly and easily. He sways along with popular opinion.

At meetings, the SuperFollower is the one who is listening very attentively. Who is saying what? What does the speaker *really* mean? What is *not* being said? Where does the power lie? Which way is the decision likely to go?

The SuperFollower does not grasp that it is better to have a mediocre decision implemented than an outstanding decision never implemented. If the SuperFollower is chairing a meeting and a consensus cannot be achieved, he will probably postpone the decision by establishing a subcommittee to study the problem further. In reality, he is waiting for a political consensus to emerge. But his procrastination can have a high price. While he waits, opportunities disappear. Sometimes the consensus he's waiting for will not surface until the situation has become a crisis and the organization's survival is at risk.

An (---I) also has trouble comprehending that once people agree, that does not necessarily mean they are actually going to implement a decision. They may appear to be agreeing in order to show political loyalty, but if in reality they feel their concerns and interests have not been fully addressed, they may actually try to undermine the plan.

The SuperFollower hires people like himself, who are politically intuitive; they have a good nose for how the political power base is moving. They are the first to identify it and to jump on the band-wagon. What do they spend their time on? "What's going on?" "Who said what?" "What does it mean?" "Where is the power base?" I call them informers, or oilers.

Their main job is to keep the boss up-to-date and make sure everybody is happy. It is their duty to feed the boss the latest office "news"; no gossip is too insignificant to relate.

The SuperFollower's subordinates know that loyalty to him is paramount if they want to be promoted. In his presence, the (---**I**)'s subordinates appear peaceful and accepting, remembering that their boss prefers people whom other people like. This often requires them to keep their true feelings hidden from him, which can easily lead to their feeling manipulated and emotionally exploited.

The SuperFollower has no particular goal; or rather, the goal is whatever is most desired at a particular time by a consensus of his co-workers. This is, of course, a very limited attitude toward corporate goals, and as a result, short-range interest groups and cliques flourish under the SuperFollower.

When a SuperFollower leaves an organization, the superficial (**I**)ntegration he established will rapidly deteriorate. At that point, an (**A**)dministrator is often called in to resolve the problem. This solution can be traumatic, as it replaces the (**I**)ntegration of people, the development of appropriate compromises, with a rigid set of regulations to force order.

Or sometimes a (**P**)roducer is called in to inject some energy and clarity, and to clean up the confusion that the SuperFollower's political maneuvering has created over the years. But any change of styles is stressful, because people must change their behavior and learn to follow different organizational cues to be successful.

THE COMMON DENOMINATOR

For all their differences, the four mismanagerial styles, (**P**---), (-**A**--), (--**E**-), and (---**I**), have one trait in common: They are all inflexible stereotypes. The managers who exhibit these styles have uni-dimensional, one-track minds. They have only a limited perception of who they are and of what they are supposed to do in life.[3] They are not well–rounded individuals.

Anyone who exhibits an exclusive, single-role management style is in danger of becoming Deadwood (----), a fanatic, or a martyr.

THE DEADWOOD (----)

Each of the previous styles of mismanagement were three quarters deadwood (**P**---),(-**A**--),(--**E**-) and (---**I**).

When change happens, a mismanager can either adapt or "die" – that is, become Deadwood, with a (**PAEI**) code that looks like this: (----). The mismanagers loose the only role they could produce. The Lone Ranger is not a person with twenty years of experience. He is a person with one year of experience repeated twenty times. He does not train his subordinates nor himself. The (-**A**--) manages by the book, Change the books and see the bureaucrat turn into a deadwood. The (---**E**-) as an Arsonist starts one fire too many and looses it all and the (---**I**), when there is need for real time decision that might need some arm twisting to implement, looks for consensus that takes time, is ignored and pushed aside. He too turns to be deadwood.

The common denominator is: *Change*. One track minds in time of change loose the only track they have.

Deadwood is agreeable, friendly, and non-threatening. He is liked, much as a friendly old uncle is liked, but he is not respected. So people endure him and do not want to hurt him. In the meantime, the organization suffers.

Deadwood is apathetic. He waits to be told what to do. He might work hard, like the Lone Ranger, but the results are not there; he does not get involved with power intrigues, like the SuperFollower; he does not provide sparks, as does the Arsonist. If he has any good ideas or opinions, he keeps them to himself. Unlike the Bureaucrat, Deadwood cares about following the rules only insofar as doing so will help him survive until retirement.

His only goal is to keep intact the little world he has created. He knows that any change threatens his position. To maximize his chances for survival, he avoids change by avoiding new jobs or projects. He does not resist anything. Resisting will expose him and make him vulnerable. So he agrees to everything and takes action on nothing.

DUNAGIN'S PEOPLE - By Ralph Dunagin

"And I remind you that I have served you for two terms without causing any harm."

In his free time, the Deadwood looks for successes that he can take credit for. He is usually out of the information network, but if he does get access to any information, he cherishes it and uses it at every conceivable opportunity, even when it's irrelevant – just to prove that he's still plugged in and kicking.

Four characteristics mark Deadwood as distinct from any other mismanagement style:

No. 1: "Low managerial metabolism"

Deadwood very likely started out as one of the other four types of mismanagers, and he still evinces his former dominant personality traits. One can still see in him traces of the enthusiastic Arsonist or the meticulous Bureaucrat. But by the time he has become Deadwood, his No. 1 characteristic is a "low managerial metabolism."

He smokes or drinks a lot. He coughs, hums, and nods his head in agreement – "Uh huh"; "Oh yes, sure"; he confides to you how well he is doing, or how well he did in the past, or how well he will do, but nothing is happening. He is only going through the motions.

No. 2: Deadwood has no complaints

Each of the previous four types has a typical complaint: "The day is too short" (**P**); "It's not being done the way it should be done" (**A**); "The most urgent priorities are not being followed" (**E**); "They did not understand what I really wanted to say" (**I**).

Deadwood? If you ask him, "How is it going? Any problems?"

"No, no! Everything is fine."

To be alive is to be always working on something. That is how you grow and develop. You're trying to resolve or improve something. If there are no problems, then there are no opportunities either.

But Deadwood thinks a complaint would reflect badly on him or perhaps result in changes he cannot handle. He might actually be asked to solve the problems he is complaining about. To avoid threats to his existence, he never complains.

No. 3: No resistance to change

Each of the other styles will resist change for one reason or another. If you go to the Lone Ranger and say, "This item needs to move from here to there," what will he say? "I have no time. When am I going to do it? I am so busy, I'm falling apart!"

If you go to the Bureaucrat and say, "We need to move this item from here to there," he's going to yell "No!" before you even finish the sentence. He will tell you there is no way to move this item – "*unless*" – and the "unless" will be so complicated that you will either give up trying to get it done, or else do it without telling him about it. He "knows the cost of everything but the value of nothing;" he sees the possible repercussions of change, but not its potential value.

Now let us go to the Arsonist. "We would like to move this item from here to there." The Arsonist says, "What a great idea! A fantastic idea! But you know what? While you're moving this item from here to there, why don't you move this other item as well from there to here, and also take this third item and put it over here, and then drop that building down …" His technique for approving change is to insist that it has to be his idea. And usually it is not one idea but a whole lot of them, and some of them are pretty bad.

Now we come to the SuperFollower: "We'd like to move this item from here to there."

"That is a great idea," he'll say. "I am really proud of you for coming up with that idea. But you know what? It's not the right time; the people are not ready yet. Let's wait and see. Let us think about it a bit more."

In contrast, if you go to the Deadwood and say, "We would like to move New York to the Sahara," he'll say, "Sure. Great idea. Let's do it." He'll show *no* resistance.

A year later, if you ask him how the project to move New York to the Sahara is going, he'll tell you, "We hired consultants. We have researched the subject; we have a study. We have a committee working on it."

Everything is being done except one thing: Not a pebble from New York has been moved anywhere. He will have reams of papers, reports, studies to show he is working on it, but there will be movement. Why? Because he will take no risk of failing and whenever you do anything new that risk always exists.

The irony is, the person I'm describing is every manager's favorite subordinate! You say, "How's it going?" He says, "No problem; everything is fine." You give him an assignment; he says, "Sure." This is the person you always wanted, right? You don't want someone who says, "No, that can't be done," or "I have no time," or "That's the wrong thing to do." You want someone who says, "Fine," no matter what.

But think about it: Where is the quietest place in the city, where no one ever complains?

The cemetery.

No. 4: Deadwood's subordinates

Who works for Deadwood? Other Deadwood.

Why? First of all, Deadwood's hiring practices reflect his strategy for survival. He favors not-so-bright subordinates, even to the point of promoting those who produce less than he does. He wants to survive; he certainly does not want his job security threatened by a too-competent subordinate who could replace him. Like the adage says, "First-class people hire first-class people. Second-class people hire third-class people."

Also, any subordinates who wish to grow and develop are completely frustrated by a Deadwood manager. He does not grow, nor does he let anyone under him grow. Either the Deadwood's subordinates get out, or they mentally die in their jobs, becoming Deadwood too.

Even those who are not quite Deadwood themselves can create full-fledged Deadwood. The gofers who work for the Lone Ranger and the yes-yes clerks who work for the Bureaucrat become Deadwood. The claques who work for the Arsonist eventually learn to suppress their own aspirations; they learn to make lots of noise but do very little. They become Deadwood.

The SuperFollower's subordinates become Deadwood, too. They are never sure what really needs to be done, and they become sick and tired of the politics, so they give up and just follow. Where? Nowhere, since the SuperFollower gives no direction.

The worst disaster is to have Deadwood at the top of an organization. He no longer wants to change; he is happy with what he's previously accomplished. Although such management sometimes tries to disguise itself as conservative, it is in fact moribund.

Deadwood almost never leave an organization on their own; either they die on the job, or they retire, or they are fired. They aren't missed, but by the time they leave, the organization is usually dead as well. No purposeful activity, no creativity, no (**I**)ntegration of people is evident.

WHAT NOW?

So here we are. We can see why the old paradigm of individualistic, ideal management is a futile search for the nonexistent. No one is perfect. Most of us humans are, more or less, mismanagers.

Does this mean that every organization everywhere in the world has to be mismanaged?

Let us see.

NOTES

1. Wouk, Herman: *The Caine Mutiny* (New York: Bantam Doubleday Dell, 1951), p.131

2. "Work expands so as to fill the time available for its completion." C. Northcote Parkinson, *Parkinson's Law: The Pursuit of Progress* (London: John Murray,1958).

3. I am grateful to Bob Tannenbaum of UCLA for having directed my attention to this common characteristic.

Chapter 5

Working Together

PROBLEM: If the roles are incompatible but we need them together nevertheless, what should we do?

THE WORKABLE ALTERNATIVE: A COMPLEMENTARY TEAM

If the ideal manager, executive or leader is non-existent, then what should we be looking for?

We know that in order to make decisions that create and maintain effective and efficient organizations in the short and long run, four roles must be performed. Every company needs individuals who possess the (**E**)ntrepreneurial and (**I**)ntegrating qualities that can guide a united organization into new courses of action; (**A**)dministrators who can translate the ideas of the (**E**)ntrepreneurs into operative systems that (**P**)roduce results; and (**P**)roducers who go and make it happen – in short, (**PAEI**).

But we also know that the four roles are incompatible; it's very difficult to be result-oriented and at the same time to be detail- and efficiency-oriented; a visionary; and finally people-oriented. It's too much to ask. We know that kind of manager exists only in textbooks.

We described what happens when only one role is being performed and the other roles are not: You get pathological extremes like the Lone Ranger, the Bureaucrat, the Arsonist, and the Superfollower.

But it is possible to find good managers who have mastered at least one role and meet the minimum needs of the others. I would code such managers as at least a (**Paei**), or (**P**)roducer; a (**pAei**), or (**A**)dministrator; a (**paEi**), or (**E**)ntrepreneur; and a (**paeI**), or (**I**)ntegrator.

Thus, in order to have good management, organizations must realize and accept a new paradigm, based on the reality that a group effort among people with complementary styles is the only workable solution. We need a team of leaders, managers, executives, whose styles are different, who complement each other, who can work together and balance one another's biases, who excel in at least one of the four roles which are different from each other, and who are above the minimum threshold of competence in the other roles. Instead of talking about a single individual who manages it all the roles of (**P**)roducing, (**A**)dministrating, (**E**)ntrepreneuring, and (**I**)ntegrating must be fulfilled by a *complementary* managerial team, because no one person can perform them all.

I want to emphasize the word *complementary*, because normally when I say to a manager, "We need a team," he replies, "Yes, you're right. I am going to hire several more people like me."

That is not a team. That is cloning.

Look at your hand. Every finger is different. The pointing finger is the most flexible and versatile; few would consider the fourth finger, the "ring finger," to be as functional. But can you imagine a hand composed of *five* pointing fingers? It would not work as well. What makes a hand a hand is that every finger is different and that they complement each other.

Hiring more people like ourselves, no matter how skilled we are, isn't a good idea either. We need to hire people who complement us where we are weak – and we are *all* weak in some area! We need a team in which the members are *different* from each other, not similar to each other as far as their style is concerned.

And when I use the word "team" of people whose styles are different, I'm not talking about hiring somebody who *knows* marketing and somebody else who *knows* finance and a third person who *knows* accounting. These are differences in knowledge. I'm talking about differentiation in style, in behavior. We need diversity of styles, not only of religion or color or gender or race, etc. Each person's style should complement the others' by balancing their naturally biased judgments. If a team is composed of people whose judgments are all the same, the team is very vulnerable. If it is completely incompatible, it's also vulnerable. What makes a team strong and viable is when it has different styles which act united.[1]

If you analyze the history of any successful organization, you will see that its success was due to a team of people whose styles, behavior, and needs were different but who worked together well nevertheless. Although organizational success is usually attributed to one person, there is almost always a team behind that person that enables him or her to perform well.

For example, many people think of the Ford Motor Company as Henry Ford's individual success story. But according to Peter Drucker, during the period when it was growing into a success – that is, from 1907 through the early 1920's – the company was, in effect, run by a top management team, with James Couzens co-equal to Ford in some areas and acting as final authority in others. It was only after Couzens left in 1921 that Ford became the lone top manager. It is hardly surprising that Couzens' departure impaired the company's competitive capability. [2]

THE MANAGERIAL MIX

A managerial mix can occur successfully at all levels of the organizational hierarchy, but it does not evolve naturally all by itself.

So how do we build managerial teams in which the players are different from each other, and how can we encourage and support their ability to work together, avoiding the unproductive trap that I call "management by committee?"

Not every team of managers is workable or competent. In an ideal managerial mix, each individual team member must possess specific qualities. Then, the team itself must be capable of achieving certain goals.

What are the necessary characteristics for each member of such a team? First, in addition to excelling at one or more of the four roles, he must have no dashes in his (**PAEI**) code. Thus, the combination

(**P**---) plus

(-**A**--) plus

(--**E**-) plus

(---**I**)

will not work. Any manager with even one blank in his code will be incapable of working well with the person who excels in that role in the team. He will be inflexible and will have difficulty developing and inspiring mutual trust and respect with that person.

A manager as a team member should have no blanks in his (**PAEI**) code, and can achieve a minimum threshold of competence in any managerial role. This means he will be familiar with and capable of recognizing excellence in areas in which he is relatively weak, and he will accept and even support others' differences.

He will realize that he himself is, by definition, imperfect – which suggests that he understands and appreciates the value of his strengths as well as the cost of his weaknesses. Thus, he actively seeks to complement his strengths and weaknesses with those of other team members. In doing so, he knows and expects that there will be a certain amount of conflict, and he works hard to manage that conflict when it arises.

When individuals join together and become a group – it doesn't matter what kind of group – we know that in addition to being individuals, they become part of another entity with its own distinct identity, which, like any identity, is rooted in one's developed values, tendencies and habits.

As an entity, then, the ideal managerial mix will demonstrate certain values and behavior. What are they?

In order to be functionally successful, the most basic requirement is that the team must have a style, or "personality," that will be allowed to flourish in its organization's climate. This can be tricky. For instance, a bureaucratic organization probably needs an (**E**)ntrepreneurial team to head its marketing department, but will a bureaucracy really tolerate an (**E**)'s intense, aggressive style? Probably not. Often, it is necessary to change the environment, perhaps by restructuring the organization, before a managerial team – even a great managerial team – can be productive. We're going to get into that in more detail in Chapter 8.

Second, in every team, the buck has to stop somewhere. In other words, among the team members there must be an acknowledged leader.

This may seem contradictory but it is not. In a (**PAEI**) team, all the team members are not equal; our paradigm of a (**PAEI**) team actually supports, rather than discourages or eliminates, the role of individual leadership. In fact, group decision-making without a leader produces a structure "that can lead to delays or impede the decision-making process," as Aetna's management complained after it unsuccessfully replaced its company president with a team of people. A complementary management team whose members are all equal could lead to stalemate and eventually disintegration. What the (**PAEI**) model does suggest, however, is that the leader needs the rest of the team to help him make decisions. So we need to choose a leader who is capable of maintaining a team environment and team operations.

Finally, each team must be composed of members whose strengths specifically complement the others' weaknesses. This can only be determined on the most personal, individual level. Let's say a prospective team member is a (**Paei**); he is not only strong at (**P**)roducing, but he has the ability to perform whatever other combination of managerial roles may be required. But if none of the other team members excels at (**I**)ntegrating, as an example, the team as an entity will be weak in (**I**) and thus unsuccessful.

To determine whether or not a manager's style is appropriate for a specific team, one has to analyze all of the team members as if they were components of a whole (which, as I explained above, is true.)

Thus, this hypothetical (**Paei**), despite being an excellent manager and even a good team player, may not be appropriate for this particular team. What is needed is a manager who excels at (**I**)ntegration.

Some Classic Combinations

There isn't one magical combination of managers that produces an ideal team. There are at least several configurations that can work. One simple model, easily grasped, is:

a (**Paei**), and

a (**pAei**), and

a (**paEi**), and

a (**paeI**).

Even better would be a team composed of:

a (**PaeI**), and

a (**pAeI**), and

a (**paEI**).

In this latter configuration, all the team members excel at (**I**)ntegration as well as some other role; thus each has the potential to transcend good management and become leaders. Each can lead – but with a different orientation. (Nevertheless, only one of them should have authority over the group's decisions.)

As Ford's success shows, a successful organizational team does not have to be composed of four people; there could be three, or even two.

One traditional model of a complementary team – the typical "mom-and-pop store"– consists of a (**PaEi**) and a (**pAeI**). The "poppa" opens new stores, finds new products, and sets prices, while the "momma" takes care of the books and deals with the customers.

But it doesn't have to be a store; it could be a multinational company with billions of dollars in revenues. Years ago I lectured to the top management of Phillip Morris. The CEO approached me afterward and said, pointing to the gentleman next to him: "Dr. Adizes, I would like to introduce you to Mama."

Why don't you ever hear of a "momma store," or a "poppa store?" Because there is no successful poppa without a successful momma! It takes a complementary team to build a store (or, for that matter, a family). Show me any successful organization, and I'll show you a complementary team.

Although success is never guaranteed, there are certain combinations that seem by nature doomed to failure. One example is if a (**PAei**) supervises a (**paEI**) in the hierarchy. What will happen? The (**E**)ntrepreneur will be suffocated under the (**PA**). The (**paEI**) needs to dream and to communicate his visions. But the (**PAei**) is so focused on order, on peace and quiet, that he will feel threatened by the (**paEI**)'s dreams. If the (**paEI**) wants to survive, he will have to stop giving wings to his creativity and completely give up his dreams and aspirations.

Conversely, a (**paEI**) cannot successfully supervise a (**PAei**) either. I believe we saw a tragic example of that in the Watergate scandal in the 1970's. Richard Nixon was President, with H.R. (Bob) Haldeman and John Ehrlichman under him in charge of the White House staff. Nixon had ambitious visions of statesmanship – (**E**); but he was also an insecure person badly in need of support – (**I**) – as was indicated by his bitterness toward the critical media. So he found himself some (**PA**) types who would support and serve him blindly.

The result could have been a fantastic misunderstanding: Nixon, an (**EI**), gave directions that may have been too general, which were interpreted and implemented by Haldeman, a (**PA**) type without any real vision or ethical considerations.[3]

One reason the partnership of a (**PAei**) and a (**paEI**) is potentially disastrous is that both the (**P**) and (**A**) roles are exclusively concerned with short-term goals, while the (**E**) and (**I**) roles are focused on the long term.

Another theory is that the problem has to do with left- and right-brain thinking. The (**P**) and (**A**) roles, I suggest, are performed on the left side of the brain, which operates logically, sequentially, rationally, analytically. (**E**) and (**I**) roles depend more on the right side, which is more random, intuitive, holistic, and subjective. Thus, combining two managers – one with left-brain strength alone and the other with only right-brain strength – will cause too much confusion, miscommunication, and conflict.

To be a competent team player, one must have a bit of both orientations. That's why the combination of a (**PaEi**) and a (**pAeI**) can work well, as long as the (**pAeI**) doesn't object to playing the supportive role. Hospitals, operas, theaters, and universities are often run by such partnerships.

A (**PaEi**) is more function-oriented, while a (**pAeI**) is more form-oriented. But instead of being focused on one to the exclusion of the other, each of these managers makes decisions based on a consideration for both short- and long-term goals. The (**PaEi**)'s role should be to look at the what, in both the short run, (**P**), and the long run, (**E**); while the (**pAeI**) should concentrate on how, mechanistically in the short run, (**A**); and organically in the long run, (**I**).

While the combination makes sense, it is also crucial that function lead form; thus in this model, the (**PaEi**) must be the leader.

THE BAD NEWS

By now it must be obvious that creating and sustaining a complementary team abounds with pitfalls: We need each other, but can we stand each other's differences? Differing styles, though they are both complementary and essential, aren't necessarily compatible. Fundamentally, working together means accepting variations in style and opinion; acknowledging that those variations will lead to conflict; and recognizing that conflict is an inevitable and even desirable facet of managing.

But I'm not telling you anything you don't know. Consider your spouse, for example: I bet his or her style is very different from yours. If you are creative and excitable, you've probably chosen a partner who pours cold water on your head from time to time and cools you off; someone who thinks the details through. And it drives you crazy, doesn't it? The reasons you married him or her might be the same reasons you sometimes contemplate divorce.

The typical couple is incompatible in a hundred ways. Peter Blumenthal, once listed the ways in which he and his wife, Laura, see and do things differently. Peter is quiet; Laura is talkative. He is undemonstrative; she is effusive. He hates to talk problems out; she likes to shout her way through them. He prefers a quiet night at home; she likes a big party. He is thorough and meticulous; she hates details. He likes to plan things in advance; she is spontaneous and impulsive. He tends to be indecisive, but when he makes a decision it is after thorough review of the facts, and then he sticks to it. She is quick to decide, but may change her mind tomorrow. When purchasing a new car or determining a color for their home décor, he prefers the staid and conservative; she wants color and pizzazz. When they collaborate on a project around the house, he works at a slow, consistent pace; she is quick but erratic. His spending is governed by a carefully constructed budget and savings plan; she is more of an impulse buyer. He tends to be severe and consistent with their children; she is spontaneous and warm, gives them lots of freedom, and often does clandestine favors.

Here is another example – from my own family. On a trip to the Far East, we bought a new camera, a digital type that none of us knew how to operate.

The (**P**) in the family, my wife, tried right away to operate it by using trial and error. The (**A**), one of my sons, immediately got upset. "Read the manual!" he shouted at her.

The (**E**) – that would be me, ladies and gentleman – was totally uninterested in the manual or even in taking the picture. I, the big (**E**), wanted to decide on the appropriate angle, direct who was going to stand where, and choose which person would shoot the photo. And I wanted to make absolutely sure I was in the picture.

Why is this peculiar phenomenon, also known as "Opposites attract," so common? The answer is that it only *seems* peculiar; in fact, it is natural and necessary.

Why are we instinctively attracted to just the kind of person we're going to have conflict with? Because a family, in order to raise children, requires both the "feminine" and "masculine" (the "yin" and the "yang") energies. The child needs you both. Even in same-sex partnerships, there is a difference in styles between the partners; despite the conventional wisdom, such differences are not gender-specific.

That is why it's so difficult to raise a child as a single parent, whether you are a man or a woman. No matter how these energies are actually determined, both are necessary for raising healthy children – and equally necessary for building a company or an organization.

When you have a problem, whether it's business-related or personal, you will find somebody who is different from you to consult with, won't you? You want somebody who's going to see the holes in your argument, who's going to make you think about what you're saying. We always look for complementarity.

In the Bible, "the perfect spouse" is defined as *ezer keneged*, which literally means "helpful against." Rabbis have argued about this phrase for centuries: How can she be helpful if she is against? If she is against, then she's not helpful; if she's helpful, she's not against. My explanation is that she is helpful precisely by being against. That's exactly what we're looking for, because we cannot embrace the total argument all by ourselves. It's too difficult to do. In order to feel secure and comfortable, we need someone who's going to complement us. In fact, the bigger our (**E**) is, the bigger the (**A**) we are looking for.

THE INEVITABILITY OF CONFLICT

We behave as if we expect peace and harmony to be normal, and conflict to be abnormal. Actually, the opposite is true. Organizational conflict emerges naturally from the diverse styles of its members and thus is inevitable.

In a real complementary team, each member is strong at something and weak at something else, which means they are human. But because they are human and different from each other – and especially because one is strong just where the other is weak – they are also going to have difficulty communicating and reaching agreement.

Now, obviously this is true of *mis*managers. We know that unmanageable conflict will develop when the managerial group is composed of people who lack the ability to perform all four roles – who are "blind" to one or more roles. Why? Because such managers will be unable to perceive the value of what the other managers contribute to the joint effort.

However, even an excellent managerial mix, perfectly suited to its tasks, whose individual team members are mature and capable of handling differences, cannot run an organization without experiencing some conflict. In fact, there will be conflict even if the goal, the information, and the reward system are clearly defined and understood – the three factors that the Nobel prize winner in economics, Herbert Simon, believed to be the causes of conflict.[5]

Think about it: Let's say one member of your team is a great extrovert, charismatic and visionary; and another is careful, conservative, slow, and needs to think things through. These two people are naturally going to get into conflict when they try to decide something together, right?

And there's the rub: Because if a decision is to be fully analyzed and implemented, it *must* reflect all four roles. In other words, there *must* be conflict.

When will an organization operate totally without conflict? It will operate without conflict if it is composed of one individual who makes all the decisions himself and implements them alone. But in that case, there is no organization. (But even here I am not so sure because he will be in conflict with himself. The four roles still need to be performed and the roles are still incompatible even if they are in one head.)

An organization composed of Deadwood can also operate without conflict. All of the decisions would be programmed and predetermined, and no one member would want to change anything. No one would complain, but no one would care, either.

Finally, conflict can be avoided in an organization in which all the members of the managerial team have the same style: They are all are (**A**)s or all (**P**)'s. Such managers would have the same outlook and play the same role, and thus have no conflict.

But in both of the above cases, the organizations would experience significant problems meeting their goals in a changing environment. They would become stale.

So part of our new paradigm should include the notion that conflict is a necessary and indispensable component of good management, and, like any other component, must be understood and legitimized.

If you are a manager and don't like to mediate between people, if you are upset by friction and differences of opinion, then you're in the wrong profession. It's the same thing as saying, "I want to be a doctor, but I can't stand the sight of blood and I don't like sick people." As President Truman said: "If you can't stand the heat, get out of the kitchen."

Let us now, in the next chapter, study how the different styles miscommunicate before they are so different. Once we understand the difference we can proceed to deal with, how to make those differences work well together.

NOTES

1. On the subject of teamwork, see also Rensis Likert, *The Human Organization: Its Management and Value* (New York: McGraw-Hill, 1967).

2. As reported by Ernest Dale, *The Great Organizers* (New York: McGraw-Hill, 1960), pp. 50-51.

3. Bob Haldeman was a highly respected associate of Adizes Institute until his death. He and I spent many hours trying to analyze what combination of circumstances caused the Watergate fiasco, which led to the impeachment of the President of the United States. Bob is sorely missed.

4. Gottman, John M.: *Why Marriages Succeed or Fail, and How You Can Make Yours Last* (New York, Simon & Schuster, 1994).

5. The commonality of individual goals, the clarity and consistency of the reward structure, and the compatibility of individual rewards are the factors that effect goal differentiation among individuals and subunits in organizations. See James G. March and Herbert A. Simon, *Organizations* (New York: Wiley, 1963), p. 125.

Chapter 6

Can We Talk?

PROBLEM: To avoid destructive conflict,
can we define and predict the sources of
organizational conflict?

A WINDOW ON MANAGERIAL STYLES

Since a manager's style determines so many of his decisions, let's try to look at the four styles systematically and see if we can predict where conflict will probably occur.

Look at the Figure below. Think of it as a French window – one big window with four smaller windows in it. The four sides of the window give you the four variables in the style of any individual's decision-making: Priorities, speed, process and focus. For each of those variables, there is a continuum.

On the horizontal line at the top, which measures priorities, the continuum goes from being exclusively task- or result-oriented, to being exclusively process-oriented. Does this manager attach more importance to the task (what we're doing and why) or to the process (who does it and how)?

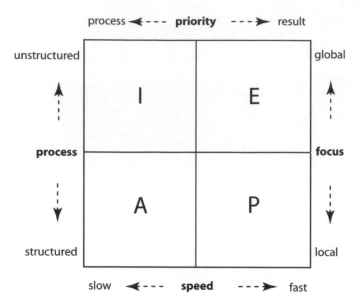

Across the bottom of the window, we are measuring the speed at which people make decisions: From slow, on the left, to rapid, on the right. Some people are slow and methodical in their decision-making; a joke about Bureaucrats, for example, is that you should never tell a Bureaucrat a joke on Friday because he might burst out laughing – on Sunday in church!

On the opposite end of this continuum is the Arsonist, who probably won't let you finish telling your joke; it reminds him of another joke, so he'll interrupt your joke to tell his.

The right side of the window addresses focus, from a global orientation, at the top, to a local orientation, at the bottom. The diagram itself is a good illustration of focus: If the four styles of manager were looking out of that French window, each would focus on a different view. An (**E**)ntrepreneur would see the flowers, the mountains, and the horizon from the window; an (**A**)dministrator might only notice that the window frame was dirty. Every manager's typical perspective can be mapped somewhere on this chart.

The left side of the window presents the last variable: The process by which people make decisions. Some managers attack a problem in an unstructured way; others are structured.

The unstructured type will start out talking about A, which reminds him of Z. Z reminds him of Q, which he relates to B, then to C, and finally to X. In his holistic view, everything is interrelated, thus there is no particular predetermined sequence in which the whole must be understood.

Structured thinkers are linear. They don't like to start talking about B until they fully understand A; they'll put off talking about C until B is fully understood; and so on.

STYLE DIFFERENCES

Looking at the diagram, we can see that the four (**PAEI**) styles – (**P**)roducer, (**A**)dministrator, (**E**)ntrepreneur, and (**I**)ntegrator, as well as their corresponding mismanagement archetypes – fit neatly into the four quadrants of the window.

The (**E**)ntrepreneur, or Arsonist, depending upon how extreme his style is, has the global, or big-picture, perspective; he thinks and acts quickly and without structure; and he is result-oriented in his decision-making.

(**A**)dministrators (or Bureaucrats) have a local perspective and a structured, slow-moving style focused on process and details. They pay attention to the *how*.

That tells you something immediately, doesn't it? You are mixing water and oil when you put these two people together to work. Their priorities are different; their speed of decision making is different; their focus is different; the way they organize facts and draw conclusions is different; the way they communicate is different.

When an (**A**) and an (**E**) get together, the (**E**) quickly becomes exasperated with the (**A**)'s incessant harping on details. Sometimes he'll simply leave the room in the middle of a discussion. This causes the (**A**) to feel ignored, abused, and abandoned. He's convinced no one cares about his problems. If he were the type of person (he isn't) who understands and can communicate in metaphors, he might tell you he feels like he's working with a sea gull: The (**E**) appears from above out of nowhere, lets out a shriek, drops a shot on the (**A**)'s boat, and disappears, only to reappear later on.

Natural Adversaries

The diagram also shows that each style will be in conflict mostly with the style diagonally across from him. Thus, (**P**)s and (**I**)s don't get along any better or like each other better than (**A**)s and (**E**)s.

(**P**)s (or Lone Rangers) are fast, local, structured, and focused on tasks, details, and results. They are our railroad engineers. They are the ones who say, "Show me the tracks and get out of the way." In meetings, they are the ones who interrupt the discussion to say: "Look, what do we need to do? Let's just go and do it. Right now. We have a business to run. What we *really* need is to talk less and do more."

(**I**)ntegrators (or Superfollowers) are process-oriented, slow, and unstructured – which is why they are so politically astute. They have a global view; they see the big picture, and they can easily change and adapt.

Seen from this perspective, the potential conflicts are obvious. The task-oriented, quick (**P**) is not generally very personable or sensitive. This upsets the (**I**)ntegrator, who wants to slow down and pay attention to how people feel. The (**I**) thinks the (**P**) is an insensitive and "macho" "hatchet man," who steps all over people without regard to their feelings and needs.

The (**P**), on the other hand, thinks the (**I**) is insensitive to what the *organization* needs. He perceives the (**I**) as weak and slow – even effeminate. (Nevertheless, this is not a gender issue. A woman can be a (**P**) and a man can be an (**I**). In fact, I have observed a real flip-flop from traditional sexual stereotypes in the United States over the last twenty years.)

So between these two types also, there will often be hard feelings and a lack of mutual respect. They need each other but at the same time they cannot work together without difficulty – like a marriage of two people who love each other because of their differences, but sometimes find those differences unbearable to live with.

What kinds of conflict do these different approaches create among managers, and are they inevitable?

One source of conflict is miscommunication, which occurs because we think and perceive reality differently: (**A**) is conservative and looks for ways to control, whereas (**E**) looks for ways to make changes. (**P**) requires short-term feedback, whereas (**E**) takes time to develop his ideas and looks to the long term for feedback. (**E**) prefers to talk, whereas (**I**) wants only to listen. (And in any case, very few people can both talk and listen effectively – that is, communicate well.)

The different styles also focus on different components of the decision-making process. And even if they use the same vocabulary, it is often meant to convey opposite meanings.

In other words, the four styles simply speak different (**PAEI**) languages! Thus, naturally, they have difficulty understanding one another.

The Inevitability of Miscommunication

Miscommunication, like conflict, is not an aberration but the norm: Inevitably, a team of people who are dissimilar in style will not communicate to each other or comprehend each other very well.

Let's take the words "yes," "no," and "maybe" as an example. For (**E**)ntrepreneurs, "yes" actually means *maybe* – or "Hmmm, why not?" But when they say "no," they're definite.

It is just the opposite with an (**A**). When an (**A**)dministrator says "no," it's a *provisional* "no;" you can still come back and try to convince him. Thus it is a "maybe." When he says "yes," however, he definitely means *yes*. For a (**P**) "yes" is "yes" and "no" is "no." For an (**I**) "yes" is "maybe" and "no" is "maybe."

I saw a classic example of this miscommunication while working with a CEO in Australia, one of the biggest (**E**)s I've ever met. He was talking to one of his vice presidents as we walked down a corridor of his office. "Why don't we have a manufacturing facility in Brisbane? What's going on?" he said.

The vice president, an (P) type, said, "Well, should we have one?"

"Yeah, why don't we?" the CEO responded.

The vice president got right on it as you would expect a (P) to do. Two months later, the CEO heard about the plans and was apoplectic.

"Why the hell are we putting up a building in Brisbane?" he wanted to know.

"But you said we needed a facility in Brisbane!" the VP answered, stunned.

"What? I was just asking why *don't* we have it? I didn't tell you to start *doing* it!"

This is a chronic problem when dealing with an (E)ntrepreneur type: People can't tell whether the (E) is thinking or deciding. Was that "yes" really yes, or was it actually a *maybe*? Or was the "yes" a "why not?"

Sometimes he's just thinking, but his subordinates believe he's deciding. They act on the "decision;" then when it's too late, they discover that what they had taken to be a decision was just musing aloud, a frequent component of the (E)'s thinking process.

They're called on the carpet for that mistake. And the result? The next time the (E) says something that although it sounds like a directive, they conclude, "That wasn't really an order; he's just thinking out loud again." And they don't act on it. But the (E) boss gets nevertheless angry again: It was not an idea. It was a decision and he'd expected them to deal with his concern right away so how come that nothing has been done.

Living in that twilight zone causes an (E)'s subordinates a lot of suffering. They begin to feel that they can never win: No matter what they do, it's going to be seen as wrong. And why? Because the word "yes," when spoken by an (E)ntrepreneur, does not really mean *yes*.

For whom is "yes" *yes* and "no" *no*? That's a (P)roducer type. For him, it's all very clear. If he says "yes," why, then, it's *yes* he means. If he says "no," it's *no*. He cannot comprehend why the people around him seem to have trouble understanding and communicating with him; it's all so simple and obvious. But in reality, in interpreting his colleagues' words literally, he is going to misunderstand and make mistakes more often than not.

Now, for whom is "yes" *maybe* and "no" also *maybe*? For the (**I**)ntegrator. For this type of manager, a political animal, everything means maybe.

AGREEMENT AND DISAGREEMENT

Another source of misunderstanding is the way different styles express agreement and disagreement. If an (**E**)ntrepreneur disagrees with an idea, he will typically be very expressive about it. He's expressive even when he *agrees*. He loves the back-and-forth of debate and habitually speaks in an argumentative, confrontational tone, very much as if he's disagreeing. As a result, people have trouble discerning whether he dislikes an idea or actually approves of it.

(**A**)dministrators, on the other hand, express disagreement by being silent and apparently very calm. They just look at you, lower their chins, and freeze. That incongruity alone can easily cause miscommunication, because an (**E**) will interpret that silence as agreement with his idea, when in fact the (**A**) is dead set against it.

In practice, how might this misunderstanding play out? Let's look at a hypothetical meeting between an (**E**)ntrepreneur and an (**A**)dministrator.

First of all, the (**E**) frequently won't bother to set up an appointment; the moment he has an idea, he wants to discuss it. He just shows up, impromptu, in the (**A**)'s office.

But an (**A**) hates surprises. He has his day organized, his desk organized, his files organized, his life organized, his vacation organized, his year organized. When our unguided missile the (**E**)ntrepreneur arrives, unannounced, he messes up the (**A**)'s carefully planned schedule.

Meanwhile, on his way to the meeting, the (**E**) has been busy formulating plans, discarding plans, and formulating more new plans. By the time he hits the (**A**)'s office, he's moving at 150 miles an hour. He hits the (**A**) like a ton of bricks.

(**A**)s are slow – not because they are stupid, but because they are thinking about the repercussions of the (**E**)'s ideas. It takes them time to process each idea. For an (**A**), listening to an (**E**) free-associate ideas is like drinking from a fire hose. For any single (**E**) idea there are at least ten repercussions that matter to the (**A**): *How* is this plan going to work? *What* are the details? *Who* will do it?

The (**E**)ntrepreneur, however, never gets around to talking about such details; he really doesn't care about the *how* or the *when* or the who as much as he cares about the why not.

You can see that this is not going to turn out well. The (**A**)dministrator can't handle the load or the speed. Very soon he concludes that the (**E**) is full of hot air. He stops thinking, stops listening, and just lets the words float past him.

And the (**E**) will take the (**A**)'s silence for agreement.

If you ask the (**E**)ntrepreneur later, "How was the meeting?" he'll probably say, "It was fantastic! It was great! I totally convinced him; he didn't say one word against it."

But if you ask the (**A**)dministrator he'll tell you, "It was a complete waste of time. The guy's totally crazy! He's going to burn the company down! He came in here, dropped a hundred ideas, and left. I don't know what the hell he was talking about, but he didn't give me a chance to open my mouth and ask a question. Nothing got resolved."

IS, WANT, AND SHOULD

The three little words *is*, *want*, and *should* signify very different perspectives that create a tremendous amount of conflict and frustration in human life. Why? Because we often confuse *is* with *want*, *is* with *should*, *want* with *should*, etc.

Let's define *is*, *want* and *should*. What *is*, is reality: What is going on right now. What you *want* is in your heart, while *should* is in your head: What your conscience or sense of obligation dictate. The three words, used precisely, correspond to Freud's theory of the ego (*is*), id (*want*) and superego (*should*). And, like Freud's ego, id and superego, *is*, *want*, and *should* are often in conflict: You *want* to eat this whole box of cookies, but you *are* overweight and you *should* be on a diet.

That these perceptions of reality will conflict, even within a single person, is normal and actually helps us to reach decisions based on more than one perspective. What creates a real problem is the confusion factor: Sometimes consciously, sometimes unconsciously, people often use one word when they really mean another.

"We hold these truths to be self-evident, that all men are created equal," America's founding fathers wrote in the Declaration of Independence. Let's look at that statement carefully. *Are* people, in fact, born equal, or *should* they be born equal, or do we just *want* them to be born equal? This country's earliest leaders, brilliant as they were, confused *is* with *want* and *should*.

Here's another example: For years, we've heard that "America is the leader of the free world." Well, *is* it? *Should* it be? Do we still *want* it to be?" The answers to these questions would determine our foreign policy, yet we don't often attempt to clarify and differentiate our reality from our desires, our desires from our obligations.

In organizations, if you sit in a meeting and listen to the way people talk, you'll find they continually misuse the three words. Instead of saying, "I *want* this," which sounds arrogant, they say, "We *should* do this." But if you carefully analyze their position, you will see that what they really mean is that they *want* to do whatever it is they are saying *should* be done. What is being labeled as necessary does not *have* to be done; it is not a *should* situation.

I often hear in meetings: "We *are* the leaders of our industry." Actually they *aren't*; they just think they *should* be because they have invested enough money to become one.

The result can be costly to an organization. Sometimes change is necessary; what *is* must move toward what *should* be. But how can we move toward change when we are so busy pretending that what *should* be is what already *is*?

TRANSLATOR NEEDED

To add further complexity to the issue, each of the four (**PAEI**) styles attaches a different meaning to the words *is*, *want* and *should* – based on his own idiosyncratic world view.

The (**E**)ntrepreneur typically perceives events – and makes his decisions – through the prism of *want*. He confuses *want* with is: "Since I *want* it, it is."

In contrast, the (**A**)dministrator's style comes from the *should* direction: "Since it *should* be, it is." If you ask an (**A**)dministrator, "Do we have a solution to this problem?" he might say, "Of course we do. We spent a million dollars on it, didn't we?" Well, perhaps it's true that we *should* have a solution because we spent a million dollars. But that's not the question. The question is: "*Do* we have a solution?"

Now, which style's perspective is: "What is, *is*. Never mind the *want* and the *should*." That's the (**P**)roducer. The (**P**) is very reality-oriented; he understands what *is*, and that's all that interests him. He is not concerned with what *should* be or what somebody might *want*. If this is the way it *is*, then this is how he *wants* it and this is how it *should* be. *Is* equals *want* equals *should* – period: They are all the same. He is proud of the fact that his feet are planted solidly on the ground, and that his decisions are practical, based on what is and not on what *isn't*.

And finally, who is continually moving around from one perception to the other? The (**I**)ntegrator. The (**I**) is capable of understanding the differences; because he doesn't have any single avenue through which he comes at reality. *Is*, *want*, and *should* are irrelevant to the (**I**)ntegrator. His views and his decision-making are determined by his concern for *other* people's opinions, not his own.

These huge differences in the use of language create a lot of unnecessary confusion, anger, and conflict.

For instance, in a meeting, an (**E**) might say, "We sold a million-dollar contract."

"Where is it?" the (**P**) asks.

"The clients are meeting next week to sign it," says the (**E**).

"Then we really *don't* have the contract," says (**P**).

"But we will! They like it!" The (**E**), feeling that (P) is challenging his credibility, is getting angry.

"But in reality, they might not," (**P**) retorts. The (**P**), is from Missouri, show me state. He believes it when he has it in his hand. Nothing less.

"But they *will*, because it makes perfect sense for them!" (**E**) almost screams. What is really happening? The (**E**) has confused what he *wants* and *should* be with what is: "Since I *want* it and *should* be, it is." But the fact is, it *isn't*; It isn't signed.

The (**P**) in this meeting is totally frustrated and disgusted. All he wants is to get to the bottom line, the decision, so that the meeting will end and he can get back to work. "Listen, guys, do we have the contract or not?" he asks. "What the hell is going on here?"

More Conflicts

Of course, conflicts will also occur between managers whose styles are not diagonal on the chart. For example, conflicts may arise between the (**P**)roducer and the (**E**)ntrepreneur if the (**E**)ntrepreneur is the manager and the (**P**)roducer is the subordinate. Under those circumstances, the (**E**)ntrepreneur will typically give instructions to the (**P**) in generalities, or "big-picture" ideas. Since the (**P**)roducer is extremely literal and has difficulty translating the general into specifics, there is the danger that he might misinterpret and make a big mess out of the (**E**)'s vague directions. As I said in Chapter 5, that may explain Watergate and other political scandals in this country's history.

On the other hand, if the (**P**)roducer is at the top and the (**E**)ntrepreneur is the subordinate, very little will get done. Why? The

(P)roducer won't delegate and the (E)ntrepreneur will wander off to do his own thing. The (P)roducer will try to do all the work himself, thus limiting the company's production and growth.

Now let's take the other side: The (A)dministrator and the (I)ntegrator. The conflict there is about implementation, but again, little gets done. The (A)dministrator occupies himself creating all kinds of regulations and rules. The (I) protests: "Cool it! Not everything conforms to rules. You don't have to be so mechanistic, you don't have to make a million laws and put every single thing in writing. You can just talk to people. If you just convince them to make something work, it *will* work."

But the (A) doesn't trust people. He *wants* everything in writing so that it can be organized and enforced and so that those who deviate can be punished.

What it Means

The diagram and anecdotes above add up to two conclusions: First, in order to know what is actually being communicated – what is really meant by words like "yes" and "no," "we are" and "we need to" – we cannot rely on the definitions in our own dictionary. We must look at *who* is speaking.

And second: In decision-making, there must be a complementary team. The (P) will naturally focus on reality: What is, *is*. The (E) will provide the *want* elements of the discussion, the ambition; while the (A) will keep reminding everyone of what *should* be done. (I)ntegrated and motivated by the (I), and properly managed, a complementary team will be able to reach a strategy that is based on reality (*is*), reflects the company's goals (*want*), and also takes into account its obligations and responsibilities (*should*).

Thus, our analysis of the different styles shows not only how difficult it is for a team of dissimilar managers to communicate with each other; it also demonstrates why it is *essential* that they do so. All three perspectives are necessary in decision-making, yet any single manager alone does not possess them in equal measure.

CONFLICTS ON THE IMPLEMENTATION SIDE

We've seen that in the decision-making process, different styles have different priorities, are focused either on the long range or the short range; move at different speeds; and deal with the process differently. All of this causes miscommunication, which causes conflict, which causes further miscommunication, and so on.

On the implementation side (remember: "To manage" means both "to decide" and "to implement"), any team of managers may simply lack a commonality of interests. In other words, I might agree with your logic, I might fully understand what you're saying; but I am not going to cooperate. Why not? Because I believe the course of action you are suggesting will benefit *you* at *my* expense.

You often hear talk in managerial training and seminars of fostering a "win-win climate." It's a wonderful idea, but let's face it: It's utopian to expect to have a win-win climate 24 hours a day, 365 days a year. It doesn't always happen between parents and children, or between spouses, so why would it happen in an organization?

In the absence of a win-win climate, those with the power can undermine those with the authority; they can "pocket-veto" decisions by simply not implementing them, later claiming that they misunderstood the decision. This can make implementation very inefficient.[1]

SUMMING IT UP

Conflict is inevitable and necessary because of change. Whenever there is change we need to decide to do and implement those decisions. To make decisions we need a complementary team which by definition means miscommunication from time to time. To implement we need commonality of interest which is often too much to ask for.

Now what?

When it is appropriately managed, conflict can be useful and productive. But if it is mismanaged or not managed at all, conflict can be destructive, sapping the organization's energy and causing us to make bad decisions, or implement our decisions badly or inefficiently.

The challenge is to harness conflict and turn it into a positive force.

The question is: How does one prevent the inevitable conflict from becoming destructive?

Here is a hint which we will develop in the next chapter: A study by the Gottman Institute of 130 newlywed couples, conducted over six years, undertook to find the characteristics that, when matched, will result in a long-term, successful marriage.[2] But what marriage expert John Gotttman and his researchers found was that there are *no* particular personality traits, or combinations of traits, that will result in a successful marriage.

It's not the differences in personality between two people,
but how each couple handles those differences.

In other studies, they also found that the reasons people get married are the same reasons they get divorced. People are fascinated by each other's differences. When we fall in love, we become infatuated with the other person's strengths, which are very often our own weaknesses. We love seeing our weaknesses reappear as a strength in the other person. And that is wonderful – until we get married. Then what happens? On a day-to-day level, what was so fascinating – the differences between us – becomes a source of irritation. How do you handle them? It is always stressful to manage differences, and many couples eventually find it unbearable and split up.

So, why some style differences make for stronger relations and others for a breakdown?

Let us see.

NOTES

1. For an in-depth discussion of conflicts of interest, please see: Adizes, Ichak: *Mastering Change: The Power of Mutual Trust and Respect in Personal Life, Family Life, Business and Society* (Santa Barbara, CA: Adizes Institute Publications, 1992).

2. On conflict as a manifestation of good management, see also Davidson, Sol M.: *The Power of Friction in Business* (New York: Frederick Fell, 1967), pp. 83-139.

Chapter 7

Constructive Conflict

PROBLEM: How can we harness conflict
and convert it into a constructive force?

GOOD CONFLICT, BAD CONFLICT

A complementary team's strength comes from its united differences.
But to get to the unity, you have to cope with the differences, which
create conflict.

We have said that conflict is inevitable, and moreover a sign of
good management. But it is not always desirable. It can be constructive or it can be destructive. It can be functional or dysfunctional.

Dysfunctional conflict is dangerous to any organization; it can
stymie an organization, sap its energy and even destroy it. Organizations need to focus all their available energy on external marketing:
Finding the clients, satisfying those clients' needs, and anticipating
their needs for the future. When managers are at odds with each
other, the energy that should be conserved for building the company
is gobbled up by internal marketing.

Thus, an organization that wastes precious energy on internal
conflicts will necessarily be handicapped. I believe this factor alone
can determine whether the company succeeds or fails. In fact, if the
ratio between external and internal energies spent is known, I believe
it is possible to predict the success of any system.

So, the next ingredient in our new paradigm for management is
a formula for success that discourages internal waste of energy, leav-

ing the fixed disposable energy available for building the company. In order to build managerial teams in which the team members are different from each other and yet can work together, a team leader must be able to harness the natural tensions that inevitably surface in any diverse group.

How do we ensure that those differences will work *for* us instead of against us?

The key lies in how we as managers deal with conflict: We must legitimize it as a learning tool; channel its energy; and focus it on being constructive.

Note that I did not say we must *resolve* conflict. In fact, that is exactly the wrong attitude; those who try to *resolve* conflict are, again, barking up the wrong tree, working from the mistaken assumption that conflict itself is inappropriate or wrong: "We should not have disagreement." "We should not have differences of opinion and differences of interest." But this common perception ignores the reality, which is that differences, and thus conflict, are natural and normal.

Before we can start to reap the benefits of our differences, however, we must accept that conflict is appropriate and necessary, and we must render it functional.

Now, how do we do that? There is one way that I know of, and that is to create an environment of mutual trust and respect. A good manager does this by fostering a supportive learning environment, one where conflict is perceived not as a threat but as an opportunity to learn and develop. (For more on Mutual Trust and Respect, see Ichak Adizes: *Mastering Change; The Power of Mutual Trust and Respect*, Adizes Institute Publications 1992.)

In a learning environment, differences of opinion are seen as opportunities to learn new perspectives, instead of as threats or challenges or annoyances. We grow *through* disagreement rather than in spite of it. When you have points of view that I don't have, I might feel uncomfortable with that, I might not like it, but whe I respect those differences I might learn something I id not think about.

If I don't respect and trust you, then our conflicts will necessarily be dysfunctional. Whenever you disagree with me, instead of learning from you I will feel that you are stopping me or bothering me or preventing me from doing what I want to do. But as long as I respect and trust you – whether I agree with you or not – I remain open to what you're saying, and if I rarely come around completely to your point of view, at least I have honed my arguments in response to yours.

Better still, more often than not, the conflict ends with a decision that both of us support and that decision is superior to the ones that either of us could have reached alone. Why? Because we learned from each others disagreement and improved our decision in doing so.

When members of a complementary team learn from their disagreements instead of suffering under them, their joint decision-making will reflect the capability of the group, which is greater than the capability of any individual.

In addition to being a knowledgeable achiever, then – a person who excels at finance, accounting, marketing, a good manager must be able to command and grant trust and respect as a member of a team. A manager who cannot command and grant trust and respect will be incapable of resolving the conflicts that inevitably arise in working in a complementary team.

Please note that I am talking about two separate abilities: The ability to command trust and respect and the ability to grant it. They are not the same, and they do not always go together. Some people command trust and respect but don't grant it. Some people grant trust and respect but don't command it. What is needed is a person who can both command and grant mutual trust and respect.

HONORING DIVERSITY

Let's define respect as the willingness to listen to and learn from any-one who has something to contribute, no matter how different he or she is.

The United States was founded on this fundamental appreciation for diversity, and I believe it accounts, at least in part, for America's enormous success and prosperity. People often credit this country's vast resources, but that cannot be the whole answer; after all, Latin America is also rich in resources. What America has in addition to resources is its climate of mutual respect: We try to recognize and honor the differences among us. When the natural order presumes respect for differences, instead of discriminating by creed, religion, color or gender, then the sky's the limit. The result is an environment in which equal opportunity is the ideal we constantly strive for. That's why so many people come here from all over the world.

Mutual respect is also characteristic of Japanese culture. In Japanese culture, to cause someone to lose face is a serious misdeed that compromises your own honor as a person. When someone loses face, he may be humiliated enough to commit *hara kiri*, suicide; even so, it is worse to cause someone else to lose face than to lose face yourself. Only in a society that puts a premium on mutual respect would that be true. Japan has a high (**I**) culture. That is not true for countries with (**E**) culture like Greece, Israel where mutual respect is difficult to come by.

We noted earlier that when we have major decisions to make in our personal lives – new situations, new conditions, new complexities – we like to get a variety of opinions, preferably from people whose perspectives are different from ours.

But would you go for advice to just *anyone* who disagrees with you? Of course not. You would only approach someone for whom you have respect, who is different from you but whose differences you understand and can learn from. If *this* person disagrees with you, he or she will be able to show you the holes in your argument and make you think harder about what you're saying.

What would happen if you spent a lot of time listening to someone's opinions, but found that at the end of the discussion you hadn't learned anything new or accepted arguments that made you change your position; that your thinking had not expanded into new perspectives? Over time, you would lose respect for that person.

Some people have something to say.
Some people have to say something
Avoid the second group.

ANONYMOUS

On the other hand, if two people agree on everything, one of them is dispensable. So we need to find people whose opinions diverge from ours and yet who retain our respect. These people, if we are lucky enough to find them, are called "colleagues," and they are essential to making good decisions.

What I'm going to say now may sound very simple and obvious, but it took twenty years and a lot of personal pain to discover it. I wish it *were* obvious.

A colleague is *not* someone who agrees with you. A colleague is someone who *disagrees* with you but for whom you have respect. Why? Because you don't learn from those who agree with you. You learn from those who *disagree*, in the course of the debate that evolves out of the conflict between you. Learning from differences is painful, but we also enrich ourselves through being different.

The root of the word "colleague," in fact, comes from the Latin word "Collegum," which means "to arrive together." In other words, we started with different points of view, but through interacting we have arrived at the same point.

And in Hebrew, the words "colleague" *Amit* and "conflict" *Imut* derive from the same root. Words that share the same root are interrelated; in this case, the connection is that there are no collegial relationships without conflict. And the reverse can happen: Good conflict can make people to become colleagues, if they learn from each other because and not in spite of the conflict. Used appropriately, it can help legitimize and unite our differences. Like a spouse, who is *ezer keneged* (helpful against), colleagues help each other cross-fertilize ideas and expand horizons – through conflict.

Without conflict, then, you don't have a colleague. For good decision-making, team members who both respect and disagree with one another – colleagues – are essential.

In Commonality We Trust

If mutual respect is necessary for good decision-making, what is required for good implementation?

The implementation side is very interesting. For efficient, effective implementation, a commonality of interests – a win-win climate – is of course ideal. But a permanent win-win climate isn't a realistic goal. Why not? Because it simply is not going to happen all the time. People will naturally have different and often conflicting interests, depending on their positions and sphere of responsibility in the organization as well as their personal styles and perspectives.

Recognizing that reality, we need to come up with a reasonable and viable alternative that will achieve the same goal: Good decisions, well implemented. One workable alternative is to create an expectation of common interests *in the long run*. And to do that, we must establish and nurture mutual trust.

What is mutual trust? It is a vision, a long-term belief and hope that even if we do not have our individual interests met in the short run, we still share the same basic interest for the organization over the long run. Having that certainty – that we are all, ultimately, working toward the same larger objectives – ensures that there will be give and take among us. Even if the group makes a decision today that is not to my advantage, I am confident that eventually I, too, will benefit.

Trust means you take into account the interests of other people because in the long run they are equal to your own, and that you expect the same thoughtfulness from others.

That's what happens in a good marriage: We are here for the long run, aren't we? We have each made a long-term commitment. Once we've made that commitment, we assume that the partner who loses today will win in the near future. In the long run, it evens out.

Trust develops when there is faith in a win-win climate *for the long run*. If I don't trust the people with whom I am in conflict, then I have no faith that they'll cooperate with me in the long run. And if I don't believe that, why should I cooperate with them now?

Without trust, managers cannot – and probably *should* not – rely on the long term to balance their own interests against those of others. In a distrustful environment, especially in an era of rapid change, no one can predict what might happen in the long run. One result is that people only feel comfortable with short-term thinking and planning. Another result is that each member of the group will protect his interests at any expense – because if he doesn't, who will?

PATIENCE, PAIN AND TOLERANCE

Mutual trust and respect are all about accepting others who are different. It sounds simple, but in fact it is a huge task, very difficult to do. Why? Because when someone is different, you don't understand him; you have difficulty communicating. You might feel you're losing control. At the very least it's annoying, and often it's painful.

To accept someone who's different from you, you must be patient enough to hear and listen to him or her although their styles are different from yours. That patience is the first step toward tolerance.

In Hebrew, the root consonants of the word "tolerance" (*SoVLanut*) are "SVL" – and interestingly, there are two other words that derive from that root: "Patience" (*SaVLanut*) and "pain" (*SeVeL*). How are these three related? Think about it: Tolerance cannot exist without patience. But to be tolerant of other people's opinions – and patient enough to listen to those opinions even when you strongly disagree – can be quite painful.

Why should we make such a sacrifice? Why should we have to be so uncomfortable? Because the pain has a payoff: You might learn something!!

Organizations that have achieved mutual trust and respect function in a way that is measurably and even visibly different from organizations that have not. You can see it in the body language of the team members. When there is mutual respect, people seek each other out when they need to make a decision. They meet and discuss and decide together, leaning toward each other and watching each other's faces for reactions to their ideas.

Once a decision is made, team members in an environment of mutual trust turn away from each other and become engaged in implementing their piece of the job. They can *afford* to turn their backs to each other, because they know they're not going to be stabbed in the back. Thus their energies can be devoted wholly to the task.

What would you see in an organization that lacked mutual respect and trust? You'd see just the opposite: When managers who don't respect each other need to make a decision, they will turn their backs to each other and isolate themselves.

And when will they face each other? When it's time to implement their decisions: Lacking trust, they'll feel the need to keep an eye on each other.

Do you want a simple way to find out how well managed your own organization is? Just make a note of which way you are facing and where your back is during decision-making and during implementation.

Here is another way to measure the quality of management: The time dimension. To make a decision together rather than alone will obviously take a lot longer. On the other hand, implementing that decision that is owned and supported by the team necessary for the implementation, is easy and quick, because people trust each other and leave each other alone to do their jobs.

Well-managed organizations may spend a long time arriving at a decision because they make it together, but once they've decided on a plan of action, implementation is swift, because they don't try to back-seat-drive each other.

In a badly managed organization, decisions are made quickly because "the fastest way travel is alone," an individual made the decision and it was thus fast. But how long does it take to implement the decision? Looks like it is going to take forever. Managers who have no confidence in each other will quickly "back seat drive each other" become enmeshed in other people's areas of responsibility, interfering with and slowing down the process, or not carry out the decision either because they do not understand it or because they do not support it.

For example, how does the decision-making process in the United States compare with Japan's? We make decisions fast, but it takes us forever to implement. Their decisions are reached painfully slowly, but it takes them no time at all to implement. People often ask me: "Why are the Japanese so successful? Why are they so fast?" You know what my answer is? "Because they are so slow."

BACK TO THE PARADIGM

We know that in organizations, in the short run, respect for people whose opinions differ from ours and shared interests are the exception rather than the rule. So we know there will be plenty of conflict. This presents two great challenges for organizations: They must train their employees to respect diverse opinions; and they must promote an expectation of "win-win" in the long run, despite the obvious short-term conflicts of interest.

Thus, our paradigm of good management must include these twin goals as missions of management. But no manager can single-handedly create mutual trust and respect; trust and respect grow – or fail to grow – in the context of an organization's climate. It should be an all encompassing value of the organization: How they treat each other, their customers, their suppliers, their investors, their community etc.

There are four factors, or categories of factors, that determine whether a culture of mutual trust and respect can thrive in a given organization. I will summarize them here and then examine each one separately and in depth in the next few chapters.

1. People

This factor is the easiest to "sell" because it is the flavor of the decade. Most books and speaker preach the importance of people, of human resources, of human capital.

I agree and share that people are an asset, an extremely important asset.

Think about it: If someone gave you the choice, to loose all your people and have to start again, or loose all you machinery and structures and start all over again, what would you choose? The answer is obvious: It is easier to replace machinery and physical structures than people who know what they are doing, especially if they know how to do it well together.

This explains why the German nation could flourish after World War II. They lost their machinery and buildings but they have not lost the German people and their German culture and dedication to quality. This explains why Israel flourished and became the third internet empire in the world: It had a huge inflow of Russian Jewish engineers.

What kind of people do we want? People who command and grant mutual trust and respect. And what should we do with a person who works for us, but one that does not grant nor command trust and respect? The usual answer I get is: "Fire him!" I disagree. I say: "Recommend that person to your competition. Why should you be the only one to suffer? As the competition gets entangled in internal intrigues and fights that this kind of person will start, as they turn their energies inwards, you can take their market away."

What should you do with a person who is extremely knowledge-able, take an indispensable engineer, but one who trusts no one and shows no respect for anyone. He demands it but does not grant it. (There are many geniuses like this.) You should treat them like monkeys: You keep them in their cages, and whenever you need information you give them a banana and extract the information. But you don't let them out in the corridors, and you never promote them to a managerial position. They are not managers; they never can and never *should* be managers. They are only there to provide the professional know-how that you need in order to manage.

Producing a culture of mutual trust and respect takes more than having people we trust and respect, we learn from. It is like cooking a gourmet dish; it takes more than just outstanding ingredients. You can destroy a dish in spite of having excellent ingredients, if you do not know how to cook it together; if you do not have a recipe, a process of how decisions should be made together, not in spite of being different, but because we want people to be different.

That is where process as the second necessary factor for building MT&R comes in.

2. Process

An aspect of "process" is effective communication. To manage well, you must be able to understand what people are telling you (as well as what they might not be saying); and you must also be understood. In other words, good managers have to speak and comprehend all the (**PAEI**) languages. As we have already discussed it, different styles use the same words but they mean different things like the word "yes" and "no."

Until this crucial piece of the paradigm is in place, there is no guarantee that a team's decisions will be implemented at all, much less implemented as they were intended to be.

In Chapter 10, I suggest a number of strategies for communicating with each of the (**PAEI**) styles one on one, while Chapter 11 addresses the problem of communicating with groups: Is it possible to modify your language in such a way that you can be understood by all four styles simultaneously? Volume 3 in this series goes deeper on how to conduct dialogues with people whose style is different than yours.

Is having excellent ingredients and a recipe good enough for preparing a gourmet dish? No. We need appropriate hardware and that is an appropriate organizational structure.

3. STRUCTURE

"Good fences make for good neighbors."

ROBERT FROST

An organization's structure determines how it distributes and measures responsibility, authority, and rewards. To achieve good decision-making the organizational structure of responsibilities has to recognize that short-term tasks have to be separated form long-term task or the long-term tasks will never be sufficiently addressed. And that is necessary for the organization to be effective in the short and the long-run. Thus marketing and sales should report to two different vice presidents. (More about it latter in the book) We need to start with – or evolve into – an organizational structure that allows people to be accountable for the short and the long run, to have the necessary authority, discretionary authority to get results, and to be rewarded to act in their best interest, the interests of their team or unit as well as in the interests of the larger enterprise.

If its structure enables people to align their own interests with those of the larger group, an organization will foster a climate in which mutual trust and respect can grow. In contrast, a structure that does not make a priority of creating mutual trust and respect will eventually become dysfunctional; its managers, with competing interests and no sense of a win-win context in the long run, will continually sabotage each other and interfere with any effort to treat the dysfunction. (See Chapter 8 for a thorough discussion.)

How does the organization match its employees' styles and skills with the tasks they are best capable of achieving?

4. SHARED VISION AND VALUES

This is a large component of the role of (**I**)ntegration, and fundamental to any organization that wants to promote mutual trust and respect. As we discussed earlier, without (**I**)ntegration, an organization can never become greater than the sum of its parts. Lacking a universal sense of shared values and a common goal, the organization will always be in danger of falling apart if its Founder dies or leaves.

Leadership plays a crucial role in this new construct. Whereas a good manager can excel at any of the four basic (**PAEI**) tasks, a leader must be an outstanding (**I**)ntegrator in addition to his other skills to create a culture of MT&R by hiring the right people, learning and teaching how to conduct meetings so decisions can be made with MT&R, structure the company's responsibilities, authority and rewards correctly and develop a common vision and nurture common values. (For a more in-depth definition of leadership, see Chapter 12.)

Slowly but Surely

On the highway of conflict, when you come to the fork in the road where one road leads to destructive conflict and the other to constructive conflict, there is a very small sign that points in the direction of constructive conflict. Inscribed on it are the words "Mutual Trust and Respect" – but the sign is so inconspicuous that only people who slow down at the intersection will be able to read it. Those who speed up will probably end up in destructive conflict.

Why? Because when people experience the pain of conflict, their usual tendency is to speed up. They get hot under the collar; they raise their voices; they start shouting and interrupting each other; they pound the table; they become more entrenched in their own arguments.

The result? Destructive conflict. And – at least when we ourselves are not upset – we can easily see why: The more tense, angry, or strident someone's behavior, the less he will succeed, because the other party, feeling that he's being disrespected, will harden his position instead of trying to work out a compromise.

Working with the CEO's of many companies around the world, I have noticed that the best, most successful managers seem to grow increasingly relaxed as the conflict gets tougher and more difficult. From this observation, I derived my "duck theory" of management: On the surface, a duck looks calm and unperturbed as it floats along in the water; but *under* the water its feet are working fast – *very* fast.

In other words, a good manager stays calm in the midst of conflict. He does not lose his head or become emotional. He does not lose his objectivity. He is considerate and respectful of others – even those with whom he strongly disagrees.

In Hebrew there is an expression that sums up what I am trying to say: "Slow down so I can understand you fast." Whenever there is a conflict or misunderstanding, take a deep breath and slow down. In fact, the more pain you feel, the slower you should go. Don't try to get *out* of it; try to get more deeply *into* it, by slowing down. Take a cleansing breath, as it is called in yoga and Lamaze technique: A deep breath in and a slow one out. By taking slow breaths, you create the necessary condition for patience. It is as if you are saying, "I realize this is going to take time, so I'm prepared to be patient."

Summing Up

To have a healthy company that is effective and efficient in the short and the long run, we need all the (**PAEI**) roles to be performed. For that, we need a complementary team. But such a team can experience conflict. In order to make that conflict constructive rather than destructive, managers, leaders of organizations, countries, families, need to create an environment of mutual trust and respect. Building such an environment involves four factors: The right people, the right process, the right structure and shared vision and values. These issues will be addressed in the next few chapters.

Chapter 8

Structuring Responsibilities Right

PRROBLEM: Is a complementary team sufficient to achieve good decision-making and effective, efficient implementation?

ORGANIZATIONAL ECOLOGY

We have discussed what management is, and how to put together a complementary team of managers with a diversity of styles and viewpoints. But that is only part of the picture.

Staffing an organization with well-trained, well-rounded managers with complementary styles – who have no zeros in their (**PAEI**) codes, are suited to their tasks and even work together admirably – will not necessarily make an organization well managed. That is a starting point and a necessary condition – but it is not sufficient.

What else is necessary? The organization must be structured to attract and nurture those complementary managerial styles; in other words, to allow people to be accountable, so that they can get results and act in the best interests of their team or unit as well as in the interests of the larger enterprise.

And this structure must be able to operate in a compatible climate of mutual trust and respect; the organization's style must fit and support its management.

Structuring requires a complicated formula that is unique to each company, because it must take into account such diverse factors as the company's product mix and market segments; its geographical distribution; its available managerial resources; the degree of innovation it needs to generate in the marketplace; as well as its phase in the organizational life cycle.

So it's important to read this chapter as no more than a basic template, a platform composed of broad strokes that should be adapted according to lots of other variables. (On the other hand, in making those adaptations, it's crucial to preserve the integrity of this basic platform, in addition to maintaining the organization's long-term effectiveness and efficiency.)

Think of this process as a kind of organizational ecology: Organizations must be structured so that there is an environment in which (P) types, (A) types, (E) types, and (I) types can thrive. Without that essential supportive structure, even an ideal complementary team will eventually become twisted and distorted by the biases of the existing structure.

I had this insight many years ago when my second son, who is now an associate of the Institute, was a small child. I had bought him a globe. He looked and looked at it and then asked, "Dad, why is the globe inclined? Why is it not this way [he put it into a horizontal position] or that way [he turned the globe into a straight vertical position]?"

"Because if the Lord had made the globe vertical or horizontal instead of inclined," I replied, "we would not have many different climates."

"Imagine what would happen if the whole world were subject to one long, forever winter," I continued. "Only the polar bears would survive. If a camel wandered by mistake into this North Pole weather, it would have very few choices: It could get the hell out of there, fast, while it was still alive; it could die; or it could adapt and grow polar bear fur in a hurry."

That was when I had my insight: When you look at the culture of an organization that has become bureaucratized to the core, you might think you're looking at polar bears, when what you're really seeing are camels in polar bear fur. In other words, the Bureaucrats who manage Bureaucracies may actually be (**E**)ntrepreneurs who have, somewhere along the way, given up fighting a losing war. They were hired to be (**E**)ntrepreneurs, but when they came in and started learning the ropes, they discovered that if the company would not change its culture to accommodate the new (**E**)ntrepreneurial style, then they would have to change their style to fit into the culture. And guess what happened? Eventually, even hard-core (**E**)ntrepreneurs will behave like bureaucrats.

Outside their workplace, these managers might be very (**E**)ntrepreneurial. They might even have a business on the side. But when they come to work, they mirror the behavior expected in that organizational climate.

How can you get those camels in polar bear drag to start acting like camels again? Many organizational development facilitators make the mistake of trying to teach Bureaucrats (**E**)ntrepreneurial skills experientially of trusting others and taking risks – perhaps by taking them to a weekend retreat, where they practice wall climbing and falling backward into each other's arms.

But even if these managers truly want to make changes, even if they remain enthusiastic throughout their training, what are they going to see when they return to work on Monday? It's snowing there. All day long. They experience a painful disillusionment: Yes, they participated in a wonderful, heartwarming weekend – but in reality, *nothing has changed*. So they retreat into their polar bear fur, and worse, they lose all hope that change can come. The next time a change is attempted, they will be even less responsive.

The only effective way to change a polar bear into a camel is to tilt the globe, to change the environment. True camels will immediately migrate to the Sahara and true polar bears will stay in the north pole. The structural change should create areas that are cold and areas that are hot; thus, every kind of animal will have a place to live and survive. There must be areas in the organization that are structured responsibility, discretion in decision making and rewards wise, for each of the (**P**), (**A**),(**E**),(**I**) styles because each one of them requires different type of responsibility, discretion in decision making and reward structure.

Why Structure Matters

Good structure is necessary for fostering mutual trust and respect. Why? Because good structure provides boundaries, which we all need in order to focus our energies appropriately: As Robert Frost wrote in a famous poem, "Good fences make good neighbors." [1] Unless you know what you have to do, what I have to do, where our responsibilities intersect and where they conflict – in other words, how our jobs affect each other – you're bound to interfere with other people's decisions and create a mess. Who is doing what, when, and to whom? It is everyone's' guess.

The precise definition of "structure" is a question that philosophers have been debating for two thousand years. But they all agree that structure is to form as process is to function. Structure is like the bend in the river through which water flows. It is continuous, consistent, stable, repetitive – and thus predictable: If I know where the river bends, then I can figure out where the water is going to go. If I know what the structure of your personality is, I can predict how you're going to behave.

Architecture is a perfect (**I**)ntegration of form (structure) and function (process): If you tell an architect what you need to accomplish and how you want to live, he will know what kind of a home to design for you. How many rooms do you need? What will happen in each room? How many people will generally occupy each room? Which rooms should be directly connected, and which should be separated? Where will access to each room be necessary? Where will you need privacy, and where will you want the family members to congregate?

With this and other information, the architect begins to imagine a division of space into one or more levels, with walls, doors, windows, and stairs – *boundaries*, in other words – that is aesthetically pleasing even as it facilitates the tasks his clients need to perform.

Structure is as crucial to organizations as it is to buildings. When it is weak or absent, obvious symptoms develop, just as they do when one of the four roles of management is missing.

When I come into an organization where people are being accused of interfering, micromanaging, or being "empire builders," I know immediately that the company's managers lack a clear idea of where their job ends and someone else's job begins.

An effective structure, by contrast, would set clear and exact limits around each manager's responsibilities. And ironically, it is precisely within the narrow confines of a detailed job description that managers become free to focus their energies appropriately. Why? Because when the boundaries are poorly defined, a manager cannot rely on others to carry out specific tasks – he cannot even figure out who, if anyone, is responsible for getting them done. Thus he is hostage to every little detail of implementation, leaving him with less time and freedom to make decisions and act on them.

Is Restructuring Always Necessary?

Sometimes it's possible to make valuable changes in an organization without redesigning its structure. If the prevailing environment is already relatively accepting of change, we can sometimes deal with issues such as motivation, strategy, vision, and information flow *without* touching the structure.

But if what you want is a paradigm shift, a change in the company's mission and direction, then a structural adjustment is crucial. Organizations are like motor boats: They have a power system, engines. If you tell me what the engine settings are, I can tell you which direction the boat will take. To change the direction, you need to change the settings.

For example, companies that have traditionally made money producing electronic devices for the military have been rethinking their mission in recent years, as military budgets have dwindled with the end of the cold war.

Let's say such a company decides to venture into consumer electronics. Simply designing a new strategy will not work. Why? Because the organization's power structure has historically been based on its managers' ability to produce military electronics. A change in the organization's primary mission sets up an inherent conflict of interest: Those in the company with power, who must initiate the change, are precisely the people with the most to lose when the company's direction changes and new skills and technologies are needed. Naturally, they would want to obstruct any change that would shift power away from them.

In one company I counseled, they kept making that same mistake year after year: They would bring in some new minted MBA and make him a project manager in charge of consumer electronics. He would write lots of reports, cry, shout, smoke a lot, cough a lot, and cry some more – but nothing would happen. Eventually he'd leave or be fired, and they'd bring in the next victim of their ignorance, and then the next person, and the next.

The problem was that the project manager position, as it was conceived, had no clout. The manager could talk as much as he liked, but he had no army behind him to enforce his decisions. The big engines were going to the right. To turn the boat to the left, they put a small, very small engine that hardly could move a bicycle much less a power boat, to turn it to the left.

My solution was to transfer the entire engineering group, which had been under military electronics, to consumer electronics. This was a radical organizational change, which forced a shift in direction.

Now, that was not an easy thing to do. The military guys did not like it at all. Structural change is painful change. As an analogy, I sometimes compare myself to a chiropractor of organizations, rather than a masseur. Why? A masseur works with your muscles; a chiropractor deals with the alignment of your bones. My task is to realign your bones so that you function much better, but it's a much more painful process than getting a massage.

Another analogy I like is the difference between psychotherapy and self growth weekend retreats: Psychologists and therapists try to change your long-term behavior, while self-growth weekends try to change how you behave *now*. The latter do have an impact, but it's like a Chinese meal: After twenty minutes, you're hungry again. To make a long-term change, you have to change the structure of the personality, which can be painful.

Nevertheless, that pain is sometimes necessary, and trying to avoid it will only lead to other, different kinds of pain in the long run. Changing the process without changing the power structure has a very limited, short-term impact. If the organization is not structured properly, you might end up placing camels at the North Pole or polar bears in the Sahara desert. Lacking a compatible structure, you could start out with all the right people in place to create a complementary team, but eventually they will have to adapt their styles to bend to the existing structure – and that complementary team will be lost.

This is a common mistake companies make when they try to do reengineering: They're trying to change the river flow (process) without changing the river bends (structure). It doesn't work: What they often get instead is destructive conflict.

ELEMENTS OF GOOD ORGANIZATIONAL STRUCTURE

A well-designed organizational structure contains three distinct elements:

- the structure of responsibility;
- the structure of authority, power, and influence;
- the structure of rewards.

Each of these elements is necessary and together they are sufficient to provide an effective structure. Why? Because they ensure that every person can be held accountable for his role in the organization. In other words, the organization must be able to identify who contributed to its success (or lack of success), and in what manner.

The first element is responsibility: What are the tasks each person is expected to perform?

People often interpret being accountable and being responsible as meaning the same thing, but there is actually a big difference between the two concepts.

I define responsibility as the results a person is *expected* to deliver for the task assigned.

Accountability is more than responsibility. True, you cannot be accountable unless you know exactly what you are responsible *for*. But being given the responsibility does not, by itself, make you accountable. People will certainly *expect* you to be accountable, but the truth is that you aren't going to *feel* accountable (nor should you) unless you are *able* to deliver what you've been given responsibility for delivering. Being able means that you have sufficient authority, power, and/or influence to carry out your responsibilities and are you getting rewarded for carrying your responsibilities successfully.

Thus it is crucial that the boundaries of each person's authority and power be defined. How far should his authority carry? How much power can or should he use? (Influence, which relies on persuasion and is available to everyone, does not require boundaries.)

The third component involves structuring a system of rewards that will motivate the person to use the authority he's been given to accomplish his assigned tasks. Although a person can be held accountable if he understands his responsibilities and has sufficient authority, power, and/or influence to carry it out, he will not *feel* accountable unless he also feels he will be rewarded for accomplishing those tasks. We also need to learn how to motivate and reward people, both for group effort and for individual effort.

The rewards should correspond logically with the assigned task, and also be satisfying to the particular managerial style that is likely to be performing that task.

To demonstrate this point, let me tell you about my experience consulting to a fast-food restaurant chain.

One day, the founder/CEO complained to me that the company lacked (**E**)ntrepreneurial spirit. His employees were content to just do what they were told, he said, but that was not good enough for him. He wanted people like himself, who would take initiative and help build the company.

I happened to know that this CEO was adamantly opposed to giving any ownership to his employees, so I asked him how he would feel about working for a straight salary.

"Absolutely not," he said. "I want equity. I want to benefit from the growth of the company I contributed to building."

"Exactly!" I responded. "Don't you see that the rewards system you've established attracts the wrong kind of people? If you want (**E**)ntrepreneurs, you have to entice them with (**E**)ntrepreneurial reinforcements; otherwise they won't come to you. In fact, if you *did* manage to hire any (**E**)ntrepreneurs, they would soon leave you, because what you're offering is not what they want."

Accountability, then, cannot be assumed until all three requirements have been met: The worker knows what he is responsible for; he has sufficient authority, power and/or influence to carry out his responsibilities; and he feels he will be adequately rewarded for doing so.

Once all three criteria are met, I can and should hold you accountable if your responsibilities are *not* met: You knew *what* to do, you *could* do it, and you were *rewarded correctly* to do it. So why *didn't* you do it?

STRUCTURING FOR ACCOUNTABILITY

Can a manager have clear responsibilities and yet not be accountable? Unfortunately, because of poor organizational structure, this situation is not uncommon.

As an example, let us look at the debacle of Enron, which went bankrupt in 2001 amid charges of investor fraud. When Enron collapsed, there were calls for government regulation as a cure for corporate "creative accounting." But I believe a better solution lies in restructuring organizations to ensure accountability.

Theoretically, Enron CEO Kenneth Lay should have been accountable for any irregularity in Enron's accounting and reporting. But was he?

I suggest that although CEOs *should* have all of the authority, power, and influence they need to carry out their responsibilities, they rarely do. If the organization is structured incorrectly, the CEO may be deprived of information that would be the source of his power, authority, and influence.

When that occurs, the CEO is like the emperor in the children's story "The Emperor's New Clothes": He parades through the company's offices and corridors believing himself to be adorned in full CEO regalia, in possession of all the authority, power, and influence in the world; and everyone applauds and genuflects when he passes, as if he really does. But in reality, he is nude. Why? Because the information that would allow him to truly guide the organization is not reaching him.

In order to get the information that provides him with the power to drive the organization and be responsible for its behavior, a CEO must always have two sources of information. If he only has one source, he loses his discretionary power to make decisions, in effect ceding all his power over to the other person and becoming totally dependent on him. He becomes a virtual prisoner of that source.

A perfect demonstration of disastrous structuring can be found in the phenomenon of the CFO, a position that's been embraced with almost religious fervor among American industries. Treasury, investor relations, budgeting, and controlling the bookkeeping(accounting) all report to the CFO; in many organizations he also supervises the administrative functions: The Legal Department, HR, and even IT.

This structure puts control of all the company's financial data in the CFO's hands. Because he is responsible for showing profitability, the temptation will be great for him to "spin" the information, interpreting and presenting it in the most positive light. And because he alone controls access to this information, it is easy for him to manipulate the numbers – to impress investors, show profitability, or demonstrate return on investment.

Instead of a CFO, two people – a Finance VP and a corporate controller – should report directly to the CEO. The Finance VP should determine whether the company is getting a good enough return on its investment, how best to handle cash flow, and what the company should do with its money. The corporate controller's focus is on collecting adequate and precise information and ensuring its integrity.

Naturally, these two will be in conflict. Finance will constantly challenge the information that the corporate controller provides, and the corporate controller will disagree with how Finance is interpreting the data. It is precisely through such conflict that the CEO will hear a variety of perspectives and be able to judge them for himself.

CEO accountability will derive from structuring the information hierarchy to ensure that he receives dissenting information, which in turn will enable him to judge the merits of different opinions and make decisions. Until that happens, we can throw one CEO after another in jail, but it won't change anything. The next CEO won't do any better unless we make him feel accountable.

WHEN THE TAIL WAGS THE DOG

Ideally, an organization's strategy should direct its structure. That is what Alfred Chandler taught us already in 1948 and it became the guiding light of all consultants: Strategy precedes structure. As in the architecture example above, once an organization has set the functions it wants or has to perform, its (**P**), it can determine which structure will best support those objectives. If the strategy is to move to the right, for instance, then we need to change the engine settings, reducing the power on the right and increasing it on the left. That is what should happen but not what is happening.

But more often than not, it is the other way around: The structure determines the strategy. What is happening – not what *should* be happening, what is happening – is that the way the engine is already set is what's going to steer the boat, regardless of how much you shout that the new strategy dictates a change in direction. Basically the form is leading the function to behave in a certain way.

Why does this occur? One reason is that changing the power structure is extremely difficult and painful, in any organization – and risky to those who initiate or support it. Some people's power positions will inevitably be challenged, and anyone who gets into that cross fire could get hurt. Any time you want to decrease power on the right and increase it on the left, the left side will be delighted, but the right side is going to fight you tooth and nail because it's losing ground. That is why Machiavelli said, "It must be remembered that there is nothing more difficult to plan, more doubtful of success, nor more dangerous to manage, than the creation of a new system. For the initiator has the enmity of all who would profit by the preservation of the old institutions, and merely lukewarm defenders in those who would gain by the new ones."[2]

By contrast, changing strategy is relatively easy: You look at the environment, you look at a map, and you make a decision. But the bottom line is that changing the strategy – standing at the top of the boat and shouting new instructions into the wind – is not going to change the boat's course by even one degree. The only effective way to change the direction of the boat is to change the power settings.

Nevertheless, here's what happens in many companies: The managers relax on deck and talk about which way they think the organization should go. Then they see rocks ahead, and they panic: "Oh my god! Pull to the right! Come on, people, we can do it! Turn to the right, all together! Let's see some teamwork! Let's get motivated! To the right!"

But who is actually adjusting the dials to shift the boat's course to the right? Nobody!

This kind of strategy is the equivalent of doing a rain dance in the Sahara. Unless you change the power structure – unless you tilt the globe to bring rain into your area – the desert is going to remain a desert. All this talk about process, teamwork, quality of people, vision, values – it's all useless if the power settings are stuck in one place.

How and why do those power settings get stuck? When the same process is repeated and repeated and repeated, it becomes a habit;

eventually, after more repetition, the habit becomes a form. And if the form isn't regularly examined and analyzed and tweaked or changed, it becomes petrified.

When that happens, structure (form) and process (function) exchange places. In the beginning, the process dictated the structure; by the end, when the structure is petrified, it takes over and impacts the process.

Picture water trickling down a mountain. Slowly, gradually, it is sculpting the river bend. But as it repeats and repeats itself, working deeper and deeper into the ground, it slowly becomes a canyon. At that point, it is no longer the water that influences how the river bends; it is the river bend that directs how the water flows.

"Sow a thought, and you reap an act;
Sow an act, and you reap a habit;
Sow a habit, and you reap a character;
Sow a character, and you reap a destiny."

SAMUEL SMILES (1812-1904) IN
"LIFE AND LABOR" (1887)

This phenomenon is so common in organizations that, usually, once I've analyzed the power structure of a company, I can tell what strategy it is going to implement, regardless of its stated goals and desires. The present structure has become so overwhelming and powerful that it tends to dictate nearly every future decision.

To avoid that situation, it is essential to consider *all* of the pieces of the organizational whole – *and* in the proper order. There is a generic template to the desired structure. That is how I start all my restructuring efforts. That in itself relaxes the setting on the engines of the motor boat. That creates space for (**E**)s and (**A**)s and (**P**)s and (**I**)'s, than we go forward and adapt the template to the specific needs the organization has in the future. These adaptations are more easy to be accepted by the organization because in the first draft of the restructuring I have already created organizational ecology for all (**PAEI**)s to have their adequate power bases. I am not alone in making change. I have allies.

Back to the Functionalist View

To determine the correct structure, then, we must start at the very beginning: What is the function of this organization and of its employees?

We know that the function of management is to make sure the organization can achieve its goals effectively and efficiently in the short and the long run. But how does that break down in terms of individual responsibilities?

To return to the boat analogy, above, we would ask, "What do these engines do? What is the responsibility of each engine?" And we would discover that one engine's task is to move us to the left; another's job is to move us to the right.

As soon as we know the purpose of each engine, we can determine what percentage of the final product it is responsible for; and thus how much power it should have. This is why we always start with responsibilities: The power structure should be driven by the responsibility structure. Until you know what a manager's responsibilities are, how can you know how much power and authority are appropriate? And the reward structure – in other words, what achievements do you choose to reward, and in what manner? – should come last.

In fact, the authority and reward structures should fall into place naturally as soon as you understand the structure of responsibilities. But they don't, and the reason they don't is because very often, responsibilities are divided incorrectly.

That's why this chapter is so important. Dividing responsibilities appropriately is the key to making an organization function at its optimum level. Essentially, structure is a tool I use to achieve that goal.

CLASSIC EXAMPLES OF POOR STRUCTURE

We have talked about the dangers of creating a CFO position that encompasses both accounting and finance. It is one of numerous popular and traditional structures that lead corporations into disaster.

Here is another: When an organization has one vice president for both sales and marketing, I know immediately that this company's marketing efforts will be dysfunctional.

Why? Here's a hint: It is a fact that you rarely find a "vice president for marketing and sales." It is invariably the other way around: "Vice president for sales and marketing." This is not happenstance.

As a second hint, let us codify marketing in (**PAEI**) terms: First, it must analyze what changes are likely to occur in the market over the long run. That is the (**E**) role. Then, it has to recommend a course for action for the company in response to those changes – the (**P**) role. The marketing department must also have some (**a**) and (**i**) abilities in order to work well with other departments, but those roles can be met at the threshold level only. So the (**PAEI**) code for marketing is (**PaEi**).

Now, how about sales? Above all, the sales department must see to it that sales happen, that revenues come in, that clients are satisfied. That is (**P**).

Second, these sales efforts had better be efficient; we want maximum bucks for minimum bang. This requires training and allocation of sales territories, which is the (**A**) role.

The sales department's code, then, is (**PAei**): Results-oriented and efficient.

In marketing, the most important role is (**E**), which is focused on the long run; for sales it is (**P**), which has a short-run perspective.

Now, we know, because Herbert Simon and James March pointed it out forty years ago in their book *Organizations*,[3] that the short-term orientation always squeezes out the long-term orientation. It's human nature, after all, that the expedient will squeeze out the significant.

Thus, when you have a VP for sales and marketing, he is very likely to be sales-focused, and the marketing staff will be consigned to doing sales support activities, such as analyzing which products were sold and measuring how many more were sold compared to previous years. Instead of making innovations as it was designed to, the marketing department just follows along, measuring the effectiveness and efficiency of the techniques already in use.

The same applies when you have R&D lumped with production/manufacturing under the same vice president. R&D should be (E)-oriented, of course; while production/manufacturing is focused on (P). But very soon, R&D's priorities will be crushed by the urgencies of (P).

Similarly, if engineering and production are combined, the engineering department will end up doing maintenance work for production. (E) will be sacrificed for the benefit of the short-term (P).

What about the (I) subsystem? The most common function of the modern-day human resources department – a fancy and misleading name for what used to be called personnel – is (A): Staffing the organization, organizing salary scales, (A)dministering benefits and performance reviews; coordinating downsizing; as well as some training and a lot of filing. If there is any actual human resources development activity, it is weak and probably discouraged.

Why? Because there is an innate conflict between (A)dministration and (I) development. To develop an organization and its human resources as an organic entity that responds well to change, both (E)ntrepreneurship and (I)ntegration are essential. But (A)dministration, which exists to serve the organization's (P)roducing role, is the natural enemy of any activity that takes up valuable time and/or promotes change (E).

In a heavy (A) environment, those who try to adapt or develop human resources are going to threaten the order that (A)dministrators wish to maintain. Before long, they will find that their plans are being obstructed and their opinions ignored, and gradually their jobs will morph into something far more (A)dministrative than (E)ntrepreneurial of the (I) role, which is what the Human Resources Development activities should be all about.

A Template for Good Structure

Here is the structure I recommend as a basic template. (However, as I have already said, it must be customized for every company's unique goals and resources and current phase in the corporate life cycle.)

To emphasize the critical driving role for each task, I have listed only one (**PAEI**) role for each. By now you should understand that the other roles must also be present, at least at a threshold level of competence. There cannot be any dashes in the code of a good manager. In fact, it is much better if *two* roles are performed well; thus marketing should ideally be (**PaEi**), sales (**PAei**), and new product development engineering should be (**PaEi**).

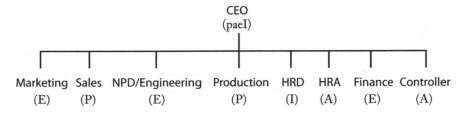

I have over-simplified the chart above in order to put one point into sharp relief: In order to have the diversity of styles necessary for a complementary team, you must also have a complementary structure that nourishes diversity. The reward structure should be different too, but before we get there, let's talk about how to organize small start-up companies that cannot afford many vice presidents.

Structure for Young Companies

In a small company managed by its founder, there will probably be a salesman to do the selling or help the founder do the selling, so the (**P**) role in client interface can be delegated. But who decides what to (**P**)roduce, which market to go after, how much to charge, and how to promote – "product, place, price, promotion," the famous "four Ps" of marketing? The founder decides, of course.

The founder might hire someone to supervise (**P**)roduction or assembly or operations – but who decides what technology should be used, where to locate the plant, how big the industrial park will be? Again, the founder.

What about finance? Even if the company has a vice president for finance – even if he is called the CFO – who *really* decides whether to take loans, what kind of loans, and what amount? Who woos investors? Once again, it is the founder, the CEO.

If there is a human resources department, it might also have a vice president; however, this person is usually one level above a secretary and would not normally attend the executive committee meetings. As to human resources development, it probably does not exist.

How would this structure look?

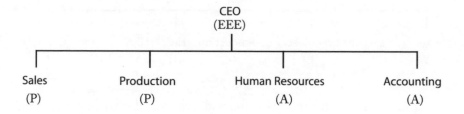

As you can see, the (**E**) role is monopolized by the founder or CEO of a start-up company.

The danger, which I call "Founders trap," is that when the founder leaves or dies, the company's (E) dies with him – and the ill experience seizure.

Summing it Up

The various techniques for structuring a company so that complementary teams can emerge and be nourished could fill several books. At the Institute, we have hundreds of pages of manuals on how to build a complementary structure in order to get a complementary team; and then even more pages and manuals on how to (**I**)ntegrate the team – since by definition, the styles of the team members will be different from each other and these differences will inevitably lead to conflict, which can become destructive. In the next chapter, I will discuss a few techniques for fitting a manager's personal style to a particular task; and creating a complementary team from the disparate talents of your staff.

NOTES

1. Frost, Robert: *North of Boston* (New York: Dodd Mead & Co., 1977).

2. Machiavelli, Nicco: *The Prince* - reprinted from the 1640 translation by Edward Dacres (London: Alexander Moring Ltd at the De La More Press, 1929).

3. March, James G., and Herbert Simon: *Organizations* (New York, London: John Wiley & Sons, 1958).

Chapter 9

Matching Style to Task

PROBLEM: Once we've structured the
organization appropriately, how do we put
together a complementary team and match
the right manager to the right job?

Diagnosing a Type

We all have default personality styles, probably from childhood, but
we can perform differently, if not quite as competently, when necessary. Most people have multiple traits. I'm a (**P**) when I wash my car,
I'm an (**A**) when I'm in the office, I'm an (**E**) when I'm with my clients
and I'm an (**I**) when I'm with my kids. All of us have all of these traits
to some degree, but which one predominates will shift depending on
the situation.

Still, we all lean toward one or another style; for instance, I am
predominantly an (**E**). I can do (**A**) work, but let me tell you, after
a few hours I'm exhausted. For me, being a bookkeeper would be a
punishment. On the other hand, for a bookkeeper to stand in front
of a crowd and speak would be a punishment.

Now, we know that the way to avoid miscommunication is to
match your communication style to the style of the person you're talking to. But if we all behave differently according to the circumstances,
then how can you know the best way to communicate?

People often ask me if there are tests they can administer that will
determine a person's style. As a matter of fact, I discovered after my

first book was published that the four basic management styles I had outlined closely matched Carl Jung's four personality types.

There is a test available at www.adizes.com that measures (**PAEI**) style. It's called the Adizes Management Style Indicator Questionnaire as you believe it is, you want it to be and what you believe your task demands it to be.

Such tests can be useful as an aid in the hiring process. But aside from that, I do not believe that testing is an effective strategy or solution for knowing someone you are already working with..

Why not? First of all, you cannot simply refuse to talk to someone until he's taken a psychological test. But more to the point, testing is the (**A**)dministrative, bureaucratic, mechanistic method of learning about people; in other words, it is precisely wrong.

What is the approximately right way? Simply being sensitive to people. Try to understand who they are and how they behave. *Feel* them. Watch them, listen to them, and try to communicate, and if you are misunderstood, assume that you guessed wrong about their style and try something else.

It isn't as random as it sounds, because it's also dictated by the situation. If you've worked with someone for a long time, you come to recognize his basic working style. I can tell that the president of my institute is an (**I**), and everybody there knows it, not only me. My chief (**A**)dministrative officer is an (**A**), my sales manager is a (**P**). Everyone at the institute knows this and can see it in the way these people handle various situations.

For example, my sales manager always has a very simple answer, no matter what the question is. Everything is very simple, very short and to the point. "Done. Next question?" He's a (**P**). I hired him because he was a (**P**). If you know what they are, you know how they'll behave and whether they will fit the position you need to fill.

Still, there will be times when a person's customary style changes in order to adapt to changing conditions. When you sense that happening, try to use the language for the style that's being exhibited. You too have to be adaptive.

What should you do if you don't know the person very well or at all? In that case, ask questions and observe closely. Ask what job he performs. Look at the organization chart; it can tell you a lot. If the manager is in marketing, he is likely to be (**E**)-oriented. If he is in sales, he should be (**P**)-oriented. If his job is in accounting, he will probably have an (**A**) orientation. This is not foolproof evidence, but it's a clue.

From there, try to assess his style by observing his office, his desk, how he dresses, his posture, his level of energy.

Again, what I am really suggesting is that you try to be sensitive to the other person. That's the best test. Watch carefully to see whether he understands you or not and continue to adapt your style to his until you see that he is comfortable with the style you are using and clearly grasps your meaning..

If the conversation happens to be a job interview but for some reason you are unable to administer a style quiz, there is a trick you can use during the interview that will cover the same ground: Tell the prospective employee that he is allowed to ask you ten questions about the position – not nine and not eleven; exactly ten. You will answer these questions fully so that he will have all of the information he needs to decide whether to take the job or not if it is offered.

Then sit back and classify your job candidate's questions in (**PAEI**) terms. A (**P**) question for instance, will be "What would my responsibilities be, exactly?" An (**A**) type question is: "What is the compensation package?" An (**E**) type question is: "Explain the company's goals and forecast its future." And an (**I**) type question is: "Tell me about the people who work here."

The sequence of the job candidate's questions, and how many (**P**), (**A**), (**E**), or (**I**) questions he asked, will give you an approximate picture of his style.

The Managerial Mix

We noted in Chapter 5 that for good management we need a complementary team in which each member is himself a good manager. The team members must complement one another and thereby form a (**PAEI**) team. There are innumerable combinations of skills and personality traits that can add up to a (**PAEI**) team; it might be composed of a (**Paei**), a (**pAei**), a (**paEi**), and a (**paeI**), for example. Even better would be a team composed of a (**PaeI**), a (**pAeI**), and a (**paEI**), since all will perform well in (**I**)ntegration. Such teams lead to an effective and efficient organization in the short and long run.

But if there are only (**PaeI**)s on the managerial team, no matter how many of them there are, the organization will be mismanaged.

Some organizations, having accepted the view that one person cannot do the management job alone, have tried to develop the concept of "chief executive office" – several executives who jointly should manage the organization. Very often this approach fails, however, because the executives make the mistake of appointing people like themselves to be on the team: An (**A**) executive will hire other (**A**)s; a (**P**) executive will hire other (**P**)s. This is a prescription for certain failure; in order to effectively perform the complex task of managing for the short and the long run, a team must have style differences among its members, and those differences must be accepted and respected.

The Complementary Team Jigsaw Puzzle

The following four questions must be answered for each prospective team member before he can be identified as appropriate for the position:

1. What does the organizational climate require? Will the organization be tolerant of this person's preferred style?

2. What does the team require; in other words, what are the styles of the current team members that must be complemented?

3. What are the characteristics and demands of the task?

4. What degree of discretion in decision-making does this task require?

Question 1 refers to where the organization is on the lifecycle and – if this manager's unit is a profit center – where the unit is on the lifecycle. (If it is a not a profit center, then this question isn't relevant.)

Let me explain: Every system has a lifecycle, and that includes organizations as well as families.[1] Managing systems is like parenting children: We take for granted that a parent's techniques and disciplinary methods will constantly be changing as he adapts to the child's growing emotional maturity. You should not parent a baby as if it is an adult, and you should not treat an adult as if he is a baby.

Well, good leaders, just like good parents, should have at least a basic understanding of the organizational lifecycle. To be functional, a leader's style should take into account where the organization is on the lifecycle.

Thus if we are going to hire a CEO, we must first ask ourselves where the organization currently is on the lifecycle. That, in turn, will determine what style CEO the organization *should* be looking for. (I have deliberately chosen to use and emphasize the word *should*, instead of addressing what the organization may actually *be* looking for – because the reality is that organizations will often seek the leadership they feel comfortable with, rather than the leadership with the style needed to guide the organization into the next desirable stage of its lifecycle.)

The same principle applies all the way down the managerial line, whether we are looking for a CEO or for a manager to run a specific profit center unit within the organization. For start-ups up to the Go-Go phase, you will want a (**PaEi**) style. Later, in adolescence, the organization will briefly require a (**PAei**) style, but should move quickly to a (**pAEi**) style. Prime organizations need a (**paEI**) style.

When the organization begins to age, in its aristocracy, you should be looking for a (**PaEi**). In a crisis, when the organization is losing market share and sinking rapidly, it's time for the turn-around style of a (**Paei**) leader.

This part of the book needs more elaboration than space allows. Interested readers can find a thorough discussion of the lifecycle phases in my book Corporate Lifecycles.[2]

Complementarity to other team members

In putting together a complementary team, it is important to remember that the final product must include representation of each of the four basic roles. No team will function properly if it is missing a manager who excels in (**P**), or (**A**), or either of the other roles. So once you've chosen one or two team members, your choices for the rest will to some extent depend on the choices you've already made.

Thus, even if the person you are considering has all the abilities that are needed to perform all the necessary roles of management – that is, he or she is a (**Paei**), a (**pAei**), a (**paEi**), or a (**pael**) – and even if his abilities fit the team's requirements perfectly, he will not be an appropriate team member if his style adds too much of one role to the team's makeup, or if it does not supply a role that is weak.

For example, a person with extra (**I**) may be needed if the other team members are weak in (**I**).

Or suppose you've picked a (**pAEi**) for one position, a (**PaEi**) for another, and a (**paEI**) for a third. You may want to avoid choosing yet another team member with strong (**E**) instincts. Otherwise, your team will always be at risk of being hijacked by its (**E**) contingent, who will introduce endless digressions to the decision-making process.

Task demands

The next condition is that each team member be placed in a position in which his respective style can be most useful. Finding someone whose style already fits the task will obviate the need for expensive development and permit immediate training.

In addition, each of the styles has certain needs that must be met in order to find any job satisfying. Intuitively, we would not expect someone who is very comfortable in his accounting job to be excited about a transfer into sales, or vice versa. A (**P**)roducer, who likes functional involvement, will resent the time he spends on (**A**)dministration. This is a complaint frequently made by people who have been promoted to (**A**)dministrative jobs from positions in which they were expected to (**P**)roduce. For example, there are many artistic directors who would much prefer to direct productions themselves, instead of hiring others to do it. Senior architects may suffer at having to (**A**)dminister, solicit new projects, and motivate others to do the designing that they would love to do themselves. Becoming the chairperson of a university department can be personally costly to those who love research.

On the other hand, there are those Department Chairs in academia who love (**A**)dministration and suffer "re-entry blues" when their terms expire. If they've felt gratified by (**A**)dministering others, they will have a difficult time getting back into research.

So before filling any position, the first step is to analyze the tasks that will be required to effectively do the job. The following are some questions to consider; the answers will help you evaluate the (**PAEI**) requirements of the task.

1. Is the task programmable? (How easy is it to train people to perform it?)

Answer: If the answer is that it is easy to train people in the task, then you will not want to assign (E)s or (I)s there. The endless routine will bore an (E) or (I) to distraction. The task is a better fit for an (A) or a (P).

2. How much ability to do abstract thinking is required to perform the task?

Answer: If a lot of abstract thinking is required, an (E) or (I) would fit well here.

3. Does the task require working under pressure?

Answer: The (P) style thrives under pressure.

4. How structured or unstructured is the task?

Answer: The more structured it is, the more it calls for an (A) or a (P).

5. How much initiative is required to perform the task?

Answer: If initiative is needed, you want an (E) style manager.

6. How much long-term uncertainty is unavoidable in dealing with the task?

Answer: The more long-term uncertainty the task involves, the more you want an (E) assigned to it.

7. How much short-term uncertainty is unavoidable in dealing with the task?

Answer: A (P) style manager copes best with short-term uncertainty.

8. Does the task require coping on a regular basis with change?

Answer: The more change is necessary, the more an (E) manager is also necessary.

9. Does performing the task effectively require taking risks? How much risk, and how frequently?

Answer: Of the four styles, (E) is best able to deal with risk; in fact, he enjoys it.

10. How much interrelationship with and cooperation from other people is necessary to do the task?

Answer: If the answer is "a lot," then an (I) should be your choice.

11. Does the task require attention to detail?

Answer: If yes, then choose an (A).

12. Does the task require substantial follow-up?

Answer: If substantial follow-up is required, again, you'll want an (A) for the task.

13. Are the results long-term or short-term?

Answer: If the task is relatively short-term, a (P) would be appropriate. For a more long-term orientation, choose an (E).

14. Can success or failure in the task easily be attributed to an individual?

Answer: A (P) responds well to situations that are direct, easy to grasp, do not involve subtlety, sees short-term results, and for which he can take direct responsibility.

TEST YOURSELF

Take the following exam to test yourself.

Match each need to one of the four (**PAEI**) styles.[3]

   Need to achieve   —

   Need to control   —

   Need to affiliate   —

   Need to self actualize   —

Discretion in Decision-Making

The higher a person ascends in a hierarchical organization, the more power, authority, and influence he is expected to have – therefore the more discretion in decision-making he *should* have.

On the other hand, if the organization is relatively decentralized, some of that decision-making discretion will be granted to lower levels of the organization.

Thus, in two organizations where one of the organizations is centralized and the other is decentralized, the same task will require two different styles of management. The more decentralized an organization is, the more initiative it will expect and the greater its (**E**) and (**I**) should be.

CODING JOBS: A BASIC TEMPLATE

We have already covered the (**PAEI**) styles of CEO's and profit center units managers, whether they are product managers, strategic business units managers, or division heads. What style is appropriate for the COO as an Executive VP or President? It should be (**PAei**) – or, even better, (**PAeI**). The (**E**) role should be the domain of the CEO.

Now let us look at the most desirable styles for the other members of the managerial team.

Finance

I differentiate between finance and accounting. Finance should look into the future, toward the coming financial needs of the company. What cash flow, what resources will be necessary so that we can finance what we want to do?

Its main function is (**P**) – but the (**P**) is return on investment, not products or sales. Who are the clients of finance? They are the stockholders, the owners, the investors. The role of finance is to make sure that investors are happy. They really should not care so much what we (**P**)roduce, for whom we (**P**)roduce, or how we (**P**)roduce, as long as return on investment is competitive.

What belongs to finance is investor relations, relations with the banks and the investment community, and analysis of financial results. Finance should be free to challenge marketing and new product development by asking whether a new product is worth the investment – because that is its role. (**A**) and (**I**) are less important. Its code, then, should be (**PaEi**).

Accounting

While finance is looking into the future, accounting has to look from the past into the present: A balance sheet of profit and loss is actually a present picture summarizing past activities, as of today.

It's a totally different orientation. Accounting concerns itself with accuracy and following the rules; in other words, its function is, first and foremost, an enormous (**A**).

What is the next most important role? This goes with a joke: A small firm was going to hire an accountant. Three people showed up for an interview, and each was asked the same question.

The first candidate was a young graduate with a brand-new degree. When they asked him, "What is 2 plus 2?" he said, "Absolutely, without question, 4."

The second guy came from a large accounting firm. He said, "I'll have to call the home office first."

The third guy had a lot of experience in the street – the street of hard knocks. When he was asked, "What is 2 plus 2?" he answered: "It depends. Are you buying or are you selling?"

In other words, for accounting, the second most important role should be (**E**). Why? Because an accountant's job is not only to provide data but also to provide information. What is the difference? Information is data organized for making decisions. Your accounting department should be able to give you information, not just data that you are not sure how to interpret. Accounting should be able to organize the data for you, so you can make decisions. The department's job is not only to collect data for the IRS. Its clients are whoever needs information in order to make decisions. Accounting should be able to tell (**P**)roduction, for example, what it costs to (**P**)roduce each of its products or services.

The code for accounting should be (**pAEi**), with (**I**) in third place and (**P**) last – a style that I have nicknamed the "pain in the neck." A good accountant is supposed to be a pain in the neck: Whenever you try to make strategic changes, a good pain-in-the-neck accountant should show you where the costs are and why you should be careful. On the other hand, if you do not often initiate change, the same accountant should challenge your propensity for staying in place, which could do damage to the company over time.

Basically, a good accountant is a good contrarian.

And that brings me back to my first point: Why I am against putting finance and accounting together. Suppose Finance opposes an investment idea Since accounting is viewed as contrarian all the time on anything, the oposition Finance is making against the investment will be viewed as the opposition of accounting, something everyone is used to and thus it will be ignored. Finance will not have the credibility; accounting will undermine it. Its opinions and recommendations are likely to be ignored; after all, everyone knows that accounting always disagrees with everything – "So what else is new?"

If Finance were separate from accounting, the inputs of the Finance department would be taken more seriously.

Human Resources

A range of styles might be appropriate here, because the function of this department varies in different organizations. The most important role of the human resources department is usually (**I**), but the role that ranks second is not always clear. If the department's task is primarily one of "files administration," as is true for many human resources departments, the role that ranks second would be (**A**). If the department is used by management as a tool to increase productivity and efficiency, then (**P**) would rank second.

I differentiate between human resources (**A**)dministration and human resources development, which means developing new capabilities. Most human resources departments were once called Personnel; the name was changed because it made the department seem boring and maintenance-oriented. The new name, however, doesn't change the fact that companies continue to need human resources, such as (**A**)dministration, performance reviews, and training for its people. These (**A**) functions are indispensable and cannot be ignored. So I code human resources (**A**)dministration as (**PAei**).

Human resources development, on the other hand, is (**paEI**): It develops new horizons for its employees, and also does executive searches, hiring, coaching, and organizational development that changes the culture of the organization and its staff. It creates and manages change.

For human resources (**A**)dministration, I recommend hiring a person whose background is labor law, while for human resources development I recommend sociologists, specialists in OD, and organizational or industrial psychologists.

Because the field has not yet accepted my (**PAEI**) theory, many of the people who work in human resources (**A**)dministration today have styles that are far more compatible with human resources development. If you want to see frustrated people, people who are hardly ever recognized for their contribution and value to the company, people who are completely mismatched to their jobs, look at the people in

Human Resources. Although the department is called HRD, in fact what they are doingis (**A**)dministration. That not only frustrates them; the rest of the organization suspects them because they say one thing but do something else.

Production

In (**P**) roduction, (**P**) ranks first; (**A**) second, (**I**) third, and (**E**) fourth. Please note that this doesn't mean (**E**) is unimportant. Remember that we are only ranking the relative importance of each role and (**I**) is very important but not as much as (**P**) and (**A**).

The tasks of the (**P**)roduction department are assembly, manufacturing, and other labor-intensive operations. The focus is on effective and efficient operations, or (**PA**). Their client is the sales department, and what do the salesmen want? They want the product (or service), on time, at the quality and quantity that was agreed upon. That is (**P**): What are you going to (**P**)roduce for me? The next priority for them is (**A**): They want to (**P**)roduce the product for the least possible expense, with no waste.

Naturally, for the department to run smoothly, its manager must ensure that people work together, which is (**I**). So (**I**) would be the third priority. There is typically the least amount of focus on the (**E**) orientation, change and innovation, and the reason is that in order to achieve results, many variables must be kept under control for extended periods of time. Thus, those who work in (**P**)roduction typically resent changes, which require painful adaptations on their part.

Marketing and Engineering

Marketing's function is to deal with the long run: What is the future environment in which the organization will operate? What will be the future needs of our clients? The role of marketing is to discover opportunities and threats, and to recommend which risks to take in dealing with that future to produce future results. Thus its code would be (**PaEi**).

In engineering, the four roles have the same sequence of importance as in marketing. The (E) creativity of engineering is directed toward results (P): Whether that involves creating new products (if we are talking about new product development engineering); or designing new processes (new process engineering), or searching for disruptive technologies not yet commercialized (new technology). (I) is important – but not so important that it is allowed to interfere with (E) or (P). And (A), which hinders creativity and replaces it with routine, is the least significant of all.

Thus, both the marketing and engineering departments share an identical code, despite their very different tasks and perspectives: (PaEi).

Sales

Many executives believe the most important role of sales is (P), followed by (E), because a salesperson must be highly creative and flexible to get clients to commit to buying. But I disagree. I don't think companies want a salesman who is only thinking about getting the contract signed; if you were a sales supervisor, you would want people on your staff who were conscious of and sensitive to the clients' needs and were honestly trying to make sure the client was satisfied.

So when we talk about individual salesmen, the second most important function after (P) should be (I), followed by (E) and then (A): (PaeI).

On the other hand, the sales manager and the sales department as a whole are responsible for keeping track of thousands of salesmen and possibly millions of dollars. The sales department organizes schedules, assigns territories, provides training, and figures out how to repeat successes across the board. Its second letter, then, is (A), followed by (I) and then (E); thus the code for the sales department is (PAei).

Please note something very important here, which is that the tasks and style characteristics of a sales manager are much more akin to those of a (P)roduction manager than to marketing. It would be a whole lot easier and more pleasant to take a (**P**)roduction manager and make him a sales manager than to take a good marketing manager and make *him* a sales manager. If the marketing manager was a lousy marketing manager, there might be hope that he was mismatched in his marketing job and really belonged in sales. He might surprise everybody. But if he excelled in marketing, there would be trouble when he arrived in sales. Why? Because his success at marketing signifies creativity, flexibility, and a long-term perspective. Sales, on the contrary, is on the opposite end of the continuum: Salesmen prefer to stay put so they can stay focused until the purchase order is signed. That is not a task that creative people are generally good at.

Another common mistake is taking a highly successful sales manager and promoting him to a senior position – in marketing! No matter how brilliant this salesman is, he might not have the vision or flexibility that the new job requires. He never needed it for his previous job, and the company never gave him the opportunity to develop it – so where and how is he suddenly going to find it now?

He won't. Cases like that usually end up with the marketing person accompanying the sales people on sales calls and interfering in their attempts to do their jobs because they want to make the sale.

Of course, some people do make the transition: Those who are well-rounded enough to change their styles easily. But they are also rare. If you manage to find someone like that, you should really try to hold on to him.

Information Technology

IT used to be known as MIS: Management information systems. It is not in the (**P**) business, as (**P**)roduction and sales are – although some of its sub-divisions are, such as the data center and tech support: Tech support needs (**Paei**) and the data center needs (**PAei**). Other subdivisions, like systems development, need (**PaEI**). In light of the above mixture of expected styles You could say that IT's basic function is (**pAEi**), but the truth is that IT encompasses such a diversity of (**PAEI**) responsibilities that it's hard to stay focused on its commonalities – those characteristics that help the department develop a sense of unified identity and purpose.

This is a department where it becomes very obvious very quickly that no one can do it all. If you want an IT head who can supervise systems development, supervise tech support, and supervise data centers, you'd better get yourself a big (**I**) and you will not be happy because he will not be productive. If you are small you will have to autsource a lot.

If the organization is big enough, I prefer to split data centers and tech support away from systems development. Why? It is much easier to find and match the leadership you need with the style you need when all of a department's functions have more or less the same (**PAEI**) code.

SUMMING UP

The right process really consists of two different processes.

The first, covered in this chapter, involves an organization's ability to match its employees' styles and skills with the tasks they are best capable of achieving. This includes finding a workable system for hiring competent people who complement each other in abilities and styles; and promoting the right people into the right positions.

The second process is effective communication. To manage well, you must be able to hear and comprehend what people are telling you, and you must be able to make yourself understood, both one to one and in groups. Communication will be covered in the next two chapters.

NOTES

1. Adizes, Ichak: *Corporate Lifecycles* series of three books (Third revised edition Adizes institute publications 2004.

2. Adizes, Ichak: *Corporate Lifecycles*, op cit.

3. Answers: Need to achieve: (**P**). Need to control: (**A**). Need to affiliate: (**I**). Need to self-actualize: (**E**).

Chapter 10

The Right Process: The Dialogue

> PROBLEM: In a complementary team, what is the best way to communicate one on one with those whose styles are different from our own?

THE MANAGERIAL TOWER OF BABEL

Once we have learned to recognize and diagnose other people's predominant management styles, and have also made sure that the organization's structure will support and nourish all four of them, the next step is learning to communicate with each style effectively.

We all know how easy it is to get off on the wrong foot when we're explaining something, and how another person can seem to hear something entirely different from what we thought we said. Miscommunication is a major source of organizational conflict. The best way to avoid it is simply to match your style to the style of the person you're talking to.

Too often, we expect others to adapt to us. But if you genuinely want to be understood, you'll be the one who adapts. You'll remember that (E)ntrepreneurs are global in their views; result-oriented; fast-moving; and unstructured. (P)roducers are also result-oriented and fast, but they are local, or task-oriented, in their views; structured; and detailed. (A)dministrators share the (P)roducers' interest in detail and immediate results, but in contrast to (P) types, they tend to be organized; slow; and process-oriented. Finally, (**I**)ntegrators, like (**E**)ntrepreneurs, take a global view of things and are unstructured. But like (**A**)s, they are process-oriented and slow. They wait for others to blaze the trails.

Again, I'm not teaching you anything new. If you were trying to get a loan from a bank, for example – even if you were a very high-flying, esoteric, (**E**)ntrepreneur type – you would not dress in jeans and a T-shirt for your meeting with the bank officer, would you? You'd probably dress conservatively, walk slowly, sit quietly, and speak to the banker in calm, precise and polite language. Why? Because you're attempting to be responsive to his or her style. You are trying to act like a banker.

In order to manage well, you must convince others to cooperate. In essence, management means selling your ideas. If you can't sell ideas, you can't manage. Thus, if you can't communicate and convince, you cannot manage.

Now, in order to sell your ideas/manage effectively, you need to know to whom you are selling. Every salesman will tell you that in order to be successful, you have to know your clients. If you don't know what they need and what they want, how will you be able to convince them to buy your idea?

Before you talk to people, it is important to ask yourself, "*Who am I talking to?*" When people talk to you, you have to ask yourself, "*Who* is talking to me?" Then you can correctly interpret what they are saying.

And equally important, you must be conscious of your own style; you must be able to answer the question: *Who am I?*

Why? Because you also need to pay attention to what impression you are giving to others. If you know you are an (**E**) type, for instance, then you know that your style of communicating is apt to be problematic for the other styles. Being aware of your own style means being able to compensate for it. What is the first prescription for an (**E**) type dealing with an (**A**), for example? *Slow down.*

Book 3 of this series, *Leading the Leaders - How to Enrich Your Style of Management and Handle People Whose Style is Different from Yours* is dedicated entirely to prescriptions for each style: Quick, easily remembered ways to compensate for the weaknesses implicit in each style.

For now, it is important to understand that you can't interpret "yes" and "no" according to your own dictionary. You have to look at who is saying it.

Let me explain what I mean by that. All religions – Buddhist, Jewish, Christian, Muslim – have a principle that is known in the West as the Golden Rule: "Do unto others as you would have them do unto you." Its corollary is: "Don't do to others what you'd hate to be done to you."

It's a good rule in most situations, but in organizations, communicating with others the way you wish they would communicate with you is definitely a mistake: If you are an (**E**) type, and you speak to others as if they are also (**E**)s, unless they actually are (**E**)s they are going to misunderstand you; worse, they are probably going to resent and dislike you. And that's not very effective managing.

Who's the Boss? Whoever You Try to Sell Your Idea To!

To communicate well, you must be conscious at *all* times, no matter whom you're dealing with of who is the person you are talking to. The truth is that it's irrelevant whether that person is a manager above you or a subordinate beneath you in the organizational hierarchy. Whether he is your boss, your peer, or your subordinate, you still have to sell him your idea. They are all associates and that is how you should treat them. Forget the hierarchy.

I love the story about Vince Lombardi the famous American football coach. The story form his biography is that before a game he will explain it to the team and than turn to the thickest headed player on the team, I mean not the brightest, and ask him what he thinks. Finally the other players got upset: Why the dumbest. Why not ask the smartest of us, they wondered.

Because if he understands, all of you understand the game. If he does not understand the game, he is going to run in the wrong direction, so what is the use.

Many books are written about how to lead your subordinates. What I'm talking about here is how to lead your *organization*, which you can only do by becoming a leader to all the people in your organization. How can you sell your ideas to each person whose cooperation you will need? Communicating to them in a style they can readily comprehend is far more important, in the long run, than knowing the limits of your authority in relation to each person in the hierarchy.

Try to think about each person in your organization as if he were your boss, whether he is or not. In other words, instead of falling back on your authority and power, try to use your influence. This is providing leadership – being a true thumb. (For more detail on leadership, see Chapter 12.)

Surprisingly, it is hardest to communicate effectively with subordinates. Why? Because we take our subordinates for granted. With a subordinate, we feel we don't have to try so hard, so we are often careless of how we communicate. We forget what their style is and just talk to them as if we were talking to ourselves. As a result, we often miscommunicate.

Below, I analyze some scenarios that occur frequently between managers of different styles, and offer suggestions for dealing with them.

Let's go in a sequence: First how to deal with a (**P**)roducer, then how to deal with an (**A**)dministrator, then how to deal with an (**E**)ntrepreneur, and finally how to deal with an (**I**)ntegrator. (I repeat. This is a summary. The material in more detail is in book 3 in this series.)

DEALING WITH A (P) — A (P)RODUCER OR LONE RANGER

A (**P**)roducer is fast, doesn't have a lot of time, and is usually under pressure to deal with a crisis. He is generally highly structured, detail-oriented and result-oriented.

Now, how does this affect his ability to communicate? And what is the communication style you should adopt in order to effectively communicate with him?

Think about what would happen if you called your (**P**) boss and said, "Boss, I need you for three hours to discuss a problem." Would that work? Obviously not. A (**P**) would almost certainly reply, "Three hours? Fine. How about in October 2012, maybe *then* I can find three hours. Where the hell am I going to find three hours to talk with you? I have so many crises I can't even tell you where I'm going to be tomorrow!"

So, how much time can you realistically ask for? Five minutes. Ten minutes. Fifteen minutes at most. Try to be short.

But first, you must get his attention, and in order to do that, you will probably have to disguise your problem as a crisis rather than a mere problem. Why? Because the (**P**) is so busy! Since he has more problems than he can solve, he deals only with crises. That means that if your problem is *not* a crisis, it's going to have to wait. He will tell you, "Put it on my desk," and you will never hear about it again; it will just sit there with the three hundred other problems he has on his desk, and it will never get attended to.

On the other hand, if it *is* a crisis, then for a (**P**) style manager it is a legitimate cause for concern, and he will give you time.

Next: When you get into his office, do not start your presentation back with Adam and Eve. Start from the end instead of the beginning; in other words, first give him the bottom line. Tell him what your conclusions are. *Then* give him any supporting material he asks for, and answer questions. The important point is to start from the end — with the decision you have already come up with.

Next, you should tell him that you're *already working* on this problem and all you need from him is his approval: "Boss, we have a crisis, and we have very little time to deal with it, and because of that I've already come up with a solution. All I need is your approval."

Why must you phrase it like that? Because if there isn't any time pressure, or you are not already in the midst of implementing the solution, what will he say? "Put it on my desk."

If this (**P**) is a Lone Ranger, you *really* have to take the initiative, because he's never going to delegate to you; you'll have to delegate to yourself. But to avoid taking on unnecessary risks, you'll still want him to approve what you're doing.

Thus, your presentation should go something like this: "Boss, we have a crisis, I need fifteen minutes of your time. Here is the problem; here is what I am already doing. I just need your approval so I can finish it." Done. There you go.

But imagine what would happen if you communicated this way with an (**A**). Let's say you call him and say the same thing: "There is a crisis, and I am already midway into implementing the solution." What's going to happen? You'll be fired on the spot! "Who gave you the right to start implementing the solution?" he will shout. "How dare you take initiative without getting my approval?"

With an (**A**), you can't do anything without asking permission first. With an (**E**) boss, too, you'd be fired. Why? Because what you did was not *his* idea.

So with each style, you have to take a totally different approach.

If you are a (**P**) type working for an (**A**), you've probably made this mistake. You probably saw a problem and figured out how to solve it; then you went to your boss to tell him how you solved it, and you couldn't understand why he got apoplectic and jumped down your throat. Well, the answer is, you used a (**P**) solution for an (**A**), and the (**A**) cannot tolerate that style. You have to do it *his* way.

Dealing With an (A) – An (A)dministrator or Bureaucrat

What *is* his way? Well, the (**A**) type is more interested in the *how* than in the *what*. He confuses form with function, so you have to pay enormous attention to the form. He doesn't care if something is a crisis or not. He cares about whether you are following the correct procedure.

If you want to grab an (**A**)'s attention, you must show him that your problem is actually a violation of something that had previously been agreed upon: "A rule has been broken. We agreed, and guess what? They are not doing what we agreed upon. It's not working right." The word "right" is important.

Then, to prove the validity of your proposed solution, bring as many pages as you can write – the more, the better – with lots of details and footnotes. Show him that your solution has been approved by all the luminaries and the gurus; that it's been tried before, and that there is no risk. Finally, end your presentation with a sentence that goes something like this: "This is my recommendation, and if it does not work I will take full responsibility for it."

Basically, an (**A**) wants to avoid risk. When a problem arises, the first thing you have to do is find a way in which the problem can be interpreted as a deviation; otherwise the (**A**) will not want to risk making any changes. Then, of course, your solution should also have no risk. If you can frame the problem as a transgression against the established code, and the solution as no risk, the (**A**) will have no reason to object and will probably tell you, "Fine, go ahead and do it."

How do you handle an (**A**) under ordinary circumstances, in your day-to-day meetings and communications when there is no urgent matter to be dealt with? You must follow a protocol.

When you need to meet with an (**A**), always ask for an appointment. Don't surprise him. If you do, you'll lose the first half hour of the meeting because he won't be listening; he'll be obsessing about how you've caught him unprepared.

Next: Use your "bias multiple." That is the term I use to measure and compensate for each style's idiosyncratic view of time. For instance, (E)s and (P)s move fast, while (A)s and (I)s can be very deliberate, even plodding, in their actions.

I have found that as an (E), my own bias multiple is six. When I tell my subordinates, "We can do this in an hour," how long does it really take? Six hours. If I tell them, "Ah, we can do that in a week," how long will it take? Six weeks.

I suggested earlier that we think of an (E) as an eagle, up in the sky: With one move of his wings he can cover half a mile down on the ground. In fact, the higher up in the clouds that (E) is, the smaller his movements have to be to cover the same amount of ground.

But for the people on the ground, traversing that same territory might entail going up and down canyons, mountains, and rocks; and it might take many hours. An (E) tends to overlook that fact, which is why it's important to remember the bias multiple.

So, if you are a (P) or an (E), and you need to meet with an (A)dministrator for what you estimate will be half an hour, you'd better call and say, "I need a meeting with you hmm hmmm hm ....for three hours." Why? Your tendency will be to say: "I need to see you for half an hour" but you should stop and calculate your bias multiple. An (A) would be infuriated by a manager who asks for half an hour and then stays for three hours. You must ask for a specific amount of time, and you must keep to that schedule. It is better to leave a meeting with an (A) early than to stay overtime.

Next: When you schedule the appointment, you should also make sure to tell the (A) what the agenda of the meeting is to be, so that he has time to prepare himself.

The next step, before the meeting, is to prepare *yourself*. How? By breathing. Deep, slow, breathing. The more relaxed you are, the more slowly you'll make your presentation and the more chance you'll have of being understood. In addition, the more relaxed you are, the better your decisions will be, because you'll be more aware of what your gut is telling you.

When you slow down, you can also be more observant of the person you are talking to. Watch his eyes, his eyebrows, his hand movements. Watch his body and synchronize what he says with how he says it. Body language can be the key that unlocks the meaning of what someone is trying to say. But you won't notice it if you are rushing. In order to become more observant, you need to slow down. And that means deep, slow breathing.

(**E**)ntrepreneurs and (**P**)roducers are not very good at breathing; they're always running out of breath. Why? Because they're going full speed ahead – all the time. In countries like Mexico, they joke that in an argument, the first one who stops to take a breath is the loser. It can be amusing, but it's not the most effective way to make your point, is it? The most important technique for (**P**)roducers and (**E**)ntrepreneurs to learn – especially when dealing with (**A**)dministrators and (**I**)ntegrators – is to slow down.

Even before you reach the (**A**)'s office, slow down – physically, literally, slow down. Take deep breaths. Consciously do it in the corridor as you're on your way to the meeting, because your natural tendency when you're excited or under stress is to speed up. The (**A**), waiting for you in his office, is moving at his usual speed of one mile an hour, and if you don't slow down you're going to careen into him at 150 miles an hour, which won't be good for either of you.

Another reason why it's crucial to slow down to his speed is that for every one of your ideas, the (A) is going to think of ten or even a hundred ramifications. He needs time to process that information. *So slow down.*

Begin the meeting by telling him again what you are there to discuss. Confirm your agenda. Again, no surprises.

Next: Begin with item no. 1. (It's important to go in order, with the first item on your agenda broached first.) As you present it to him, it's very important to watch his eyes: When his eyes go "out to lunch," that means he's not listening anymore. He's thinking. What is he thinking about? The repercussions of your idea. Who is he listening to when his eyes are out to lunch? To himself. Is he listening to you? No.

What should you do while he's listening to himself? Stop talking. *Stop talking!* This is very difficult for an (**E**)ntrepreneur, I know. But it's crucial to wait until the (**A**) has finished processing the information he has before you continue.

What should you do while you're quiet? If you're an (**E**), three hundred new ideas will have crowded into your mind while you waited, and you'll want to say them before you forget them. Don't. Write them on a piece of paper. You can get to it later. Once you write them down, you will immediately feel calmer, because you'll know you can go back to them any time you want. You will not have to over-burden the person you're talking to.

What happens when the (**A**)dministrator comes back from "lunch?" Usually, he will have a question. And what will that question be? It will be about some detail of implementation, which, especially if you are an (**E**)ntrepreneur, will probably upset you: Here you are trying to deal with the big picture, and here is this (**A**) type asking you about totally irrelevant little details.

Don't get upset. That is him and you are not going to change him. Take another deep breath and then acknowledge the question: "Good question; let me write it down." Even better, write it on a flip chart, so the (**A**) can see that you respect his question and are not ignoring it. Copy it down and say, "Thank you. Great question. I would like to address it later, when I finish my presentation, if you don't mind, so that it can be discussed in the full context of what I am presenting." This serves two purposes: First, the (**A**) will understand that you're acknowledging his concerns; and second, you will not feel as if you're being sidetracked.

Continue with your presentation until the next time his eyes go out to lunch. Then stop again. Take a deep breath. Wait. Acknowledge his question when it comes up. Write it down. Continue with the big picture.

What you are doing, in effect, is presenting the *what* and *why* before you address the how, or the repercussions of implementation.

When you finish explaining the big picture, summarize it for the (**A**), making sure he understands it, and conclude, "Now let me address your questions." Then it's time to deal with the details, one by one by one. In this process the (**A**) can not veto your idea, or even argue against it, until he knows what it is; thus, you must not be drawn into discussing the *how* until you've communicated the *what* and the *why*.

If you're ready with answers to the (**A**)'s questions then and there, go ahead and answer them. But beware: If you are not absolutely sure of your answer, it would be better to ask for time to consider. Make another appointment to come back and present your answers.

Honestly addressing the (**A**)'s concerns might mean that you will have to change your original recommendation. So be it. If that is what happens, the important thing to remember is that by giving yourself extra time to reconsider the details, you avoided making some major mistake. Be thankful.

How long should you stay in a meeting with an (**A**)? *Only the length of the time that was allocated to you.* Don't say, "Ten more minutes, just ten more minutes and we'll be finished." Because that's when you start rushing, and the worst mistakes are usually made in the last ten minutes of an extended meeting.

If you're an (**E**) type, it will be very difficult for you to stop in mid course. It is almost like *coitus interaptus*. But remember: Management is about selling ideas. And you're not selling them to yourself, you're selling them to somebody else. You must communicate to an (**A**) in a way he can understand you, if you want him to buy what you are saying.

There is one more important point to remember when communicating with an (**A**), especially if you yourself are an (**E**).

For an (**E**), numbers tend not to be meant literally. They're really only a magnitude. Thus, an (**E**) might say, "We sold a million," when he really means a million *more or less* – somewhere between half a million and a million and a half.

Now for an (**A**), a million is exactly a million. If it is 999,999, then it's not a million. This is a huge issue between (**E**)s and (**A**)s; it's one of the main reasons that (**A**)s mistrust (**E**)s. The (**A**) thinks, "That guy

– you really don't know what he's saying. His word is not his word. He says, 'I need to talk to you for half an hour'; then he comes half an hour late and stays for three hours. To him, numbers, time, words have no meaning. He's full of hot air, and I don't trust him!"

When you are talking to an (**A**), remember that they are very literal-minded, and try to honor that. Be careful not to confuse ideas with facts, because if you refer to something as if it is fact when it isn't, as soon as the (**A**) catches your mistake, you're dead. He won't trust you anymore, and he will dismiss everything else you've said as if it has no value.

Dealing With an (E) – An (E)ntrepreneur or Arsonist

It would be a waste of time to approach an (**E**)ntrepreneur type the way you would an (**A**) – with a 30-page report detailing a problem and its solution. An (**E**) will not read your 30-page report. He will put it on his desk and forget about it.

Furthermore, an (**E**)ntrepreneur resists any idea unless it is his own idea. If you walk into a meeting with an (**E**) and say, "Boss, here is a problem; here is the solution; I just need your approval," there is a good chance he's going to say, "Wrong problem, wrong solution." He's going to try to change it, he's going to attack it, he's going to look for a loophole, he's going to try to find out what's wrong with it. Why? Because he wants to put his stamp on it. He does not like final-ized ideas, which don't require his input. In fact, he feels threatened by them. For an (**E**), if you present an idea that's already finalized, it means you're charging ahead and leaving him behind, forgetting him, ignoring him, not consulting with him. He feels disrespected. And sooner or later, he's going to find a way to put you in your place.

So how should you approach an (**E**) when you have a problem?

First of all, don't call it a problem. An (**E**) is not interested in problems; in fact he gets annoyed when you talk about problems, because problems are something he hired you for. Instead, figure out how to transform your problem into an opportunity. When you get to his office, instead of saying, "We have a problem," try saying, "We have an opportunity to do something better," or "We have an opportunity to change something. What do you think?"

The second issue to think about is: "How do I make the solution his idea?" Here it helps to use phrases such as "I suggest …," or "May I suggest …," or "I've been thinking …," or "It appears that …," or "What do you think?" instead of saying, "Here's what I think we should do." Allow the (**E**) an opportunity to put his stamp on the solution.

Please note that I'm not talking just about your boss; I'm talking about your subordinates too. If you treat an (**E**)-type subordinate as a subordinate – "This is what you need to do; here is how I want you to do it, this is when I want it done; now go do it!" – he's going to be unhappy and resentful. The reason is that you aren't giving him a chance to use his creativity. (**E**)s like to design the train; they even like to design the route the train is going to follow, not to run it.

So you have to talk to them – whether they are boss, peer or subordinate – in the identical (**E**)-language: "What do you think?" "What would you suggest?" "How would you improve this?" You know you've succeeded in selling your idea when the (**E**) gets excited and says, "Yes, that's good, but what if we also …?" and begins to add his own thoughts to the mix. All you need to do at that point is find a way to incorporate his ideas so that he can own the solution.

Here's another technique: Explain the problem and your solution – but intentionally leave a mistake, a very obvious mistake, at the very beginning of your presentation. An (**E**) will see it immediately and correct it, and in correcting it he will feel ownership of the solution.

In the advertising business, this is called "the hairy arm" strategy: When the storyboard is designed for a TV ad, the artist will deliberately draw excessively hairy arms on one character in the ad. The minute he sees the storyboard, the client will notice the hairy arms, point them out and say, "That's wrong; fix it." This accomplishes two goals: The client will feel he has contributed to the process and thus "owns" the result of that process; while at the same time his attention has been focused away from other aspects of the project that he might have felt like changing.

One of my clients, an architect, once told me: "I listened to your crazy idea and I tried it. Now when I design something, I put an intentional error up front. It has to be very easy to identify, so that the client finds it right away and doesn't get distracted by something else. What happens is that instead of starting to make changes that I don't want him to make, he picks up this problem and corrects it – which you know he's going to do because you planted it yourself – and you're home free."

"But watch out. It can't be too stupid, or they'll fire you."

Finally, how do you give an (**E**) bad news?

If there is any hint in your presentation that he, the (**E**), is somehow to blame for the problem, he will immediately attack you: "I don't know what the hell you're talking about!" "You have completely messed this up!" "You are trying to create turmoil in this organization!" "You're totally dysfunctional!" The key is that the bad news must not reflect badly on him.

An (**E**) can easily become emotional and paranoid, so you have to be extremely careful in your choice of words: "It appears that we have an opportunity to do something better here; what do you think we should do?" Saying "it appears" is always less risky than stating something very definitively.

If he denies what you're telling him, you have no choice but to retreat. If he replies, "That's interesting, but don't worry about it," you can press a little harder: "Well, but it appears that...." But be very careful, because if he interprets the bad news as making *him* look bad, he will look for a scapegoat, and you will be the most convenient target.

Dealing With an (I) - an (I)ntegrator or Superfollower

What is an (**I**)ntegrator, or in extreme cases a Superfollower, looking for? His highest priority is agreement; in other words: "Is there a consensus?"

Thus, if you go to an (**I**) and say, "Boss, here is the problem and here is the solution and we want your authorization," what is he going to say? "It's not time yet, we are not ready, have you talked to Rudy, have you talked to Paul, have you talked to Denise?" He's going to want to assess the political climate before approving anything.

So before you approach him with a problem, cover all your bases. Talk to Rudy and Paul and Denise and Nancy and find out where they stand. Then you can go to the (**I**) and say, "Boss, *we* have a problem, *we* have discussed it, *we* all agree, *we* think this is the solution and we want your approval." The (**I**) will immediately want to know: "Who are the people who agree or don't agree with this solution? And what about Joc? Did you talk to Joe?"

If Joe is very important to him, and you haven't talked to Joe, he's going to say, "Well, I just don't think we're ready yet."

If you say, "Yes, we talked to Joe and he's going to resign unless we implement this solution," he'll ask you, "And what about Bill?"

If you can tell him, "Yes, we talked to Bill also and he's totally behind it," then the (**I**) will probably reply, "Then what are we waiting for? Let's do it."

Keeping Your Styles Straight: A Cautionary Tale

Each of these strategies can easily backfire if you misread the style of the person you're talking to.

Imagine that you are an (**I**)ntegrator with an (**E**)ntrepreneur boss. All your life you've tried to resolve conflicts, so when a problem comes up, what do you do? You go and talk to all the relevant people, you resolve all the conflicts, and then you go to your (**E**) boss and say, "Boss, we had a problem, we all met, we all agreed what the problem is and we all agreed what the solution should be. Now we want you to approve it."

How is the (**E**) boss feeling? He's probably sweating. He's thinking, "My god, this guy is building a revolution behind my back. He's trying to execute a coup d'etat against me. My staff never told me about the problem, they just went into a back room and discussed it without my input; they came up with a solution, and now they're trying to force me to approve it!"

An (**E**) will never forgive you, and he will never forget. At the first opportunity, he will fire you. This is a frequent problem for (**I**) types: They try to build a consensus, they encourage participatory management – and they end up getting fired by (**E**) bosses who feel threatened by that style of management.

If you don't know someone very well and are not familiar with his typical working style, what should you do? Ask what job he performs. Look at the organizational chart; that can tell you a lot. If this person is in marketing, you can expect him to be (**E**)ntrepreneurial. If he is in sales, he should be (**P**)-oriented, a (**P**)roducer. An accountant will very likely have an (**A**) orientation.

You can also find telling clues by looking at his office, his desk, how he dresses, his posture, his energy level. In other words, be sensitive to and observant of the other person; watch his reactions to your comments; and adapt your style to his so that you can communicate to him clearly.

Summing Up

Knowing whom you are talking to and how to talk to them is essential for success in management and, I believe, life in general.

A good manager, who is by definition a well-rounded person, should be able to communicate with anyone, of any style. It is like knowing several languages. You can't insist on speaking English in

Rome and then complain when people don't understand you. In Rome, you'll behave as the Romans do if you want to influence people and be respected.

But now we come to another problem: If adopting the "language" of the person we're talking to is the only way to communicate effectively, then how should we behave when we're dealing with several different styles simultaneously, how do we manage meetings?

Let's talk about that in the next chapter.

Chapter 11

Converting Management by Committee into Teamwork

PROBLEM: How do you communicate
and manage in a meeting, when you have a
multitude of styles in the room?

The Communication Blues

Robert Hutchins, the long-time president of the University of Chicago and one of the great social thinkers of the twentieth century, once spoke of the need for a "civilization of dialogue."[1] Civilized dialogue is essential if people of different types of interests are to come together. But without attention to other people's styles and assumptions, you cannot have a productive conversation. The diverse perspectives that should be a source of strength and wisdom become debilitating.

Let's say you want to get a colleague's point of view on an important business issue. In order to get any value from that person's opinion, you must understand his style. (E)ntrepreneurial types toss off solutions, some only tangentially related to the problem at hand. Ask them to outline a detailed solution to a problem and they will probably lose interest. (A)dministrative types, on the other hand, will invariably want more data. They can find the holes and pitfalls in any proposal, but they can also get lost in minutiae. (P)roducers often rush to judgment, just to get out of the meeting and back to work. And (I)ntegrators consider any decision reached without full consensus to be an unacceptable risk.

In addition, we have seen that different types of people understand words differently; look for different needs to be satisfied; and make decisions in different ways. To successfully communicate and sell your ideas to them, you need to adapt yourself to their style.

This is complicated, because nobody is really a perfect, exclusive (P) or an exclusive (A); we are usually an amalgam. This is why good managers must necessarily be sensitive. If a manager tries one approach and sees it's not being understood, he tries another. He's constantly watching the person he's selling his ideas to, and adapting his style of communicating until the other person fully understands.

But what happens when you are trying to speak to several people at once, as in a meeting, where several or all of the basic managerial styles are represented?

If you speak in "(P) language," an (A) might misunderstand it or resent it. And the same applies if you speak any other (PAEI) language. The problem is even further accentuated in global companies, where multiple cultures work side by side. For a German, whose style is likely to be (A), a budget is a policy that cannot be violated. For an Israeli, probably an (E), a budget is at best a guideline. For a Brit, who is often an (A) type, a delivery date is sacred; whereas for a Mexican, whom you can expect to be a (P), manana – "tomorrow"– might mean anything from next week to next year.

Even the word "decision" has a different meaning for each style. For a (P), a decision means "This is a done deal; now let's go do it." For an (A), it means, "We have arrived at something that we can now, cautiously, begin to think about implementing." An (E) reacts to a decision by thinking, "Aha, this is very interesting! Now let's see if I can improve on it"; in no way has the (E) committed to it as a finalization. And an (I)'s interpretation of a decision is, "Let's wait and see what happens."

Trying to communicate as a team while each manager is attaching different meanings to the words being spoken is like trying to play a team sport in which one player is following the rules for ping-pong, another the rules for tennis and a third the rules for rugby. How in the world could that team ever win a game?

Thus it is no surprise that such meetings often escalate into shouting matches – with some participants accusing others of lying, intentionally miscommunicating, sabotaging, or undermining a decision that's been made – or else they collapse into cold silence, in which not even the silence means the same thing to all parties. This is not what Hutchins had in mind.

In my work with organizations, I continually insist that we stop and define the terms we are using, because we cannot move forward effectively until everyone understands what is being discussed, what they are being asked to agree or disagree with, what their colleagues are saying when they make comments.

My clients often have difficulty with this practice of mine. The (**P**)s, especially, go berserk: "Oh, so we are paying you to teach us English now?" To illustrate how important it is to understand the concept behind the words, I tell them a joke, about a 23-year-old Jewish man who goes to a surgeon and says he wants a castration. "Why on earth would you want to do that?" the concerned doctor says.

"It is my religious conviction, and that's that," the young man replies.

So the surgeon, reluctant to challenge the man's religious convictions, makes him sign a release form, wheels him into surgery and castrates him.

When the young man is wheeled to the recovery room, he finds another young man lying next to him.

"What are you here for?" he asks.

"For a circumcision," the other young man says.

"Argh!!!" screams our castrated young man, "*that* is what I meant to say!!!!"

Defining Terms: "Policies," "Rules," and "Guidelines"

Although good communication is essential to effective and efficient functioning, most executives have a hard time believing that the time spent on clarifying our vocabulary is well spent. Most seem to believe that not only are they themselves excellent communicators, but that their organizations' goals and requirements are also well organized and documented and that everyone understands them.

Here is one way to test that theory. Obviously, everyone in a company, regardless of his role, must know the difference between what *must* be done under a given set of circumstances; what *should* be done (unless there is a defensible reason not to); and what is merely *recommended*.

Guidelines are instructions that can be ignored at will. They are the accumulation of a body of knowledge and experience, either written down or in someone's head – and then whoever is supposed to implement them is free to implement them or not implement them. That's why they're called guidelines.

Rules are instructions that you can violate if conditions warrant. When you're in the field and have to make a decision whether to follow a rule or not, you are free to violate the rule if you judge that the situation you are looking at constitutes an exception to the rule. However, if you violate a rule, you must inform your superior, who will need to do damage control, or else might reconsider the wisdom of the rule itself and decide, "Ah, this rule really should not be a rule, it should be a guideline."

What is a policy? A policy cannot be violated without getting an approval *upfront*.

There should be very few policies. That's why the Bible has only ten commandments, no more, because more would be too difficult to follow. Then there should be some rules, and there could be thousands of guidelines, both written and unwritten. But everyone in the company should know which is a policy, which is a guideline, which is a rule.

You would be surprised to find how often the employees in an organization, especially in global companies in the older stages of the lifecycle, cannot actually look at the company's manual and say which is which.

Yet without that knowledge, your employees might be paralyzed, believing every guideline is actually a policy set in stone; or they may be too freewheeling, confident that the rules are made to be broken. Either way of adapting is potentially disastrous for an organization.

For a big (**A**), everything will be a rule or a policy. For an (**E**), because he is impulsive and changes his mind all the time, everything in the manual ends up being treated as a guideline. A (**P**) will be totally confused. If he works for an (**A**) he will become paralyzed, and if he works for an (**E**) he will get so frustrated that he'll lose confidence in his decisions.

Another reason to periodically review the company's regulations and strictly label each one as a policy, rule, or guideline is that companies tend to accumulate policies and rules over time, without officially getting rid of the ones that have become obsolete. The difference between a young organization and an old one is that in a young organization, in general, everything is allowed unless specifically forbidden. In an old organization, everything is forbidden unless specifically permitted. The older the company (and I am not talking about chronological age so much as behavior), the more likely it is to have what I call "manualitis:" Everything must be documented; all processes must be written out step by step.[2]

When there are too many manuals, at a certain point the organizational culture changes, and employees start to assume that everything they want to do must be forbidden somewhere – unless it's specifically permitted. In such organizations, the written word becomes the dominant determiner of behavior. So everybody asks for permission instead of forgiveness. Eventually, the climate becomes so moribund that even when something obviously needs to be done, people are afraid to take the responsibility for it, thinking, "I'd better not do this unless I get specific permission, because who knows if somewhere there is a policy prohibiting it." And if they ask permission, often it is denied – because the manager who must decide is beset by the same concern: "Why take chances? There's probably a policy somewhere that prohibits this."

At that point, people are no longer managing the policy book. It is "the book" that is managing the people.

That's why, in a very large bureaucratic organization, nobody acts on their own unless they get permission. Look at the United States military or government bureaucracies, for example. For maximum efficiency, everything has been written into a manual, in a language so loaded with acronyms that you have to decode it in order to understand what's going on. But the truth is, in unusual situations that require a quick response, you may have to violate some of your efficiency rules in order to be effective. You have to be willing to be flexible, allow for deviations from the norm, take some shortcuts.

When I participate in a company reorganization, one of the first things we do is divide its documentation into policies, rules, and guidelines. In the manuals, we separate them by color: Guidelines on white paper, rules on blue paper, and policies on pink paper, so that when you look at a three-ring binder, you can easily see how many rules, guidelines and policies the company has. It's fine to have a manual even for guidelines, as long as you call them guidelines. The danger is that if you write a manual and don't label the guidelines as guidelines, they become policies.

In your company, do you know which is which? If not, then it's very likely that there are other areas in which your managers miscommunicate.

"Hard Rules"

Of course, defining each word we use is a slow and laborious process. What is really needed is a kind of Esperanto for management – a new "language" that all agree to use that is neither (**P**) nor (**A**) nor (**E**) nor

(I) language. In my work, I have developed such a universal management "language," which is based on rules of conduct.

My methodology for running meetings is taught at a five-day training seminar at the Adizes Institute. It would take a separate book and a lifetime of practice to excel at it. But let me give you some fundamental insights.

Before I begin a session, I ask everybody to take deep, relaxing breaths until their tension has diminished. I do not allow meetings to start when people are very tense. We have to breathe deeply and relax before we start the meeting.

Then during the session, where tensions may easily resurface, we must follow what I call "hard rules."

What are hard rules? First and most important, whoever is speaking can speak as long as he wants to, and nobody can interrupt him or even use body language that shows impatience. Anyone who interrupts must pay a penalty, which is donated to a charity we've chosen.

When the person who is talking stops talking, that doesn't necessarily mean he's said everything he wants to say. It often means that he's processing what he's just said, running the "tape" back to see if he's said what he actually meant to say. So we wait. Usually he will start talking again; then stop again, listen to what he has said and resume talking again. The only person who knows whether he's said everything he wanted to say is the person who's talking.

When he is finished talking, usually his eyes clear up and he refocuses on the group. Sometimes he repeats himself three or four times first. When he's truly finished, he demonstrates that he is finished by taking a deep breath and looking to the right – not to the left but to the right.

Why to the right? Because to look to the left is effortless. That is how the clock turns. That is how, in agricultural societies, the seeds were dispersed by hand in the field. You have to be conscious to look to the right. Only when you have stopped thinking about what you want to say and whether you've said it adequately will you be able to consciously turn to the right.

The moment the speaker turns his head to the right, that's a signal for anyone else who wants to talk to raise his hand. They must raise their hand. The previous speaker then will call on the *first person to his right whose hand is raised*. He must call him by his first name.

Why must he call him by his first name? Because it's more intimate, and thus it reduces the tension and potential conflict. In contrast, for example, when you are upset with your child, you might address him by the last name: "*Mr.* Adizes, it's time to go to sleep." That is how you distance yourself and make it formal.

If you call someone by his nickname in a tense situation, you might inject a tone of voice that is condescending or a putdown, or you might be misinterpreted as injecting that tone.

But it's interesting: The moment you call someone by his first name, the aggressive voice disappears. I do not know why but I have now tested it in 48 countries and it works. Even if you've spoken very passionately and said some very strong things, when you're ready to yield the right to speak to the next person, if you call out his first name it will always be in a relaxed, non-emotional tone, without any animosity and it effectively returns the atmosphere to neutral.

But it's even more important that you call on the first person to your right *whose hand is lifted – not* the first person with a lifted hand, but the first person with a lifted hand on your right. That means that the people who lifted their hands earlier have to wait. Slowly, this forces them to develop patience and tolerance, and behaviorally that is interpreted as trust and respect for other people who are talking.

Furthermore, this method keeps the (**E**)s from dominating the meeting. An (**E**) can, and often does, start talking before he's finalized in his head what he's going to say. (**E**)s interrupt others, whereas (**A**)s wait for their turn – so if there are no rules of conduct in the meeting, (**A**)s will never get a word in. This rule guarantees that everybody participates.

When I see that a meeting is becoming heavy and emotional and people are interrupting each other, I slow down the process and prevent it from overheating by calling out: "Stop! Hard rules." As a matter of fact, I don't even have to do it; usually someone else in the room will call out, "Adizes rules, Adizes rules!" and everybody will stop screaming and interrupting, take a deep breath and wait for their turn to speak.

Another rule: Meetings start on time. Whoever is late gets a penalty: Ten push-ups for each minute he was late; or ten dollars per minute – whatever people can agree to without resentment.

Next rule: No talking unless it's your turn to speak to the group. No cell phone use. No reading or signing of papers. No leaving early. If someone does leave, he is barred from returning to that session.

The sessions should never be longer than an hour and twenty minutes, which I have found is the maximum time people can stay in a meeting and remain alert and productive.

Enforcing "hard rules" isn't easy. Most managers resent them. Knowing that, before I lay out the rules I usually initiate a group discussion: "What destroys meetings?" If you ask people why they hate meetings, they will tell you for sure that meetings are not effective. And why aren't they effective? Because people come and go; they interrupt the flow of discussion; they do not listen; etc.

After that discussion, I present the Adizes rules of conduct and write them on the board for everyone to see and discuss how those rules will address their concerns. It's crucial to enforce the rules: If you don't strictly enforce the penalties, people will soon lose respect for the rules – and for you.

It is interesting that rules need to be enforced and that people resent them. Was it not them who claimed that what destroys meetings is lack of rules, the coming and going and interruptions and the lack of listening. So how come they resent now the rules that are there to prevent this from happening.

My insight on this dilemma is that people want rules but for others to follow. And that is where lack of respect starts and that is why rules must be enfoced no matter how much they are being resented.

Once we get started, I am often (by design, to tell the truth) the first person to violate the rules. So I am the first one to pay the penalty. "I am subject to the rules, too, just like everyone else," I explain. That sets the tone and is actually very helpful.

Nevertheless, there is usually somebody – often a (**P**) type – who will refuse to pay the penalty for breaking a rule. He will arrive late, for example, but when you ask him to pay the fine or do the push-ups, he is offended: "I was *selling*, and I resent that I have to pay a penalty when I was only doing what the company needs and pays me for."

In that situation, I do not argue; I simply take out my wallet and pay the fine for him – which embarrasses him so much that he won't break the rule again. Meanwhile, I explain that if we start accepting excuses for why rules have been broken, then where will it end? And how much time will be wasted in deciding which explanations are acceptable and which are not?

Accepting rules is especially difficult for companies in the Infant and Go-Go stages of the organizational lifecycle, when the (**P**) role and thus (**P**)-style managers dominate. But like children, (**P**)s (as well as other styles) need to know that there are boundaries. I have noticed that once people have truly accepted the principle of hard rules that was imposed during these sessions, their respect for rules and boundaries tends to carry over into their decision-making and other situations, such as their ability to adhere to budgets, follow up on decisions, and honor commitments.

Is, Want, and Should

In a meeting situation, where several styles are represented, one of my rules is to insist that, for clarity's sake, the words *is*, *want*, and *should* be used in the (**P**) sense – that is, literally.

If you sit in a meeting and listen carefully to the way people talk, you'll find they continually confuse *is*, *want*, and *should*. Instead of saying, "I *want* this," which sounds arrogant and thus is awkward to say, they say, "We *should* do this." But when you analyze what they said, you will find that what they really mean is that it's what they *want* to do. It did not *have* to be done.

So I insist that in meetings, people use the word *want* when they mean *want*, instead of the word *should*. The word should is reserved for those things that *must* be done because the situation dictates it. *Should* has nothing to do with what you *want*.

For instance, if an executive says, "We are the leaders of our industry," he had better be speaking in (**P**) language. If the company is *not* the leader, then I expect him to say, "We *want* to be the leaders of the industry, but we aren't there yet. What we *should* do in order to become the leader *is* …"

Questions, Doubts, and Disagreements

Often in a meeting, when someone questions an idea, the question is interpreted as a personal challenge of the person whose idea it is. This is especially true when you're dealing with (**E**)- and (**A**) style managers.

Here is how I handle it. In a meeting, when we finally reach an illumination, a working idea, I say, "All right. I want everyone to take a piece of paper and divide it into three by drawing two horizontal lines across it. Label the upper part 'questions;' the middle part 'doubts'; and the lower part 'disagreements.'"

Let me define each.

"Questions" means you're asking for more information. "What is this?" "What is that?" "What happened to this?" "What happened to that?" "How will this work?" "How will that work?" You aren't expressing an opinion and don't necessarily have one; you're simply asking for more details.

"Doubts" means you have all the information you need but you're in doubt about whether it's going to work. Here you list your concerns.

"Disagreements" means you're not in any doubt; it's not going to work, and here's why.

Next, I spell out the proposed solution in detail, while everybody writes down their questions, doubts and disagreements in the appropriate sections of the page.

Then we accumulate *only* the questions – not the doubts and not the disagreements – and try to answer the questions. Nobody feels threatened or gets upset, because we've already established that a question is not a disagreement. We take the questions one by one and we try to answer them together until they are all resolved.

By separating the questions from the doubts and disagreements, I make sure that everyone understands, "Oh, it's just a question; nobody's decided. I can relax." And as we deal with the questions – and the questions are often very legitimate – we change and adapt the proposed solution, so that it is constantly evolving, growing, changing, right in front of our eyes.

When all the questions have been answered, we again accumulate questions, doubts and disagreements (I call it the QDD list). What will happen is that the doubts from the previous list will move up to become questions in the new list, and the disagreements will move up to become doubts. And we start the process again. Again we deal only with the questions, until they are all answered.

Next we do another QDD list, and now the original disagreements have moved up to become questions. We repeat the process until, finally, when I ask, "OK, any new questions?" there are none. "Any doubts?" There will be none because they have all been dealt with. "Any disagreements?" None as well.

Sometimes we hit a question that the group cannot resolve by using this process. For that, I use a methodology called dialectical convergence, which involves looking for the assumptions behind the disagreements. We're dealing with the *why*, and we go deeper and deeper and deeper, looking into the *whys*, until we find out the source of the disagreement. Then we attack the source of the disagreement. (Unfortunately, due to space limitations – how much can one book contain? – the dialectic convergence methodology will have to be spelled out in a separate book.)

What happens if the dialectical convergence method does not resolve the problem? On the rare occasions that we reach an impasse, I postpone the discussion until the next meeting. Usually, what happens after people sleep on it is they come back much more relaxed and much more willing to change. Time is a good healer. What people cannot agree about today, they've already gotten used to by the time we meet next week or next month.

BACKUP BEHAVIOR

When people are tired or upset, they often revert to their default styles of communicating, ignoring the needs of those to whom they're speaking. That's why it's extremely important to be relaxed and well rested before important meetings. And even under the best of circumstances, there are times when a meeting should be stopped altogether and rescheduled.

How will you recognize those situations? Let's use your car as an example. You're very familiar with the normal humming sound your engine makes, so if someone asks what that noise is, you can say, "Oh, nothing. That's normal."

Once you know what a normal noise is, you can identify noises that aren't normal and might indicate a problem. If you hear such noises, what should you do? Normally, you should stop driving as soon as possible and get the car checked out.

The same is true in personal relationships. Sometimes a conflict is normal and nothing to worry about. It's even music to your ears, because you know you are both learning. It's pain with gain! But when you hear abnormal noise, it's time to intervene and stop the discussion.

If a meeting is not stopped at the point when people are getting emotional and angry, the danger is that the machine will keep sputtering until major and sometimes irreparable damage is done. What is breaking down is not the transmission or the muffler, but mutual trust and respect.

Each of the (**PAEI**) styles exhibits a typical abnormal "noise," which I call "backup behavior." It appears whenever people aren't listening to or learning from each other anymore. It usually starts when people feel intimidated and fear they are losing control.

When (**P**)s feel they are losing control, they become little dictators. They proclaim, "OK, I've heard enough! Here is what we're going to do, and I don't want to hear any more about it. Period!"

When an (**A**) feels under attack, he freezes. His jaws lock, his face becomes frozen, he's totally quiet. He just looks at you, or not even at you but through you. What he is thinking is not fit for print, but he doesn't say a word. However, he remembers everything. Ten years later, that (**A**) will say, "Do you remember what you said, Friday, the 22nd of April, at three o'clock in the afternoon?" He'll never forget. He'll keep a detailed diary in his mind and sometimes even on paper.

An (**I**) yields like a tree in the wind. He flexes himself until the wind passes and then he straightens himself up again. How does this manifest itself? He will claim, "Oh, I didn't mean that," or "That wasn't what I meant to say," or "That's not exactly it," or "I'm sorry, I didn't mean it." See what's happening? He's wiggling.

An (**E**) is the most dangerous when threatened. He will go for your throat. He will cut you to pieces, suck your blood and spit it out, he will call you obscene names and publicly demean you. What's interesting is that the next morning he will act as if nothing happened. He's forgotten about it. It's all over, done, finished, that's it. He doesn't understand why you're still upset.

This sort of conflict occurs in many marriages. (**E**)s often marry (**A**)s because they complement each other. Traditionally, although not necessarily, the (**E**) is the male and the (**A**) is the female. In an argument, he attacks her, and she withstands it silently while mentally cataloguing it. Years later, when she wants a divorce, he falls to pieces because he doesn't know what went wrong. She starts reminding him what happened on that infamous afternoon ten years ago, and he is shocked because he has very little memory of the fight. He hardly remembers what he had for breakfast, much less what happened ten years ago. But an (**A**) never forgets and never forgives.

When backup behavior occurs in a meeting, whoever is still more or less in control of his emotions needs to stop the discussion immediately. You can say something like, "Let's discuss it tomorrow. I hear you, and I want to give you the full attention you deserve, but we are too emotional right now." Refuse to continue the discussion.

Be prepared for the (**P**)s and (**E**)s in the room to object and insist that the problem be resolved immediately. They hate pain and want to get it over with. When they hear abnormal noise, they don't slow the machine down; they speed it up. Don't get sucked in.

It's also not a good idea to resume the meeting too soon. After all, what did you do with the car that sounded as if it were breaking down? You stopped it. Did you immediately start it up again? Of course not. You checked the source of the breakdown first. The same holds true for personal conflict when there is backup behavior. When the meeting has been adjourned and everyone has cooled down, try to find out what caused the backup behavior in the first place. Clear up that issue before continuing the discussion. Ask the others, "What happened yesterday? You seemed upset. What did someone say or what happened that upset you?" Only when that issue is resolved should you reactivate the machine. Then you can go back to discussing the issue you were dealing with.

Summing it Up

Meetings can be frustrating and unproductive because of the different styles and interests of those present. It is not enough, even for a strong manager, to simply "run" a meeting according to his or her own style and expect good decisions or good follow-through. Inevitably, someone will be misunderstood, and resentment, resistance or confusion will result. What's missing is a set of rules. Every participative endeavor must have agreed-upon rules of conduct; without them you get either anarchy or dictatorship.

Well-functioning groups can develop their own rules for effective participation. But it's best to have a group leader who can bring order and efficiency to meetings. Even more important, by promoting a spirit of mutual trust and respect, he can help the management team make effective decisions together.

What are the characteristics of a team leader, and how can we find or train him? The next chapter addresses these issues.

NOTES

1. Hutchins, Robert Maynard: "Seeking the Civilization of Dialogue," *Goethe Bicentennial Convocation* (1949).

2. For more on this topic, see Adizes, Ichak: *Managing Corporate Lifecycles* (New York: Prentice Hall, 1999).

Chapter 12

The Right People and Shared Vision and Values

PROBLEM: What type of people, and what kind of shared vision, do we need to ensure the success of our complementary team?

THE ROLE OF LEADERSHIP

Having a complementary team does not mean all are equal. Someone has to lead.

Let's look more carefully at the role of leadership itself. Is the character of a team leader substantially different from the rest of the team? I suggest that it is not. All good managers should command and grant mutual respect and trust; if they cannot, they should not be on a complementary team to begin with.

We've said that trust is created when there is an environment in which people have faith that they will benefit in the long run from their short-run sacrifices. Respect is created when conflicts are perceived not as problems but as opportunities to learn.

But how do you get divergent personalities to effectively communicate and ultimately come together around important decisions? That is the leader's role. A leader, then is a person who not only excels at certain roles, but also is energized by the process of collaborative decision-making – where conflict is as necessary an ingredient as smell is in an onion – and can help others to share that experience. And, equally important, he can build a climate, a system of shared vision and values, that encourages everyone to work together so that no one is indispensable. This ability, which I call (**I**)ntegration, can change the consciousness of the organization from mechanistic to organic, and turn individual (**E**)ntrepreneurship into group (**E**)ntrepreneurship.

Thus, in order to identify the leaders, or those with the potential to become leaders, in our organizations, there are certain qualities we should be looking for, and they are more about character than style.

Leadership is Being a Thumb

The best things in life are sometimes discovered in their absence. You don't know the value of love until you don't have it anymore; you can't realize the value of health until you've been sick. You don't know the value of democracy until you've lived under a dictatorship.

A good leader may also be revealed by what happens – or doesn't happen – in his absence; that's when his staff notices that everything is running as if he's around, even though he isn't around. Ralph Ablon has said: "A good manager creates an environment in which the most desirable thing will most probably happen."

Many people visualize leadership as a pointing finger. "Do this, do that!" My view is that a complementary team is like a hand composed of fingers of different lengths and capabilities, and its leader is like a thumb. Why? Because the thumb is the only finger that opposes the other fingers, yet can "work" with any or all of them – thus enabling them to perform as a hand. If you lose a thumb, a surgeon will break one of your healthy fingers and refashion it into a thumb so that you can have a hand again.

Being a leader is being a thumb: Making *different* fingers work *together* like a hand.

A good *manager* does not necessarily have to excel at (**I**)ntegration, or being a thumb. A *leader*, however, does. The difference between good management and the next level, leadership, is that a leader must excel in at least two of the managerial roles, one of which must be (**I**)ntegration. Without that ability to (**I**)ntegrate, which enables four fingers to perform like a hand, there can be no teamwork.

Of course, all members of a team should have some leadership qualities – at least the minimum level necessary to (**I**)ntegreate a department or a meeting, and keep conflict from destroying fragile agreements.

There are three archetype styles for leadership. The first is (**PaeI**), whom I call the shift-level leader, or sometimes "The Small League Coach." Then there's (**pAeI**) – a Participative (**A**)dministrator; and finally there is (**paEI**) – the Statesman. If the three of them were to comprise a team, the question of who would lead it would have to be determined by the changing nature of the tasks to be performed, as well as the always evolving mission of the organization itself.

For me, a good analogy for leadership is a relay race. Please note that I did not say a marathon race, which is as different from a relay race is night is from day. A relay race, of course, is based on teamwork, while a marathon is an individual effort.

Here is another good analogy: Good leaders are like parents who take turns supervising their children – so the kids will learn early how to adapt to different models of authority.

In the Adizes methodology there is no voting; nor are team members' proposals rejected unilaterally (if it occurs at all, a veto would take place only at the highest level of the company). Instead, the team discusses the problem until there is consensus – and I mean consensus, not compromise. The only exception is when there is time pressure, in which case the leader will make a temporary decision, to be reviewed and possibly revised later on.

What kind of leader is best for a particular organization at a given moment in time will depend on several variables, including where the organization is in its lifecycle; the styles of the other team members and on the nature of the tasks to be accomplished. The appropriate leadership style must change as the organization grows and ages, just as parenting style has to change depending on the age of the child.

Characteristics of a Leader

Understanding that no one can be the ideal, perfect manager described in management school textbooks, what general characteristics should we be looking for instead?

A good member of a complementary leadership team sees himself as a servant. He's there to serve the organization so that the people that comprise it can get their job done. He creates an environment in which people can shine.

And a good leader assumes that his people are doing their best. As K.H. Blanchard said, "Catch them doing it right. Don't catch them doing it wrong. Reinforce the positive."[2] If someone is not doing his best, a leader will sense that, figure out what is blocking his capabilities, and help him to improve. If that proves to be impossible, a leader will find another place for him to work that better fits his capabilities and style. Eventually, with the help of the leader, that person will shine somewhere.

As will become clearer in the following pages, what makes a good leader is maturity, and maturity comes from experience – from the "University of Hard Knocks." I'm very much against the "fast track" for young MBAs: It means they climb to the top based on what they *know*, not what they *are*. What they lack is the experience that brings maturity, which in turn brings humility.

Not everybody knows how to lose, for instance. Winning is easy. Losing is difficult. Show me a leader who knows how to lose and come out a winner (by acquiring some wisdom in the process), and I will show you a good leader, because the road to heaven is through hell. The person who has gone through hell knows his weaknesses and has learned to be humble. He's learned to seek the assistance and support of others. As the late Mary Kay said when she was asked the secret of her success, "Do you want to see the scars on my knees?"

What makes a winner is not whether or not he falls, but how quickly he gets up and tries again,

A good leader creates an environment in which the most desirable outcome will probably happen. He (**I**)ntegrates. He is a thumb, not a pointing finger.

I am aware that many of the attributes I ascribe to a leader are traditionally thought to be feminine rather than masculine traits. The role of the (**I**)ntegrator in a complementary team is analogous to that of one parent – usually the mother – in a family? What makes a house a home if not the feminine energy? What integrates a family, with its multiple needs and personalities, into a cohesive entity if not the feminine energy? But please notice I did not say "a woman" or "a man," because the so-called feminine energies can be possessed by either.

"A leader is best when people barely know that
he exists,
Not so good when people obey and acclaim him,
Worst when they despise him.
Fail to honor people,
They fail to honor you;
But of a good leader, who talks little,
When his work is done, his aim fulfilled,
They will all say, "We did this ourselves."

Lao Tse

Can the elements of good team leadership be broken down and generalized? In working with leaders of organizations all over the world, I have found that good leaders do have certain characteristics in common:

1. Self-awareness

Most people do not know themselves. All of us tend to be a bit deluded about ourselves, believing that we are excellent (**P**)roducers, fine

(**A**)dministrators, creative (**E**)ntrepreneurs, and good at (**I**)ntegrating others. We rarely have an accurate picture of ourselves; we are either favorably or unfavorably biased toward ourselves.

A good leader must be aware of what he is doing, aware of his style, his (**PAEI**) code. Can you monitor yourself they way you monitor others? That may sound simple but it isn't. When I describe mismanagement styles in my lectures, people in the audience laugh because they can immediately identify their bosses, their peers, their subordinates. They can say, "That one is a big (**P**)," "That one is a big (**A**)," etc.

But when they try to categorize their own style, it's more difficult. Why? Because most people are not aware of what they do. "It takes two to know one," as the social scientist Gregory Bateson once said. Being aware means being cognizant of your and other people's reactions and emotions. Can you *feel* what is going on?

2. Consciousness

What is the difference between being aware and being conscious? They are not synonyms. Consciousness to me means: "I am aware of the *consequences* and *meaning* of what I am aware of. I understand cause and effect. I am cognizant of my effect on others – the impact *my* behavior has on *other people's* behavior."

You might think that you are a wonderful (**I**)ntegrator, not realizing that you cause lots of disruptive conflicts in the organization. What counts is not only how *you* feel but *how you make others feel.*

One way to be conscious of your behavior and its effect is to watch how people react to your words and actions.

But that is not as simple as just *seeing* what happens; you have to *notice* it, *understand* it, and *evaluate* it. This requires, first of all, that you have the ability to intuit other people's feelings by observing their body language and behavior, their words and their silences.

Second, you must be conscious enough of what you have said and done, and how it might have been experienced, that other people's reactions will make sense to you.

For example, let us say you are a big (**P**) manager and you tend to order people around very brusquely when you're tense. After an episode of that kind, it wouldn't do you much good to notice that your staffpeople seem angry or subdued – *unless* you are also aware that you behaved brusquely and might have hurt some feelings.

None of this is simple. This is multi-tasking in the inscrutable arena of human relations, where knowing all the facts does not necessarily make you wise.

But this awareness beyond yourself of the meaning and impact of what you do is part of what defines us as human. Have you ever seen an animal build a temple, or worship a god, or make symbols? No: We are the only living creatures who assign meaning to symbols. We even die and kill for symbols. Animals are aware, but they do not attempt to construct a bigger picture, to derive a meaning from their acquired knowledge. That is consciousness, which goes beyond awareness.

In order to be conscious, you have to be (**I**)ntegrated in the world, understanding that there is a larger meaning beyond yourself. There must be an intention behind your actions, a purpose for what you do that transcends yourself.

Awareness is short-term; consciousness is long-term. Unless you are conscious, you will not try to build a learning environment, you will not try to be tolerant or patient. You will just do whatever you want to do, because you're not thinking beyond yourself and your own short-term desires.

I suggest that we are what we do to others; we are how we behave. This existentialist, behavioral approach implies that in order to know ourselves, we must realize what effect we have on others. We can do this best if we are open enough to hear and accept what people have to say about us – even if what they say is inconsistent with our own beliefs about ourselves.

Can you see yourself through the eyes of others? If you really want to know who you are, go ask your subordinates; they know *exactly* who you are. If you cannot bring yourself to ask, or you cannot credit what people tell you when you *do* ask, you're almost certainly going to be living with some illusions about yourself.

A conscious leader knows how his style affects the team as a whole. Thus, being conscious means you must hear, and then *listen* to and *feel* what you hear – rather than just hearing without listening, or listening without feeling. This brings me to a personal story:

Many years ago I was lecturing in Mexico, speaking in English with a simultaneous translation. And I was getting tired of simultaneous translation because the audience always laughed at my jokes a minute or two after I said the punch line; it was all out of synch. So I asked them whether they would mind if I spoke to them in 15th-century Spanish, or Ladino, which as a Sephardic Jew I had spoken as a child. (It was the only language in which my grandmother and I could communicate.) They agreed.

So I tried it and something very interesting happened. At a certain point when I asked them, in 15th-century Spanish, "Did you hear me?" they looked as if they did not understand me. So I asked them in English, "What did I say? Why are you reacting that way?"

"Well, you asked us if we *feel* you."

"No, no, no, no," I said. "I did not ask you if you *feel* me, I asked you if you *hear* me."

And they said, "Oh no, the word in modern Spanish is *escuchar*, and you were using the word *sentir*, which is really to feel." (It's interesting, however, that in modern Spanish the source of the word remains: A person who is hard of hearing is called "mal de sentido.")

That's when I had a big illumination: Five hundred years ago, the verbs "to feel," "to hear," and "to listen" were one and the same word: *Sentir*. It really meant "to sense." (That is why, in languages that developed from the same source, the word *sentir* today has different meanings. In Spanish it means "to feel," in Italian "to hear," in French "to smell.")

What has civilization, development and sophistication brought us? Now there are three words instead of one. Now I can hear and not listen: "*I heard you!*" – but I did not listen to what was said. I can repeat every word of what was said, but it went in one ear and out the other. Nothing was absorbed because I did not listen.

Then there is the next disintegration, in which a person listens to what he hears but he does not *feel* it.

Five hundred years ago, people *felt* what they were saying to each other; they were more in touch with each other. Life was more primitive but more connected. My dog, for instance, can hear, listen, and feel me just by smelling me. When I come home, he senses if I am in the mood to play or whether I am so upset that he'd better keep out of the way. I do not have to say a word. He *feels* me.

With some people, on the other hand, it might take time and effort for them to make the transition from hearing to listening and finally to feeling what I want to say. The modern world with its rapid change has caused disintegration, to disengage, separate, tune out. Thus, it is much more difficult to communicate.

Here is another example: One day I was in Chicago, driving a rental car from a client's office to the airport. There was a blizzard outside, and it was freezing.

Of course, I did not feel the cold. I was in a heated car with my jacket off; I was an inch or two from a freezing situation – and yet I felt nothing.

But that is emblematic of the new, bold world we live in. The person sitting across from us on the train may be falling apart emotionally – but we do not feel it.

So in essence, what I am saying is that a good leader has to *feel*, not just think and analyze and rationalize. He must try to understand less in his head and more in his heart.

In order to know himself, a manager must get in touch with a surrounding world that is less censored, less controllable and more direct. Can you *feel* what people tell you, not just hear and listen? For a manager to be in touch with himself, he must be in touch with others. When I work in developing countries I often enjoy it more than in highly sophisticated countries. Relationships in developing countries are more direct, without intermediary interruptions. In modern countries, there's too much thinking and not enough instinctive feeling going on.

Let me say it directly: What makes you a good manager or leader is not what you know but what you are. What you know gets obsolete over time. What you are is forever. Thus:

> *It is easier to hire a person who IS,*
> *and teach him to know,*
> *than to hire someone*
> *who knows*
> *and teach him to BE.*

3. Well-rounded: No zeros in (PAEI) code

Every manager and leader has his strengths and weaknesses; in other words, they are human. Thus, there are no perfect (**PAEI**) managers and it is useless to go looking for one.

On the other hand, a manager who has any blanks, or zeros, in his code is doomed to being a mismanager. Each zero signifies a blind spot in his perspective, which leaves him unable to properly fit any position. It is as if he were a pilot, who must distinguish among different-colored signals, and yet he is color-blind.

Thus, an (**A**)dministrating manager whose style is coded (-**A**--) cannot be a leader and in fact cannot be a competent manager either. A good manager must be at least a (**pAei**); an (**A**)dministrating leader a (**pAeI**). An (-**A**- -) style manager is dysfunctional, even if he is the best (**A**) the organization has ever had. Why? Because the other essential roles are absent.

Why must he be competent at all the roles? One obvious reason is flexibility: If, for example, there is no (**A**) type around at a crucial moment, you might have to step in and do (**A**) tasks. The individual as a team member must be able to perform the other roles when necessary. In my analogy of the five fingers, the fingers combine to create an organic entity called a hand, and part of what defines a hand is that each finger can do the job of any other finger. It might not excel at doing this job; it might be somewhat awkward – but it can do the job if it's called for.

What would happen if you were missing one of the four roles but had a surplus of another? Could you make up for your lack of (**E**), for example, by throwing lots of extra (**P**) into the mix?

No – because (**P**)'s ability to contribute to the totality will be limited by the deficiency of the other components that are necessary for an interaction. You can carry that (**P**) only so far; how far depends on the deficiency of the other letters.

This same principle can be seen in chemistry, in the concept of limiting regions: "If the reaction mixture contains one of the reactants in greater quantity than is required by the equation, the excess reagent simply does not react. The quantities of the products obtained are determined by the reagent(s) not in excess."[3]

To rephrase that more simply: If a formula requires 2 mg of one ingredient, 3 mg of another, and 4 mg of something else, then putting in 50 mg of any of these components is useless because it won't be supported; you would have to increase everything else proportionately in order to get a bigger reaction. There is an optimal interaction that is necessary in quantities.

The same thing is true in complementary teams. There is chemistry among the members of a team, and you have to watch what everybody contributes. The value of any single role to the organization must be evaluated based on the interaction with the other styles. No one can evaluate himself in a vacuum – "I'm a great (**P**)," "I'm a wonder-(**E**)" – because the fact is that your (**E**) will be worthless unless you have an (**A**) and a (**P**) and an (**I**) that enable your (**E**) to grow successfully.

Thus, if you are a very big (**E**), you will need to find an equally powerful (**A**) to complement yourself on your team, and vice versa.

A third reason you need a threshold capability in each one of the roles is because without it, you would probably be unable to appreciate the strengths and contributions of the other team members. If a manager has no competence in or understanding of a particular role, his link with the person whose major task it is might be compromised, because if you are blind to the hardships of (**A**), on what basis can you learn to respect an (**A**)? But if you can perform each one of the (**A**)'s tasks, at least minimally, then you can appreciate what the (**A**) is excelling in.

Let me emphasize again that the difference between a manager and a mismanager is not what he excels in. All of them will excel at something. But one is flexible, able to perform all of the (**PAEI**) roles if called for and over time, while the other is inflexible. What defines a mismanager is his *inflexibility*: There is an exclusive role he can perform, he is blind to anything else, and because of that he is very close to being Deadwood. When change happens, this mismanager will not be flexible enough to adapt, and he may flip over and become Deadwood.

4. Knows strengths and weaknesses; knows his uniqueness

It is important to have a balanced view of yourself. Some people only identify their strengths while denying their weaknesses. Some magnify their weaknesses and underestimate their strengths.

A balanced view means, "I know what I'm good at; I know what I'm weak at. I don't overestimate my strengths and underestimate my weaknesses, and I don't underestimate my strengths and overestimate my weaknesses. I'm aware of them and I am also aware that I am unique in my strengths and weaknesses."

Why are you unique? Because if you take each component of (**PAEI**) in any individual and score its presence from 0 to 100, you will get more permutations than there are people on this globe. We are all alike and we are all different at the same time. There are no two people who are the same. There is nobody like you, nobody in the whole world.

How do we reach an understanding of our unique capabilities and limitations? By being in regular communication with others, by being open to the assessments that others make of us. In these ways we can help determine our place as managers on the (**PAEI**) map.

This knowledge is particularly important for working well in a team. You must know who you are, so that you can find out what kind of people you'll need to complement yourself.

5. Accepts strengths, weaknesses, and uniqueness

A good manager does not try to be someone else. He knows his weaknesses and his strengths, and he accepts them. He does not have an unbalanced view of himself.

Managers are sometimes given psychological tests. One might show, for example, that a manager has a tendency to be too task-oriented. In that case, the manager is told, "You must become more people-oriented." But this type of limited feedback does not change a manager at all. It cannot. If he could be more people-oriented, he probably would be already. Such an approach only gives the manager cause to be less satisfied with what he is. Thus his level of frustration rises, without any significant change in his behavior.

Accepting oneself does not come from taking tests. It is part of becoming mature. An adolescent may act out his dreams, but adults accept reality. As adults, we know our limitations and like ourselves in spite of them.

On the other hand, accepting oneself does not mean giving up any effort to improve. Acknowledging that I will never be a perfect (**PAEI**) manager doesn't mean I should fatalistically accept all my flaws and give up hope of learning to do better. Just the opposite, in fact: Armed with a realistic assessment of their skills and weaknesses, managers can focus on removing any blanks in their code and enhancing their performance of the necessary roles, continuing to learn and grow in all roles – instead of measuring themselves against some impossible ideal of perfection.

Accepting yourself is important, because unless you accept who you are already, you cannot effectively change. Accepting your weaknesses is a condition for improving. Why is that? Because your energy is a limited resource; if it is spent on rejecting who you are, it will not be available for adapting and changing yourself into the person you want to be.

The desire to improve should be realistic; try to avoid those New-Year's-resolution-like commitments to changing your personality completely. In my work, I do not even try to change styles. I only try to *enrich* the style so that a manager can communicate and work more effectively with others. I teach and train people how to work together – not in spite of being different but *because* they are different. I also use my techniques to place people in positions that are compatible with their managerial style, and help them develop their ability to perform additional roles so that they can advance in the organization.

But to be able to accomplish this growth, a person must first know who and what he is. My definitions of these criteria correspond closely to the respected psychologist Abraham Maslow's description of "the self-actualized personality."[4]

According to Maslow, self-actualized people can accept themselves and others as they are. They do not shun those who have not become what they "ought" to be. Nevertheless, self-actualized people are action-oriented, and are neither self-satisfied nor satisfied with the status quo.

Because self-actualized people are secure, they are not afraid to reveal their feelings to others. Their interpersonal relations are very deep.

Self-actualized people tend to judge people and situations correctly and efficiently. In general, they are readily able to detect the spurious, the fake, and the dishonest.

Self-actualized people are self-reliant and make their own judgments. They are autonomous and independent in thought and action. Their decisions are guided by internal standards and values rather than by what others are doing. They respond to problems in a natural, logical manner.

Self-actualized people enter into fruitful exchanges with anyone they meet. They are willing to learn from anyone, and are not afraid to ask questions that others hesitate to ask. They do not fear blunders.

Self-actualized people generally have fresh, happy outlooks. They are filled with awe, pleasure, wonder, and even ecstasy.

Once you become aware, conscious, and accepting of your strengths and weaknesses, you have something you can work on. Are there zeros in your code? Can you perform all four roles competently?

In addition to being a prerequisite for self-improvement, the ability to accept yourself and be at peace with yourself despite your weaknesses is also a condition for accepting others who are weak in certain areas. If you cannot accept your own uniqueness, you are not going to accept the uniqueness of other people. If you don't accept yourself, you're not going to accept anybody around you. All the frustrations you have with yourself, you'll pass on to somebody else.

6. Can identify excellence and weaknesses in others

Now that you're aware of and accept your own style, strengths, and weaknesses, you must become conscious of the styles of others, and in particular you must be able to identify the strengths of other people in areas in which you are weak.

This is tricky. Big (**E**)s can identify other big (**E**)s instantly. But they do not know how to evaluate (**A**)s because this is their weakness. They don't understand (**A**)s, they don't know what criteria to apply to (**A**)s; as a matter of fact they don't even like them.

By and large, for example, big (**P**)s hire other (**P**)s. The Lone Ranger, or (**P---**), hires gofers. He suspects and despises (**A**)s, fears (**E**)s, and ignores (**I**)s. So how can he realistically be expected to identify or hire them?

This is one of the biggest challenges for managers: Can you hire and utilize and develop and cherish and nourish people who are different from you, instead of opting for the security of hiring people who are like you?

Knowing your managerial code is not enough. You must know all the requirements of good (**PAEI**) management and be able to recognize and respect the characteristics in others that complement your own.

This is where uni-dimensional people with zeros in their codes, who are blind to other roles, have enormous difficulty: In identifying, accepting, and appreciating those roles.

Successful managers recognize that all managers are deficient humans. Ray Kroc, the president of the McDonald's chain, once described himself as a "country boy," who does not even pretend to know finance or in-depth management techniques. He viewed his role as that of finding the right people to work together.

This in itself is no revelation. What is new, however, is that I am not talking here about skills or knowledge; I'm not trying to fill a position in a specific area, such as finance or operations. On the contrary, I am talking about something less concrete and at the same time more embedded in personality: Styles, behaviors. Can you identify excellence in a style component in which you are weak?

Unfortunately, many managers fear excellence in others. These are managers who have little self-respect or who are not flexible enough to deal with people whose styles are different from theirs. Such managers do not have the best people working for them. They are like the racehorse owner who fills his stable with ponies but expects to win the Triple Crown.

7. Can accept and appreciate differences in others

When we reach the stage at which we can recognize the qualities of others, the next step is to figure out how to live with them. Can you see beauty in difference? Can you accept, respect, and nourish it?

Now, accepting people doesn't mean you have to work with *all* of them. Accepting might mean accepting the responsibility for getting rid of an employee, if you discover that for one reason or another he cannot work within a team.

But accepting also means understanding that you're never going to find the perfect person. So can you work with someone who is different from you, despite his inevitable weaknesses? Are you aware that since you cannot be superior in all four management roles, your subordinates will ideally be superior to you in some respects? Each time one of them excels, it reinforces how weak you are in that role. Can you experience that and not feel threatened? Can you accept that you are human, that you have weaknesses, and that it is OK and even desirable that someone else can do what you cannot?

The superior-subordinate-superior type of relationship is common in research and development (R&D) departments. An R&D manager may have "under" him Ph.D.s who are geniuses in certain areas. These "subordinates" may be fantastic (**E**)ntrepreneurs, whereas the R&D manager may be only an (**A**)dministrator. A problem will arise only if the (**A**)dministrator wants to be both the best research director and the best researcher — if he wants to compete rather than support.

8. Knows how to slow down and relax in difficult situations

In Chapter 7, I mentioned my "duck theory" of management: If you look at a duck as it's floating along in the water, on the surface it looks unperturbed and calm, but under the water its feet are working fast, very fast.

A good manager should and a good leader *must* be relaxed when conflict arises. He remains objective and respectful of other people. In fact, one common characteristic of the best managers I've known is that the more intense the conflict, the calmer they've become.

On a basic level, being a good manager or leader means knowing how to disagree without being disagreeable. Some people actually *agree* disagreeably. We've probably all had the experience of finally reaching agreement with someone, after many hours of discussion, but feeling that the process was so painful that we never want to deal with that person again. Whether it's your marriage, your family or your business, you often forget the content of a conflict — *what* were you fighting about? — but if you felt abused by the discussion you will never, ever forget *how* it was handled. The *how* is more important than the *what*.

The same thing is true in international relations. How we handle our enemy is extremely important. Never disrespect your enemy, because you will never find peace that way.

9. Creates a learning environment in which conflicts can be resolved, by both commanding and granting mutual trust and respect.

Conflict is necessary, indispensable. Show me an organization without conflict and I will show you a cemetery. Show me a marriage without conflict and I will show you a marriage that has died, is dying, or will soon die. Show me a society where conflict is forbidden by law, such as a Communist regime, and I will show you a stymied society that cannot change easily.

A leader must be able to command and grant respect; he must be able to create a learning environment in which conflict is used constructively, as a tool, rather than destructively. Thus he must have a lot of (**I**) in his code. He must be able to (**I**)ntegrate his followers to follow.

Finally, a leader must have patience and be tolerant of the conflicts that inevitably arise among colleagues with different styles and strengths. He must be able to harness conflicts – accepting the pain that this process requires. For me, good management is not about how much financial theory you know, or how well you read financial statements, or how good you are at strategic planning. To me, good management is about how much pain you can take in working with others. The higher you go up the ladder, the greater is the pain.

I often joke that one way to identify a good leader is by the depth of the scars on his tongue. Leaders have to bite their tongues: They must know what to say and how much to say, and they must be able to handle the frustration of *not* saying what's on their minds, when that is appropriate.

SHARING VISION AND VALUES

Consider a marriage. A good marriage enables children to grow up healthy and well-developed. But what defines a good marriage?

In a healthy marriage, the spouses complement each other's styles. They have a process and a culture of mutual trust and respect so that their inevitable conflicts do not become destructive.

Each of them grants and commands respect and trust. There is a clear structure of domestic responsibilities; each knows what tasks are his or her own responsibility, and what belongs to the other.

Is that enough ? No. Why not? Let's go back a step. What if the two partners have different ideas of what a marriage is all about? One might want an open arrangement, sexually, while the other wants a traditional, monogamous marriage. These two definitions of marriage are mutually exclusive. So what now?

That's simple. It is not going to work.

For a team to work together as a team, there must be a shared vision and shared values as well.

(Conversely, sharing a vision and values is not sufficient either. Many companies that started out with exactly that – the Body Shop, for example,– eventually failed commercially because they lacked the right structure, and process. To achieve success, all four ingredients – structure, process, people, and shared vision and values – must be in place.)

Values are what we believe in.

Vision is a statement of the desired in light of the expected: Where do we want to go, given where we are right now and how far we can reasonably expect to get in the time available? In this construct, of course, the first clause – desire – is the domain of the (**E**), and the second – reasonable expectations – the domain of the (**A**).

IMAGINING ONES IDENTITY

How do you design the vision and determine the values of a company?

At the Adizes Institute we train people to do it. The detailed methodology is in manuals, and the process takes about six days.

But here are some pointers:

Defining the Market Product Scope

When I taught at universities, students used to come to ask me for help in deciding on a future career. I noticed that the students who knew who they were also knew where they wanted to go. Those who were less sure of their identities were also less sure of their destinations.

Thus we should start with "Know thyself," which also happens to be the first item on my list of leadership characteristics.

How do you know yourself? Let's return yet again to the functionalist, or (**P**) view: You are what you do for and to others, period. So if you want to know who you are, watch what you do to others.

How does an organization "know itself"? Again, start with the (**P**) function. An organization is what it does for or to others, period. So:

Who are our clients and what do they want? Which of their needs do we satisfy? Which don't we satisfy?

That gives you a continuum.

Now, ask another question: What are our core capabilities – what do we know how to do?

Now put these two continuums next to each other:

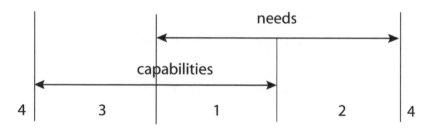

You should now see four distinct sectors. Area 1 is where we have the ability to satisfy our clients' needs – and we do satisfy them. Area 2 is where our clients have needs that we do not satisfy, or satisfy adequately. Area 3 is where we have capabilities whose potential is not being realized. Area 4 is the unknown: Clients' needs that we do not know about, or that we do not have the ability to provide.

A startup company is all in Area 1. As it grows, the fields of Areas 2 and 3 increase as clients develop other needs that the company does not attempt to satisfy, and the company develops capabilities it doesn't exploit.

When a company ages and becomes bureaucratized, the organization gradually loses its market and Area 1 shrinks. (When another company comes into the market to compete against an aging company, they don't start by going after Area 1. They penetrate Areas 2 and 3 first. After building up business there, they use those areas as a base from which to attack Area 1.)

Now we can answer the question "Who are we?" The answer is that we are what we *do* (Area 1); what we *should* do (Area 2); and what we *can* do, if we choose to (Area 3).

This is called the company's "market product scope," and it is applicable not only to businesses but also to not-for-profits, which also have clients and capabilities.

THE VISIONING PROCESS

The next step is to map on this same chart all of the company's activities, according to which ones are currently satisfying clients (Area 1); which are not (Area 2); which ones we have not yet found a market for); and which are unknown (Area 4). In doing this exercise, organizations in the GoGo phase of the lifecycle will find that they are literally all over the map, with activities, investments, and Joint Ventures even in Area 4! Organizations that are becoming bureaucratized will be able to see that their regular market (Area 1) is very small. So this part of the process can also be used as a diagnostic tool.

Now the visioning process starts: Which of these activities should we keep, which should we drop and which should we develop and nurture?

In order to make those decisions, we must first analyze the changing environment – physical, legal, political, technological, social, economic, and cultural. How they are changing? What does that mean for the future of our products or services? In light of that predicted future, what should we do or not do?

Every company has some part of the environment that critically affects it. For a bank it is the economic and political environment, for the fashion industry it is the social, for the transportation industry it is the physical. But by and large my experience shows that all aspects of the environment should be analyzed, because they are interdependent and interactive.

ASSESS THE COMPETITION

Next, analyze what you believe your competition is going to do to respond to this changing environment.

CHOOSE YOUR FUTURE

It is time to put the pieces of the puzzle together and analyze what all these facts and educated guesses mean for your company.

These discussions should include what activities the company should continue; what it should undertake; what it should drop; what it should develop. The discussions also should determine marketing efforts, changes in organizational structure, allocation of budgets, changes in staffing decisions – and, perhaps, changes in values.

Now, I said earlier in this chapter that values are a belief structure that guides behavior. But sometimes that belief structure has no logic behind it.

Those values could be past decisions that worked out well and became policies by default. If their validity and effectiveness are not reviewed periodically, they can become pointless obstacles to growth.

Here is an example: Twenty years ago, when I worked with Northrop Aviation, I found out that Northrop was not selling much, if anything, to the United States Air Force. This puzzled me, because the Air Force was a natural client for Northrop, and could have been its biggest.

I started to ask questions, and here is what I eventually found out: Jack Northrop, who built the first fighter plane and founded the company in 1938, would only build two-engine fighter planes because he believed one engine was not reliable enough. With time and advances in technology this assumption was not true anymore but the original assumption did not change. It became the "policy" of the company: We produce two engine fighter planes. So who was buying them now? The planes were mostly purchased by developing nations, which did not have the budget or trained personnel necessary to maintain a single-engine plane. However, the U.S. Air Force went on buying single-engine planes from other companies.

The two-engine plane policy may have been an engineering decision originally; but by the time I consulted with the company, it was no longer an engineering decision or even a marketing decision. It was a value statement, and it urgently needed to be reviewed.

Here is another, example from my experience: One of a retail company's market strengths is that it is selling on credit. This company buys another retail company – one which grew by working on very low margins but offering no credit. The buying company installs credit in its new acquisition; after all, that is its *modus vivendi*.

What happens? The first company loses its shirt. Why? Because it kept the second company's low margins while installing credit. A system of low margins that sells on credit cannot afford any bad debt – however, bad debt is a predictable cost of doing business with credit.

I could offer endless other examples of how value systems help or hinder the development of an organization. But I think you can already see my point, which is that these belief systems need to be articulated so that they can be periodically evaluated and addressed.

THE ASSESSMENT TEAM

How is this done?

When I consult to a company, I put together a team of the organization's so-called "black sheep," or *enfant terribles* – the people who are always very loudly disagreeing with the company's policies and arguing against them. I consider them to be the most conscious.

I assign them two tasks. The first is to identify which values should be kept, which should be dropped, and which must be adapted because of changes in the marketplace. The second is to identify changes that must be implemented in the market product scope.

When all the homework is done and one team presents the market product scope, the other one presents what changes we need to do due to the cnahgin environment and the competitive predictable moves, and the values team presents which values need to change, be droped or developed, we have a discussion: *What should we do* in light of all the above. The discussion is very structured and follows a road map. At the end, each member of the team is given an assignment:

Imagine that it is three years into the future. It is the end of the year and you are writing a report to the stockholders.

And you must sum up in writing what *changes* the company has done and what those changes accomplished, what the company stands for and why.. Write this report in the past tense: "We did this, and the results were …" "We did that, and the results were…"

They read to each other their reports and start integrating the reports unitl a common report emerges.

Slowly, through this road map for discussion, there emerges a vision of the company's identity today, and what it needs to be in the future to adapt to the changing environment.

The important result is not so much that there was a discussion. The imoortant result is that there is a common vision and an agreement on the values the company should adopt, nurture or drop.

What follows this discussion is another session on the structural repercussions of this vision and values: What do we need to change structurally in the organization so that this vsion can become a reality. But that is material for a totally new book.

Summing Up

Characteristics of good managers

1. *Self-aware*
2. *Conscious*
3. Well-rounded: *No zeros* in (**PAEI**) code
4. *Knows* strengths and weaknesses; knows his uniqueness
5. *Accepts* strengths, weaknesses, and uniqueness
6. Can *identify* excellence and weaknesses in others
7. Can accept and *appreciate* differences in others
8. Knows how to *slow down* and relax in times of adversity
9. Creates a *learning* environment in which conflicts can be resolved, by both commanding and granting mutual trust and respect

A Shared Vision of Success

Successful leaders know that they cannot be right on every decision all the time and forever. They need to seek out the wisdom, expertise and points of view of those around them with different styles and perspectives.

Complementary teams hold the answers to most of the problems an organization will face. However, they also have the potential for frustration, gridlock, and dysfunction. How the team's interactions and communications are handled can spell the difference between success and failure.

Successful leaders know that to convert destructive, dysfunctional conflict, to be constructive and do it by integrating the complementary team to have shared values and a shared vision to work with. They should have the right process of decision making so they can work and understand each other and the company must have people who command and grant respect and trust and they should be assigned responsibilities that match their style in a structure of responsibilities that enables all (**PAEI**) roles to be fulfilled.

NOTES

1. Adizes, Ichak, *Managing Corporate Lifecycles* (Englewood Cliffs, N.J.: Prentice-Hall, 1999).

2. Blanchard, Kenneth, and Robert Lorber: *The One Minute Manager* (New York: Morrow/Avon, 1982).

3. Dillard, Clyde R.; and David E. Goldberg: *Chemistry: Reactions, Structure, and Properties* (New York: Macmillan Company, 1971, p. 28).

4. Maslow, Abraham H. ed.: *Motivation and Personality* (New York: Harper & Row, 1954).

Chapter 13

Nurturing the Wrong Tree?

PROBLEM: The structure of traditional management squashes potential, while management schools do more harm than good by encouraging the illusion that a single individual can excel in all managerial tasks.

THE WRONG TREE

We know that perfect executives do not exist; and that, in any case, each managerial role requires different behavior, a different style of managing. Furthermore, we know that no organization can succeed without a senior team that, collectively, can perform the four basic roles – (**P**)roducing, (**A**)dministrating, (**E**)ntrepreneuring, and (**I**)ntegrating – with excellence.

Nevertheless, for years organizations have been chasing down some mythical perfect manager. In their quest to find this incredible faultless genius, they raise salaries, increase stock options, and give all kinds of special incentives and rewards to CEOs.

But even if you could find one, it would be dangerous to rely on genius. Why? Because let's face it: Genius appears very, very seldom. Any corporation that depended solely upon the talents of one individual, even if that individual were outstandingly competent, would be extraordinarily limited. There is a military expression that illuminates this point: "Organizations should be organized by a genius so that even an idiot can run them, rather than organized by an idiot so that only a genius can run them." The reason is that there simply aren't enough geniuses to staff all organizations and all the positions in them.

Suppose an organization did have a manager who was so superior to everybody else that he naturally assumed all the decision-making power? If that man made a mistake, he could easily point the organization in the wrong direction, and even geniuses make at least one mistake once in a while. In their book *Corporate Management In Crisis: Why the Mighty Fall*, Joel Ross and Michael Kami suggest that "what causes big corporations to fail is one-man rule"[1]– even though it is also true that one-man rule has often been the key to a start-up company's initial success.

The problem is that if no evolution to a longer-term style occurs over time, eventually the company grows so complex that no individual manager can fill all the essential roles – nor is he likely to let go of them – and the collapse of such conglomerates has often been swift and dramatic.

So it's clear that organizations must make it a priority, not to scout out one all-purpose, perfect manager, but to use the innate talents of *all* of their employees to promote a cadre of managers, each with expertise in one or two managerial roles as well as the ability to perform the other roles with competence. In addition, organizations must provide these managers with opportunities to develop their lesser skills; thus ensuring a source of future leadership from within the company.

Traditional Management Squashes Potential

Ironically, however, the structure of the modern organization is more conducive to eliminating managerial talents than developing them. Instead of fostering well-roundedness, it inhibits growth.

Consider the modern hierarchical system. It capitalizes on the strengths of individuals. A person who is a strong (**A**)dministrator will be promoted as an (**A**) and will climb the corporate ladder as an (**A**). In the short run, an organization may be getting the maximum out of that manager, but in the long run, his lack of opportunities to develop (**P**), (**E**), and (**I**) will make him inflexible and uncooperative when dealing with people whose styles are different from his, and that will ultimately harm the company.

Another danger is that some potentially great leaders will remain stuck in supportive positions throughout their careers – simply because they are too good at what they do. Examples of such biases in promotion are often seen in the Army, where someone who is an excellent sergeant or staff sergeant may not be recommended for a commission because his commanding officer doesn't wish to lose a good adjutant.

Yet another breeding ground for mismanagement lies in the very rigid boundaries that corporations typically maintain between workers and management.

At the bottom ranks of most organizations, (**P**) is expected almost exclusively. Workers are not expected to be (**A**)dministrators, (**E**)ntrepreneurs, or (**I**)ntegrators, nor are they given opportunities or experience in those roles. (In particular, management regards as a potential threat any attempts at (**I**)ntegration from the lowest levels – which often manifest themselves as unionization efforts or informal, non-sanctioned leadership.)

Just above (**P**)roduction are first-line managers, who are expected to have plenty of (**A**). When a (**P**)roduction worker is promoted to first-line manager, he needs to relax his (**P**) role to (**p**) and begin performing (**A**) tasks and even some (**e**) and (**i**).

None of this is easy. In order to reduce his (**P**), the new first-line foreperson must let others do the work that he formerly did himself. This entails becoming relatively detached from tasks to which he may have been totally dedicated – and to accept the fact that others can and should do the job instead.

Lacking crucial experience in the new roles, however, the new manager will more often than not continue using his exclusive (**P**) approach. Eventually, he will end up as a (**P---**), a Lone Ranger.

This would be equally true if a (**P**)roduction manager were promoted to CEO. In any new job, people tend to repeat the style that has worked for them, and since what made him successful was his (**P**) orientation, the new CEO will probably continue to (**P**), running the company single-handedly and making all of the important decisions himself.

And it's true for those I call "financial engineers" – venture capitalists or investment bankers whose success has derived from their individual deal-making, a (**P**) task. Given the role of managing director, for example, a financial engineer would need to add some (**a**), (**E**), and (**I**) skills and to relax his (**P**) style to (**p**); he'd also have to learn how to work well with (**A**)-, (**E**)-, and (**I**)-style managers. If he could not quickly make this transition, the company he manages would soon be in deep trouble.

Paradoxically, until an employee rises to the vice presidential level, (**E**) and (**I**) are generally discouraged – but once he does reach that level, he is *instantly* expected to be creative and to facilitate staff interactions. The question is: Where will he find the skills and the emotional resources to perform these new functions when he has been harnessed, suffocated, and divested of his creative impulses for twenty years or so? Usually, the answer is: He won't. This may explain why so many companies fill their top management positions from the MBA ranks who have no experience except learning to write business plans which is (**E**).

Mismanagement Breeds Mismanagement

Organizational roles are eternally in conflict, and the style that prevails is often (not coincidentally) the style of the company's founder. If the founder's style is extreme and intolerant of other styles, he will limit the opportunities for other roles to develop and mature. Thus, mismanagement breeds more mismanagement.

Typically, for instance, corporations founded by (**P-E-**)s grow rapidly (assuming that they are successful). During this phase, they usually lack the cohesion that good (**A**)dministration provides; in fact, efforts to create controls are sometimes met by antagonism from a (**P-E-**) founder.

If the organization is to continue to grow, however, the (**A**)dministrative function has to be developed.

When the problem becomes serious enough, a (**pAei**) is usually called in to establish some order. But his chances of surviving at the company for very long with a (**P-E-**) at the top are slim at best. A (**P-E-**) tends to change accountants and (**A**)dministrative managers more often than is prudent for organizational stability.

The challenge for the organization at that point is to find a way to grow away from the (**P-E-**) founder, to reduce his control over the company. If the organization cannot do that, its (**pAei**) (**A**)dministrator will be seriously handicapped in his attempt to substitute structure for chaos.

Sometimes the only way to reduce the (**P-E-**) founder's power is to get rid of him. But since he is also the source of much of the company's (**E**)ntrepreneurship, energy, and creativity, that strategy can be dangerously self-defeating.

There are several possible scenarios for what happens next. If the by-now large corporation keeps growing at the same explosive pace, over time its founder will lose control – simply because the job, or jobs, he's been doing by himself will become too overwhelming. Various roles and responsibilities will start to shift, resulting in confusion and a power vacuum. This leaves the organization vulnerable to a takeover by an outside firm. After a takeover, the founder generally resigns, is forced out, or is shunted aside to some innocuous position.

The organization does become free of a destabilizing influence – but at what price?

During this phase of its lifecycle, the organization is exposed to other risks as well – some of which may make a takeover look good.

If, for example, an (-**A**--) takes control, bureaucracy begins to grow like kudzu. This is fatal to the organization's (**E**)ntrepreneurship: Suddenly it is open hunting season on the company's (**E**) types, who soon find themselves with exactly two choices: Either they must give up and adapt (don't make waves; don't stand out); or they will have to go elsewhere.

SCHOOLS THAT DO HARM

The 20th-century phenomenon of management, as a profession and a "science," has led to a burgeoning of business schools and training courses for both novices and veteran managers. And without question, there is a need for such training. Unfortunately, however, these schools continue to focus on the wrong goals and the wrong strategies.

In fact, most business schools of management do not teach management at all. They will teach you accounting, and finance, and the economic theory of the firm, and behavioral science. But knowing how to measure profits, optimize financial resources, or understand group dynamics and personal needs does not guarantee that you will know how to manage. Management – the art of defining what you should want and making it happen – is not just the sum of the above management skills. It is something else entirely, and it is not taught.

For one example, traditional management theory fails to differentiate among the various styles and circumstances that should be considered when managers plan, organize, and motivate. Any organization, if it is to remain healthy, must have a style and strategy that is heavily contingent on its current phase in the organizational lifecycle. Both style and strategy will and should change regularly, because what is functional and desirable at one stage in the lifecycle can be deadly at another. However, this is nowhere acknowledged in traditional theory, which tends to use the same formula for any organization, regardless of its degree of maturity.

But the schools' most outrageous failure has been to buy into and purvey the conventional – though wildly unrealistic – paradigm of the individual perfect manager. By encouraging students to believe they can manage large groups of people without the support of a complementary team, these schools do their students a tremendous disservice, setting them up for a future of perceived humiliating failure.

The schools encourage these unrealistic expectations in ways both direct and indirect. For instance, management textbooks, to illustrate good management practices, often put together a collage of the best traits of the best managers – and then present this collage as if it were a single, individual manager. This mythical creature will then proceed to manage (flawlessly, of course) all tasks – planning, organizing, training, developing, motivating, leading, organizing, disciplining – under all conditions in all organizations in the same way.

In effect, then, the textbooks present as a model for their students a manager with no weaknesses – a model who, in reality, could never be emulated, trained, or found – because he does not and *cannot* exist.

Have you ever known *anyone* who was entirely without weaknesses? No, of course not. And here's a related question: How many people do you know who attended the best MBA schools and programs in the country, who could recite the textbooks by heart; and yet weren't able to manage skillfully? Quite a few, right?

Why? *Because nobody is perfect*; people, by definition, have flaws as well as virtues, areas of weakness that balance their skills. There is no manager on earth who can perform with exceptional ability every single task within his purview.

Nevertheless, management textbooks are thick with formulas, maxims, directives, and rules for what every good manager "should" do: He "*should*" plan, "*should*" organize, "*should*" communicate, "*should*" discipline, "*should*" lead; there's hardly a single page that doesn't contain at least one "should." What you *won't* find is any hint that the degree of perfection required to qualify as a "good manager" – at least as these textbooks define it – might be impossible to achieve.

This is a simple, basic perceptual flaw – but with vast consequences: It virtually wipes out the value and effectiveness of contemporary managerial training. In this way, it closely resembles the development of economic theory, which developed an abstract entity called "the firm" to represent the group process of decision-making. Economists then put this construct to work as a research tool: By analyzing the conditions in which "the firm" tends to raise prices and those in which it tends to lower them, they could predict organizational behavior.

It is instructive to note the effect of this technique on the study of economics: While the hypothetical "firm" can be valuable in determining *why* certain decisions are made, it has been a poor device, at best, for studying the more crucial question of how the decision-makers interacted.

For the same reason, the education and training that management schools currently provide for students is doomed to be misguided at best, useless at worst. The moment the choice was made to present an abstraction, a better-than-human being, as the model for students to strive for, an unrealistic, ultimately unhealthy archetype was established. Inevitably, that archetype began to twist both theory and practice away from constructive and necessary pursuits, toward false values and unrealistic goals.

Origins of the Species

The paradigm of *individuals* as perfect managers has never worked; it is the fundamental error from which all the other management schools' flaws derive.

How did it come about? Why are millions being spent by corporations to train into being a creature who could not possibly fit the definition and still be human?

There are several causes. One simple one is that management theory has primarily been developed in the United States, where the tradition is individualistic and (**E**)ntrepreneurial. Thus it was a logical manifestation of American culture to personalize the process of management into one individual, called the "manager" or the "leader."

Reading chronologically through the major works in the development of management theory, you can actually see the (**PAEI**) code emerging, bit by bit – while continuing to focus on one individual and his behavior and effectiveness rather than on a management team. For example, Frederick W. Taylor, a pioneer in the field, was concerned primarily with (P)roductivity and specialization, the (**P**) role.[3] Both Henri Fayol and L.F. Urwick, on the other hand, were concerned with organizational structure, authority, span of control, delegation of authority, and staff-line relationships – the (**A**) role.[4]

Mathematician, engineer, and social philosopher Norbert Wiener focused on the dynamics of change – (**E**), and introduced the theory of cybernetics, which he defined as the science of communication and control in the animal and the machine.[5]

Elton Mayo, a sociologist at Harvard, did groundbreaking studies on behavioral science in the workplace and developed the human relations movement,[6] which has become the heart of contemporary management theory.

Psychologists, too, focus on behavior – in their case, on why people have the styles they have: What needs motivate them.[7] However, while understanding the why of behavior is interesting, it does not tell you what to do about it.

Whatever their ideas happened to be, all of these theorists had one thing in common: They concentrated exclusively on the individual manager – claiming, in essence, that one or two fingers equals a hand.

More recently, general management theoreticians including Peter Drucker,[8] William Harold Newman,[9] and Harold Koontz,[10] have changed their definitions somewhat, putting result orientation (**P**), structure (**A**), change (**E**), and the human element (**I**) together into a whole that they called the "process" or "functions" of management. However, they stopped short of challenging the old paradigm, which held that all of these roles are meant to be performed by a single manager.

Most or all of the research and documenting of management theory has been flawed for this reason. It's true that some management theorists have attempted to correct this error, by basing their own studies on the observation of real managers functioning in real situations. But because the premise behind the classic definition of management has never been challenged, the results of these descriptive studies are liable to be misapplied. Henry Mintzberg's ten roles of management[11] may be more specific than Fayol's four roles[12], but the individual who tries to master all ten roles is still attempting the impossible.

The Management Training Gap

That is why it is dangerous to rely exclusively upon managers who have impressive management school degrees but negligible experience: They have never been trained to make decisions by asking for input from those who complement them. Nor have they learned how to resolve conflicts among people with different interests; in fact, the importance of resolving such conflicts has barely been conveyed to them, even though they will inevitably need the cooperation of many styles of managers, in all four management roles, in order to implement important decisions.

What their education did teach them was to expect perfection from themselves and to believe that their training would enable them to solve any and all problems. Over time, this will become a serious handicap for the organizations that hire them.

In general, I've found that this "fast track" for young MBAs is a bad idea. Hired because of what they know instead of what they are, management school graduates are moved too quickly into positions for which they lack experience, while still laboring under the misapprehension that they have what it takes to lead an organization.

When an MBA begins to work in the field, he quickly discovers that he cannot live up to his own expectations. Trained to believe that he can and should be a perfect (**PAEI**), he is shocked and shamed by this discovery. First, he becomes angry with himself, then defensive; and eventually, he may start looking among his subordinates, peers, and bosses for a scapegoat – someone whose inadequacies can conveniently be singled out as the cause of any failure.

In the midst of this crisis of faith in themselves, these managers naturally lose their ability to be sensitive to the needs of others. This, in turn, leads them into a predictable form of mismanaging, which I call the Slave Driver (**PA--**).

Fortunately, experience brings maturity, which brings humility. But it can take a good three years after graduation before this kind of manager has let go of his delusions of grandeur, acknowledged that he is flawed, and learned to seek assistance and support from others.

This may be why Robert Townsend specifically advises against hiring an MBA from Harvard. According to him, Harvard's MBA students are taught to be presidents, not co-workers.[13]

SUMMING UP

Management schools have actually worked *against* organizations by promoting an ideal for managers that is humanly impossible. The schools need to revise their training based on a new paradigm of management, which recognizes that perfection is impossible and that a complementary team of managers is more workable.

In addition, we must change the nature of our organizations to support rather than discourage potential growth and development.

Training managers will not suffice: Organizations are powerful behavioral manipulators. Nor will changing organizations suffice: New organizational styles require managers who can make them work.

Both conditions must be met if effective managers and leaders are to be found and nurtured. How to do that is presented in the next chapter.

NOTES

1. Ross, Joel, and Michael Kami: *Corporate Management in Crisis: Why the Mighty Fall* (New Jersey: Prentice Hall, 1973). Other authors who oppose one-man may include: Harold J. Leavitt, *Managerial Psychology* (Chicago: University of

Chicago Press, 1964), pp. 297-99: and Peter F. Drucker, *The Effective Executive,* 1st ed. (New York: Harper & Row, 1967).

2. See my book Pursuit of Prime (Santa Monica: Knowledge Exchange, 1996)), which describes and analyzes why organizational structure, goals, managerial roles, reward systems, and strategies are contingent on where the organization is in its lifecycle.

3. Taylor, Frederick W.: *The Principles of Scientific Management* (New York: Harper Bros., 1911).

4. Fayol, Henri: *General and Industrial Management* (London: Sir Isaac Pitman and Sons, 1949); also see Urwick, L. F., and E.F.L. Brech: *The Making of Scientific Management* (three-volume set, London: MPT, 1945, 1946,1948).

5. Wiener, Norbert: *Cybernetics; or Control and Communication in the Animal and the Machine* (New York: Technology Press/John Wiley, 1948).

6. Mayo, Elton: *The Human Problems of an Industrial Civilization* (New York: Macmillian, 1933).

7. See David C. McClelland's work at Harvard on achievement motivation; and McClelland, David C.: *The Achievement Motive* (New York: Irvington Publishers, 1976; revised).

8. Drucker, Peter Ferdinand: *The Essential Drucker: In One Volume, the Best of Sixty Years of Peter Drucker's Essential Writings on Management* (New York: HarperBusiness, 2001).

9. Newman, William Harold: *Process of Management: Strategy, Action, Results* (New Jersey: Prentice Hall, 1987).

10. Koontz, Harold, and Hoinz Weihrich: *Essentials of Management* (New York: McGraw Hill International, 1986).

11. Mintzberg, Henry: *Mintzberg on Management: Inside Our Strange World of Organizations* (New York: Free Press, 1989).

12. Fayol, op. cit.

13. Robert Townsend, *Up the Organization: How to Stop the Corporation from Stifling People and Strangling Profits* (Greenwich, Conn.: Fawcett Publications, 1971).

Chapter 14

The Mission of Management and Leadership Education

SOLUTION: What kind of training will produce managers and leaders who are well-rounded and can work well with a complementary team?

I believe it is a myth that some people are born leaders and others are born followers. I call this kind of talk "managerial racism." I believe that potentially all people have all of the qualities necessary to be leaders, although these qualities may be dormant as a result of neglect. We are all, latently at least, (**PAEI**)s in different situations and over time. The environment in which we operate, and the training that is made available to us, will determine whether our latent capabilities will grow or disappear. Unless inhibited, people rise to meet challenges and exercise any of the four management roles appropriately as they are called for.

So appropriate training, whether it's in-house or at schools that give advanced degrees in management, can and should be provided. Without it, any organization's ultimate success will be compromised.

Under the new paradigm, since we start out with the demonstrated premise that a perfect leader or manager is an impossibility, that such a manager can neither be found nor trained, then we know we must turn our focus away from the impossible and toward entirely different goals – both inside the organization and as a revised mission for managerial schools.

DECISION-MAKING PROGRAMMABILITY

Before we can discuss the training of individual managers, we must clarify the concept of decision programmability and the personality requirements of the (**PAEI**) model.

The process of management is based upon the making of decisions. One cannot manage without deciding. However, decisions may be programmed or nonprogrammed.

When a predetermined situation triggers a predetermined response, we can say that a decision is programmed.

In computer terminology, a program is a ready-made decision that structures the computer's tasks. For instance, an inventory system should be a programmed decision. A certain level of minimum desired inventory is predetermined. When the inventory reaches the minimum level, the computer will "decide" to print out an order.

Here is a concrete example of a human programmed decision. You leave your office to drive home, and the next thing you know you are in front of your garage. Your last vivid memory is that of leaving the office. What happened in the meantime? What streets did you cross? Which lights were red or green? If you cannot remember, how did you drive? The answer is: In a programmed way. We can equate learning to drive with getting programmed. We are taught to stop at red lights by making certain motions. We are taught to accelerate at green lights by making certain other motions. Sooner or later, driving becomes an activity that we can perform without conscious thought.

Nonprogrammed decisions are decisions that one has to make from scratch, with conscious effort. To make a nonprogrammed decision, one must search for information, identify the problem, evaluate possible alternatives, and act. Let's stay with the car analogy: Imagine a car running a red light in front of you as you drive home. As this is not supposed to happen, you do not have a "programmed" reaction stored and ready to implement. You have to gather information: At what speed is the other car moving, and in what direction? You have to identify possible courses of action (stop, accelerate, turn right, turn left, etc.). You have to choose among the alternatives. And then you have to act.

Why is programmed driving easier than nonprogrammed driving? Those of us who have driven in a foreign country know the answer to this question. A few hours of driving in a strange place can be as tiring as several days of driving at home. This is because when we drive in a strange place we have to make nonprogrammed decisions, which demand creativity (generating and evaluating alternatives) and risk-taking (judging which alternative to choose). There is uncertainty and there is risk, and both create anxiety.

Given a choice between anxiety and security, most people will choose security – that is, they prefer programmed to nonprogrammed decision-making. However, if all our decisions were programmed, we would be bored stiff in no time. It is the balance of programmed to nonprogrammed decisions that makes us feel capable or incapable of coping with a given situation.

People who cannot cope with having to make nonprogrammed decisions – who need to have a set of rules for every situation – are highly inflexible. We all know of door-to-door salespersons who have to start their pitch from the beginning if they happen to be interrupted. Obviously their sales presentations are too programmed.

By the same token, people who have to make every decision in a nonprogrammed way (even when the routine is self-evident) are also inflexible. They are constantly reinventing the wheel. We might say that their behavior is programmed to be nonprogrammed. They get exhausted fast, and they exhaust those around them.

The four management roles involve different kinds of decision-making. (**P**)roducing results and (**A**)dministering programs involve programmed decisions. (**P**)roducing is a matter of applying a technology or a particular sequence to a task, whether it is manufacturing shoes, making sales, or raising funds. Occasionally nonprogrammed decisions will be needed in performing these tasks, but management tries to systematize and teach the best-known methods so that even a minor talent can get major results.

In contrast to **(P)** and **(A)**, the **(E)** and **(I)** roles are not and should not be programmed. There is no program that can tell an **(I)**ntegrator or an **(E)**ntrepreneur what policy to initiate, or when, or how.

When an **(E)** gets an idea, even he may not know what stimulated it. Thus it is not so strange that his work hours and staff meetings are unpredictable.

Why can't **(I)**ntegration be programmed? Because the **(I)** role deals with people, whose responses will never be entirely predictable. Even if the same group of people meets repeatedly, each member of the group will be in a different mood and dealing with a different set of circumstances each time; thus for an **(I)**, each assembly of people is a new "happening."

(I)ntegrating is even less programmable than **(E)**ntrepreneuring because **(E)**ntrepreneuring does not necessarily deal with people, whereas (I)ntegrating involves uniting individuals behind a group decision. In fact, the most difficult, most creative job of all might be trying to **(I)**ntegrate a group of **(E)**ntrepreneurs into a cohesive unity – to forge group risk-taking from individual risk-taking, to fuse an individual sense of responsibility into a group sense of responsibility.

There *are* some elements of both **(E)** and **(I)** roles that can be programmed. There are courses on how to stimulate creativity and there are courses on how to feel, understand, and relate to people. However, I strongly recommend that one not overdo this training. If **(E)** and **(I)** become too programmed, we will lose the spontaneity that is essential to these two roles. The essence of **(E)** is thinking out of the box, and the essence of **(I)** is an intuitive sense of other people. Thus it is counter-productive to try to program the box, or to become very mechanistic in our relationships. I'm sure you have met people who know how to smile, look you in the eye, listen and make encouraging, supportive remarks – but whom you somehow feel are not genuine. Instead of being accepted, these over-trained **(I)**-emulators cast doubt on the credibility of others in the organization who are (**I**)-oriented, and can poison an entire company's (**I**)ntegration efforts.

If you arrange the four management styles into a hierarchy, with the least programmable type of decision-making at the top and the most programmable at the bottom, it would look like this:

1. (**I**)ntegrating (least decision programmability)
2. (**E**)ntrepreneuring
3. (**P**)roducing
4. (**A**)dministering (most decision programmability)

Clearly, in the typical corporate hierarchy, the higher one ascends, the more nonprogrammed decision-making is required. In other words, the individual must be more and more creative and take greater and greater risks, since decisions have to be made from a more diffused and less structured database. In fact, the Peter principle – that a manager ascends to his level of incompetence – makes perfect sense when analyzed from the perspective of programmed versus nonprogrammed decision-making requirements. The reason promoted managers frequently fail is either that they lack the necessary creativity, they are afraid to take risks, or both.[1]

THE EFFECTIVENESS OF TRAINING

Many courses and training programs are actually forms of programming. That is, they provide trainees with a set of functions that can be called upon to perform a range of tasks. The training of most (**P**)roduction workers – industrial engineers, production managers, lathe operators – could be considering programming.

(**A**)dministrative decisions are also predominantly programmed, usually by a book of rules, policies, or guidelines. Historically, for example, the strength of the British Empire has often been attributed to its superior training of public servants – which amounted to programming.

This routinization and standardization of procedures enabled a few Englishmen to rule over a great many colonials without running into organizational snafus. The goal was to elicit predictable behavior: Under certain conditions, all British (**A**)dministrators could be expected to act in a certain way. An officer in the foreign service could use the same procedures whether he was posted in India or Africa, and when he was rotated to any other colony, he could hit the ground running. It was efficient.

Is it possible to train people in nonprogrammable skills such as (**E**) and (**I**)? Well, someone is always trying to, for example, the numerous books that try to demonstrate how to make a strategic plan, or how to become a millionaire in ten easy steps, are all attempting to program (**E**).

And to teach (**I**), there are workshops that offer step-by-step methods to analyzing people and situations more effectively.

Certainly an individual can be taught skills for dealing with people, but whether he will use those skills correctly will depend upon his discretion, creativity, and willingness to take risks. If he is uncreative, he may not recognize when a given situation has departed from the ordinary and thus requires a nonprogrammed decision. Many business executives have made the mistake of reacting in a programmed way to altered situations that call for a new approach.

CURRENT TRAINING IS INCONSISTENT

For (**P**)roducers and (**A**)dministrators, training is paramount and development far less so. Usually associated with a particular field or organization, training for (**P**) and (**A**) is acquired at schools. This is followed by employment and on-the-job training, which may include learning any and all organizational structures and regulations.

Obviously, the know-how needed to (**P**)roduce results and systemize effective methods are important for good management. But this type of training leaves the student without a threshold level of skill and comfort in either (**E**) or (**I**).

In some universities, management is considered to be applied (**E**)ntrepreneurship; thus business schools are part of the school of economics. Students there are trained in economic theory: To know finance, estimate value and risk, and identify opportunities in the marketplace.

But again, a highly trained (**E**)ntrepreneur will not necessarily be a good manager. If he or she does not bring in people who can capably (**A**)dministrate and co-lead the organization, even brilliant (**E**)ntrepreneurship can lead to economic disaster.

The latest trend in management training is behavioral science. Management schools now offer courses in human motivation and group dynamics, in which endless hours are spent analyzing inter-personal relations and learning how to motivate followers. At best, a successful Superfollower could emerge from this training – someone who is good at getting along with people but has no knowledge or skill at marketing, (**P**)roduction, finance, or (**A**)dministration.

Redefining the mission of education

Clearly, it is not sufficient to be trained exclusively in any one aspect of management. All aspects are necessary: One must learn disciplinary material (**P**); (**A**)dministrative methods (**A**); to identify goals, work under uncertainty, and take risks (**E**); and finally to work well with others and manage the conflict that inevitably arises (**I**).

Thus, a (**P**)roducing manager should be a (**Paei**) rather than a (**P---**), an (**A**)dministrating manager should be a (**pAei**) rather than an (**-A--**), and so on. Managers must perform all the roles – to the degree of meeting the threshold needs of the task – and they must excel in one or more roles depending on the task – but not all four. Not even the best corporate leaders excel in all four roles; as a rule, they excel in (**I**) plus one or two other roles.

If someone is incapable of performing a particular role – in other words has a blank in his code – I doubt not think that even the best management education could turn him into a good manager. It's probably about as worthwhile a project as taking someone who is tone deaf and training him to be a conductor.

The chief purpose of managerial education, then, whether it is at in-house training for top executives or at schools that grant MBAs, should not be to create a (**PAEI**), nor to remove the blanks in a person's code but to provide the tools necessary to perform each of the roles, and most important, to teach people how to work with those whose styles and roles are alien to them.

How do we do that? By making them aware of the four (**PAEI**) roles that must be performed in every managerial position; and by teaching him how to benefit, rather than feel threatened by, the unfamiliar styles and priorities of other managers.

(**P**) and (**A**), because they mainly require programmed decision-making, call for training. (**E**) and (**I**) involve nonprogrammed decisions; thus they call for development.

In order to develop, people have to let go of what they are strong at and try to do something they are weak at. They have to venture into unchartered territory, and that can be painful, because when we do that we cannot help exposing our weaknesses. People with a strong fear of failure – particularly those who are missing the (**I**) skill – will probably find such exposure terrifying. For their own sakes, those people should probably stay away from managerial jobs, since on balance the managerial role will be neither gratifying nor rewarding.

Is effective development possible? In extreme cases, in which a manager actually fits one of my four archetypes in that he is capable of performing only one role to the exclusion of the other three, the usual methods are unlikely to succeed. Such people probably need professional psychotherapeutic intervention if they are to change and become managers.

In milder cases, where only one or possibly two roles exist at the threshold level and just need to be developed, a gradual increase of exposure with fast reinforcing feedback is of value. But for everyone, without exception, development triggers growing pains, which can be minimized but not eliminated.

What Schools Should Do

Using our new paradigm, let's try to define goals for management schools. Immediately we have a new priority before us: Each student should understand that he is not and never will be a perfect executive. That premise, once it is established, can be the springboard from which other principles and strategies will naturally emerge; including:

- learning humility;
- understanding and appreciating a diversity of managerial and personality styles and feeling comfortable with them;
- developing strategies to communicate effectively with other styles;
- developing strategies to communicate effectively in meetings, where people of very different styles must be able to grasp what is being said.

In addition, of course, schools must effectively teach all four of the basic (**PAEI**) management roles.

Education for (P) and (A)

School training for the (**P**) and (**A**) roles – whether the task will require them in big letters or small letters – is very straightforward. A (**P**) has to learn the discipline of his profession – selling, engineering, accounting, marketing, or whatever job-related courses fit the bill here. Some experiential learning is necessary for reinforcement and behavioral absorption of the material; but straight, traditional teaching certainly makes sense.

For training in (**A**), the same prescription is applicable to courses on (**A**)dministration, on how to organize, systematize, control implementation, and so on. A common approach is a course that studies a decision from its inception through implementation, to see whether what was planned was actually realized, at what cost, with what success, etc.

Education for (E) and (I)

But where does one learn (E) and (I)? The roles of (E)ntrepreneur and (I)ntegrator, which are most vital at the upper levels of management, consist mainly of nonprogrammable decisions that have to rely on talent and intuition. One cannot hope to attain excellence in these roles simply by memorizing some rules.. The qualities or characteristics required at this level – risk-taking, a high threshold for anxiety, good listening, intuition – must be present or at least innate if they are to be successfully developed experientially

If you analyze the kinds of training that are available for (E) and (I) at management schools, it becomes obvious that the designers of these courses have made an underlying assumption that the student already has basic (E) and (I) skills. The purpose of the training, then, is to systematize (E) and (I) with respect to a specific job performance.

For (E), courses in brainstorming and synectics provide guidelines on how to stimulate one's creativity and to utilize it systematically.

Training for (I) includes courses on process facilitation, organizational development, change agents, sensitivity training, and leadership.

If the basic personality capabilities exist to begin with, these courses can be very effective at augmenting and improving technique. However, it is counterproductive to give (E) training to people who do not have (E) skills. Learning how to do strategic planning will not make someone better able to take risks or plan creatively in an atmosphere of uncertainty. (In fact, most (E)ntrepreneurs who have started companies did not go to business school. They may simply have been so ignorant when they began that they didn't realize how much risk they were taking.)

What schools must try to innovate are ways to *develop* the skills of (E) and (I).

Some schools are already working on that. The UCLA School of Management, for example, offers experiential courses for (E) and (I), in which, working in teams, students learn to make decisions with others and might also gain a certain amount of self-knowledge. All UCLA management students are required to take at least one experiential course during their first quarter.

At ITESM University, in Mexico, professors and business executives assist students on a continuing project. The students identify a business opportunity; then they plan, structure, and manage a business with the help and supervision of the professors and business executives. Each class of students passes its results along to the next group.

At Stanford, only applicants who have already shown leadership potential are accepted to the MBA program, which has been consciously designed to give students the tools to further develop their demonstrated talent. I think Stanford has the right answer.

What Organizations Can Do Themselves

People can become effective managers only if they are given opportunities to develop roles outside of their normal ones. So it is in the best interests of all organizations to give employees the opportunity to develop as many roles as possible. It is true that the short-run costs of this policy are quite real, and many profit-oriented organizations would consider such a practice a luxury. However, the long-run benefits will eventually outweigh them: People will learn new and practical skills, gain insight into the problems of their co-workers, and develop parts of their personalities that they do not ordinarily have an opportunity to express.

For example, since marketing is generally unaware of the realities of (**P**)roduction, and (**P**)roduction might not appreciate the pressures to which marketing must respond, exposing the staffs of each of those departments to the other's experiences will ultimately have the effect of reducing conflict between the two departments.[2]

This technique has long been a policy in the Israeli military, where an officer cannot be promoted beyond a certain rank until he has held several lateral positions and can understand the organization from many different angles, from a staff person at headquarters to a line commander in the field.

An additional benefit of moving people outside their own departments is that they can sometimes be particularly helpful when they are divorced from a problem and therefore completely objective. (It is to avoid the blindness of subjectivity that most doctors do not treat their own families.) Thus, in the Adizes methodology, people from (P)roduction are assigned to facilitate the problem-solving of the people in marketing; people from marketing (I)ntegrate people in finance; and so on.

In-house Training and Development for (P) and (A)

Obviously, to learn (P) and (A) skills, employees should be assigned a task that requires the performance of those roles. These kinds of tasks are plentiful throughout any organization; sales and (P)roduction line work would both be appropriate. For the purpose of training, the only special requirements are that success or failure in accomplishing the task should be easily attributable to the trainee; and the task should be relatively short-term, so that feedback can be given without undue delay.

The (A) role requires systematization, order, details, power, operating under certainty, maintaining a certain level of predictability, enduring repetition, and enjoying routine. Tasks that require and reward those qualities are easily found in (P)roduction scheduling, accounting, and traditional personnel jobs. Imagine how an Arsonist might benefit from a short-term excursion into the domain of keeping the system running as a system.

In-house Training and Development for (E) and (I)

The traditional structure of large organizations has worked against the development of (E) in two ways: First, the hierarchy's rigidity and bureaucratic tendencies have alienated (E)ntrepreneurs; and second, the structure has monopolized (E) tasks at the top of the pyramid, preventing (**E**) talents from developing anywhere else. Consequently, most organizations have a shortage of (**E**)s, and when (**E**) executives are needed, they must be hired from outside the firm.

Still, there have been a few attempts, using techniques like synectics and brainstorming, to teach managers how to introduce more imagination and innovation into their decision-making process: The Federal Executive Institute, for example, once offered an eight-week session in which the participants spent much of their time "just thinking."[3]

Although (**I**) is not as endangered or as beleaguered as (**E**), its growth and development are not especially encouraged either. Organizations are goal- and task-oriented. They expect results, and in order to achieve results they depersonify interpersonal relations. Professional – rather than person-to-person – relations develop in organizations, and this impairs the (**I**) capability.

Developing (**I**) means exposing people to situations that test their ability to work with others. One has to hear, to listen, to feel, and to react empathetically One must develop an inner ear for what is *not* being said, as well as a sixth sense that can accurately intuit what was really meant by what was said.

Extra-organizational activities that are open to all employees, such as artistic activities and theater productions, have proved to be useful at (**I**)ntegrating people and teaching them to tolerate diversity. There is a bank I worked with in downtown Los Angeles that had a magnificent theater – which it used only for sales meetings. If the bank took the simple step of making the facility available for entertainment events, written, produced and acted by employees as a kind of extra-curricular or even volunteer project, the participants could add new dimensions to their lives, while at the same time hierarchical barriers would be breaking down.

In recent years, there has been a growing effort to help management cultivate the (**I**) function, utilizing methods developed by the behavioral sciences: Sensitivity training, the T-group, the Forum groups, and so on.[4]

The success rate of these efforts, however, has been mixed. Why? Research has shown that if the organizational climate is hostile to the training, or to the attitudes being fostered in the training, then the impact of such (**E**)- and (**I**)-related programs will be extremely limited.[5]

Thus, an important facet of the Adizes methodological approach is modification of the environment to permit the development of (**I**) and (**E**) – in other words to create an atmosphere in which new (**I**)ntegrative approaches and creativity are fostered and supported, allowing both to surge.

Delegation and Decentralization

The best vehicle for developing (**E**) and (**I**) is probably democratization and decentralization of organizations. The simple reason is that the more often people participate in decision-making, the more (**E**) and (**I**) they will develop and use.[6]

Before we delve further into this subject, we must clarify the distinction between delegation and decentralization. They are not synonymous. To delegate is to give subordinates the responsibility for making programmed decisions. This means that (**P**) and (**A**) can be delegated.

Decentralization involves more than the transfer of programmed duties. In a decentralized organization, there are certain spheres in which subordinates are expected to take initiative, to use discretion in decision-making, and to accept responsibility for their decisions. Decentralization necessarily implies more elbow room for nonprogrammed decisions, which are inherently unpredictable.

Decentralization, then, requires that (**E**) and (**I**) be nurtured on the lower levels of the organization. Because they are not programmable, (**E**) and (**I**) cannot be delegated. They have to be nurtured.

In-house Executive Training

Traditional executive training programs make the familiar mistake of focusing on individuals rather than teams. But, beyond learning the various characteristics and roles of management, an individual working alone can do little to improve himself. Working alone is working in a vacuum. Growth occurs as we work with others. Thus, traditional executive training is unlikely to effect real and significant changes.

In fact, graduates of executive training programs are often at a loss to explain the benefit of the experience. "I really can't tell you what I applied," they will say. "It must be here. … How I got my thoughts organized was the greatest benefit."

Executive training should be in clusters of five or more people from the same organization: Teams that can work together to develop their cognitive know-how (**P**), their skill at evaluating and implementing systems (**A**), and their ability to work together to reach good decisions while avoiding destructive conflict (**E**) and (**I**).

In addition, executive training programs must be well rounded: No one discipline should be taught exclusively. Finally, cross-fertilization is essential if one is to become a member of a complementary team rather than a Lone Ranger, a Bureaucrat, an Arsonist, or a Superfollower.

THE DARK SIDE OF FORMAL EDUCATION

Under our new management paradigm, management schools and in-house training are both essential tools for producing well-rounded managers.

But formal education can also be overdone; and overschooling can be dangerous to managerial health.

Some of our most successful contemporary (**E**)ntrepreneurs had no formal education – and that may be *why* they are so successful. They did not have their (**E**) and (**I**) trained out of them. They were never told to turn to a rulebook for solutions. No one convinced them not to trust their instincts. They knew how to adapt, how to be creative in new environments – and they made their own solutions. A senior vice president of one of the largest banks in Mexico is a high school dropout, but his Ph.D. subordinates consider him a leader of stature. "Unhindered by education, he can think," one of them told me.

A good portion of any type of education involves learning models that apply to specific situations – preprogrammed solutions to problems that are expected to come up repeatedly. These models, of course, are an organization's single most effective tool for eliminating waste and promoting efficiency. However, they are also dangerous.

In the process of being educated, students learn to accept and even welcome a certain amount of programming. This presents several dangers. They may become too dependent on their supply of easy, reliable models, and forget to distinguish between decisions that can be made automatically and those that cannot.

If they rely too often on formulas to solve problems, eventually they will be out of practice at working through a difficult decision. Their ability to be patient, to be tenacious, and even to think clearly and communicate clearly will have dissipated.

Or, in the event that a nonprogrammed decision is required, they may get lazy and decide to force-fit an already available solution, even if it is inappropriate.

The famous philosopher and sociologist Ivan Illich argued that our contemporary education system, instead of teaching people to learn and think for themselves, actually programs them to live up to the expectations of the establishment.[7] Certainly it is true that our schools spend more time teaching people the "right" answers than teaching them to ask the "right" questions. If our management schools are reliably to produce great managers and leaders, this system will have to change.

NOTES

1. Peter, Laurence J., and Raymond Hull, *The Peter Principle* (New York: Morrow, 1969).

2. See Adizes, Ichak: *Dialectic Convergence for Management of Conflict,* Paper no. 10 (Los Angeles: MDOR Institute, 1977); idem, *A'SIM Method for Diagnosis of Organizations*, Paper no. 7 (Los Angeles: MDOR Institute, 1977); Idem, *Democratization of Organizations*, working paper (Human Systems Study Center, Graduate School of Management, UCLA, 1977).

3. Quigley, William S., and Ronald J. Stupak, "An Experiment in Managerial Creativity: The Federal Executive Institute and the Policy-Making Process," *Training and Development Journal,* 28 June 1974), 22-28.

4. Raymond L. Hilgert offers managers ten suggestions for strengthening their own positive thinking, in order to influence subordinates. See Hilgert: "Positive Personal Motivation: The Manager's Guide to Influencing Others," *Personnel Journal,* 53 (Nov., 1974), pp. 832-34. (The true avalanche in this field, however, has come with the advance of sensitivity training.

5. Hand, Herbert H., Max D. Richards, and John W. Slocum, "Organizational Climate and the Effectiveness of a Human Relations Training Program," *Academy of Management Journal,* 16 (June 1974), 185-96.

6. For more information, see these publications:
    (a) Adizes, Ichak: *Industrial Democracy: Yugoslav Style* (New York: Free Press, 1971). Idem, "The Developing Nations and Self-Management," Research Paper Reprint No. I (*UCLA Institute of Industrial Relations Publications Series*, 1975), translation of chap. I of the Spanish edition. Idem, "Problems of Implementation and the Role of Professional Management," Research Paper Reprint No. 2 (*UCLA Institute of Industrial Relations Publications Series*, 1975), translation of chap. 10 of the Spanish edition.
    (b) Adizes, Ichak, and Elisabeth Mann-Borgese, eds., *Self-Management: New Dimensions to Democracy* (Santa Barbara, Calif.: ABC/CL.IO, 1975).
    (c) Adizes, Ichak: "Industrial Democracy and Codetermination," in *Encyclopedia of Professional Management* (New York: McGraw Hill, 1977).
    (d) Zupanov, J., and I. Adizes, "Labor Relations in Yugoslavia," in *Handbook of Contemporary Developments in World Industrial Relations*, ed. A. Blum (Westwood, Conn.: Greenwood Press, in print).
    (e) Adizes, I.: "On Conflict Resolution and an Organizational Definition of Self-Management," in *Participation and Self-Manangement*, vol. 5: Social System and Participation, First International Sociological Conference on Participation and Self-Management, Zagreb, Yugoslavia, 1973, pp. 17-33.

7. Illich, Ivan: *Deschooling Society* (New York: Harper & Row, 1971).

Bibliography

Abravanel, E.and King, E.: *Dr. Abravanel's Body Type Program for Health, Fitness and Nutrition* (New York: Bantam Books, Inc., 1985).

Adizes, Ichak: *How to Solve the Mismanagement Crisis* (Santa Monica, Calif.: Adizes Institute, Inc., 1979).

Adizes, Ichak: *Industrial Democracy, Yugoslav Style: The Effect of Decentralization on Organizational Behavior* (New York: Free Press, 1971; reprinted by MDOR Institute, 1977, paper).

Adizes, Ichak: *Managing Corporate Lifecycles* (Paramus, N.J.: Prentice Hall Press, 1999).

Adizes, Ichak, with Griffin, Patrick H.: *Managing the Performing Arts Organization: Founding Principles in the Management of the Arts* (Santa Monica, Calif.: The Adizes Institute, 1999).

Adizes, Ichak: *Mastering Change: the Power of Mutual Trust and Respect* (Santa Barbara, Calif.: Adizes Institute Publications, 1992).

Alessandra, A. and Wexler, P.: *Non-Manipulative Selling* (San Diego: Courseware, Inc., 1979).

Bell, Gerald: *The Achievers* (Chapel Hill, N.C.: Preston Hill, 1973).

Bennett, E.: *What Jung Really Said* (New York: Schocken Books, 1967).

Bennett, J.: *Enneagram Studies* (York Beach: Samuel Weiser, Inc., 1983).

Berliner, Joseph S.: *Factory and Manager in the USSR* (Cambridge, Mass.: Harvard University Press, 1957).

Berne, Eric: *Games People Play* (New York: Ballantine, 1996, revised edition).

Blake, Robert, and Mouton, Jane: *The Managerial Grid* (Houston: Gulf Publishing, 1964).

Blau, Peter M.: *The Dynamics of Bureaucracy* (Chicago: University of Chicago Press, 1956).

Bolton, R. and Bolton, D.: *People Styles at Work* (New York: American Management Association, 1996).

Bolton, R. and Bolton, D.: *Social Style/Management Style* (New York: American Management Association, 1984).

Choiniere, R., and Keirsey, D.: *Presidential Temperament* (Del Mar: Prometheus Nemesis Book Company, 1992).

Drucker, Peter F.: *Management: Tasks, Responsibilities, Practices* (New York: Harper & Row, 1973).

Fieve, Ronald R.: *Moodswing: Dr. Fieve on Depression* (New York: William Morrow and Co., 1989).

Francis, Roy G., and Stone, Robert C.: *Service and Procedure in Bureaucracy: A Case Study* (Minneapolis: University of Minnesota Press, 1956).

Fraser, J.: *The Chinese Portrait of a People* (Glasgow: William Collins Sons & Co. Ltd., 1981).

Gordon, Dr. T.: *L.E.T. Leadership Effectiveness Training* (Wyden Books, 1977).

Halberstam, D.: *The Best and the Brightest* (London: Pan Books Ltd., 1972).

Hartman, T.: *The Color Code* (Taylor Don Hartman, 1987).

Herrmann, N.: *The Creative Brain* (Lake Lure: Brain Books, 1990).

Keirsey, D. and Bates, M.: *Please Understand Me* (Del Mar: Prometheus Nemesis Book Company, 1984).

Lear, F.: *The Second Seduction* (New York: Alfred A. Knopf, 1992).

Lowen, A.: *Depression and the Body* (New York: Penguin Books, 1981).

Lowen, A.: *The Language of the Body* (New York: Macmillan Publishing Co., Inc., 1979).

March, James G., and Herbert Simon: *Organizations* (New York, London: John Wiley & Sons, 1958).

Mottram, V.: *The Physical Basis of Personality* (Baltimore: Penguin Books, 1960).

Parkinson, C. Northcote: *Parkinson's Law: The Pursuit of Progress* (London: John Murray, 1958).

Peter, Laurence J., and Hull, Raymond Hull: *The Peter Principle: Why Things Always Go Wrong* (New York: William Morrow & Co., 1969).

Rothchild, J.: *Going for Broke: How Robert Campeau Bankrupted the Retail Industry, Jolted the Junk Bond Market and Brought the Booming Eighties to a Crashing Halt* (New York: Simon & Schuster, 1991).

Schumpeter, Joseph: *Business Cycles* (New York: McGraw Hill, 1939).

Soros, George, Wien, Byron, and Koenen, Krisztina: *Soros on Soros: Staying Ahead of the Curve* (New York: John Wiley & Sons, 1995).

George Albert Steiner: *Top Management Planning* (New York: Macmillan, 1969).

Storm, H.: *Seven Arrows* (New York: Harper & Row, 1972).

Sundberg, N.: *Assessment of Persons* (New Jersey: Prentice-Hall, 1977).

Waldo, Dwight, ed.: *Ideas and Issues in Public Administration* (New York: McGraw Hill, 1963).

Woodward, Joan: *Industrial Organization: Theory and Practice* (New York: Oxford University Press, 1965).

Additional Works by the Author

(All available from the Adizes Institute at www.adizes.com)

Books

Adizes, I. *Industrial Democracy Yugoslav Style*. New York: Free Press, 1971.

Adizes, I. and Mann-Borgese, Elisabeth, eds. *Self-Management: New Dimensions to Democracy*, Santa Barbara, CA: ABC/CLIO, 1975.

Adizes, I. *How to Solve the Mismanagement Crisis*. 2nd printing. Santa Barbara: Adizes Institute Publications, 1980. (First printing, New York: Dow Jones Irwin, 1979.)

Adizes, I. *Corporate Lifecycles: How and Why Corporations Grow and Die and What to Do about It*. Englewood Cliffs, NJ: Prentice Hall, 1988.

Adizes, I. *Mastering Change: The Power of Mutual Trust and Respect in Personal Life, Family, Business and Society*. Santa Barbara: Adizes Institute Publications, 1993.

Adizes, I. *The Pursuit of Prime*. First printing, Santa Monica, CA: Knowledge Exchange, 1996.

Adizes, I. *Managing the Performing Arts Organization*. Santa Barbara: Adizes Institute Publications, 1999.

Adizes, I. *Managing Corporate Lifecycles: An Updated and Expanded Look at the Corporate Lifecycles*. First printing, Paramus, NJ: Prentice Hall Press, 1999.

Adizes, I. *Management/Mismanagement Styles: How to Identyfy a Style and What to Do about It*. Adizes Institute Publications, Santa Barbara, CA, 2004.

Adizes, I. *Leading the Leaders: How to Enrich Your Style of Management and Handle People Whose Style is Different from Yours*. Adizes Institute Publications, Santa Barbara, CA, 2004.

Articles

Adizes, I. "The Role of Management in Democratic (Communal) Organizational Structures." *Annals of Public and Cooperative Economy*. Quarterly review of CIRIEC. Brussels: CIRIEC, No. 424 (1971): 399–420.

Adizes, I. "Administering for the Arts: Introduction and Overview." *California Management Review* 15,2 (1972): 99–103.

Adizes, I. "Boards of Directors in the Performing Arts: A Managerial Analysis." *California Management Review* 15, 2 (1972): 109 117.

Adizes, I. "Economic Changes in Yugoslavia." *East Europe* 21, 10 (1972): 8–16.

Adizes, I. "Management in Der Demokratischen Organisationen." *Annalen der Gemeinwirtschaft* 41 (Januar-Marz, 1972).

Adizes, I. "Samoupravljanje Kao Drustveni Cilj i Organizacijski Proces - [Self-Management as a Social Goal and an Organizational Process."] *Socijalizam* 11, 12 (1972): 1324–1333.

Adizes, I. "Uloga Rukovodjenja u Demokratskim Organizacionim Strukturama." [Serbo-Croatian translation of "The Role of Management in Democratic Organizational Structures"]. *Moderna Organizacija* 6 (1972): 937–951.

Adizes, I. "Uloga Vodstva v Demokraticnih (Skupnostnih) Organizacijskih Strukturah." ["The Role of Management in Democratic Organization"] *Moderna Organizacija* 6 (1972): 437–451.

Adizes, I. and Weston, F. "Comparative Models of Social Responsibility." *Journal of the Academy of Management* 16, 1 (1973): 112–129. Reprinted in F. Luthans and R.M. Hodgetts, *Social Issues in Business*. 2nd ed. New York: Macmillan, 1974.

Adizes, I. "Gerencia y Estructuras Comunales (I)." "The Role of Management in Democratic Organization" *Gerencia*. Instituto Peruano de Administracion de Empresas (IPAE) Lima, Peru, (Noviembre/Diciembre, 1976): 23–76. Adizes, I. "On Conflict Resolution and an Organizational Definition of Self-Management" in *Participation and Self-Management*, Volume 5 "Social

System and Participation," 1–73. First International Sociological Conference on Participation and Self-Management. Zagreb, Yugoslavia (1973).

Adizes, I. "Le Role de la Direction Dans une Communante Organisée Sûr une Base Democratique." "The Role of Management in Democratic Organization" *Les Annales De L'Economie Collective* 1 (Jan.-Mars, 1973): 83–109.

Adizes, I. and McWhinney, W. "Arts, Society and Administration: The Role and Training of Arts Administrators, Arts and Society." *Arts and Society*, 10, 3 (1974): 40–50.

Adizes, I. "Gerencia y Estructuras Comunales (II) Management and Communal Structures" *Gerencia*, IPAE (January/February, 1974): 36–43.

Adizes, I. "Relaciones Organizativas en la Empresa Autogestionaria [The Self-Managed Enterprise]." *Apuntes* 1, 2 (1974): 21–30.

Blame, M. and Adizes, I. "Parkview Symphony." In *Business Policy: Strategy Formation and Management Action*, ed. W. Glueck, 366–374. 2nd ed. New York: McGraw-Hill, 1974.

Adizes, I. "Autogestion y Naciones en Dsarollo [Self-Management in Developing Nations]." *Apuntes* 4 (1975): 106–122.

Adizes, I. "The Cost of Being an Artist: An Argument for the Public Support of the Arts." *California Management Review* 17 (Summer, 1975): 80–84.

Adizes, I. "Mas Alla del 'Principio de Peter': una Tipologia de Estilos de Incompetencis Gerencial." *Instituto de Administracion Científica de las Empresas* (lACE). Monterrey, Mexico (1975).

Adizes, I. "Mismanagement Styles." *California Management Review* 19, 2 (1976): 5–20.

Adizes, I. "Seattle Opera Association." *Business Policy: Strategy Formation and Management Action*, ed. W. Glueck, 610–634. 2nd ed. New York: McGraw-Hill, 1976.

Adizes, I. and Zukin, P. "A Management Approach to Health Planning in Developing Countries." *Health Care Management Review* 2, 1 (1977): 19–37.

Adizes, I. "Industrial Democracy and Codetermination." *Encyclopedia of Professional Management*. New York: McGraw-Hill, 1978.

Zupanov, J. and Adizes, I., "Labor Relations in Yugoslavia." Handbook of Contemporary Developments in *World Industrial Relations*, ed. A. Blum. Westwood, CT: Greenwood Press, 1978.

Adizes, I. "Mismanagement." *Affarsekonomi Management. Stockholm*, Sweden, 1978.

Adizes, I. "Organizational Passages: Tools for Diagnosis and Therapy of Organizational Behavior." *Organizational Dynamics* 8, 3 (Summer, 1979): 28–46.

Adizes, I. and Turban, E., "An Innovative Approach to Group Decision Making." *Personnel*, 62,4 (1985): 45–49.

Adizes, I. "Back to Basics: Mutual Trust and Respect and Productivity." *Executive Excellence*, 10, 10 (1993): 11–13.

Adizes, I. "Managing: The Business of Mutual Trust and Respect." *Manage* 45, 1 (1993): 26–28.

Adizes, I. "Twelve Tips on Keeping Your Growing Business at Prime." *Manage* 44,3 (1993): 14–17.

Adizes, I. "Corporate Lifecycles: Entrepreneurship and Integration." In *Management and Entrepreneurship*, the English version, ed. I. Vaji, 168 172. Vol. II. Centar za Management i Marketing, University of Zagreb: Zagreb University Press, 1994.

Adizes, I. "How to Convert a Committee into a Team." *Successful Meetings* 43, 2 (1994): 115–118.

Adizes, I. "Integrating Innovation." *Executive Excellence*. 11, 11 (1994): 12–13.

Adizes, I. "Keeping the Fires Burning [about TQM]." *Manage* 46, 1 (1994): 12 16.

Adizes, I. "Information Superhighway: Overloading Human Potential." *Executive Excellence* 12, 4 (1995): 15.

Adizes, I. "What Comes First? Strategy or Structure?" *Executive Excellence* 2, 9 (1995): 20.

Adizes, I. "Eight Myths [about management]: Getting Right the People Dimension of Business." *Executive Excellence* 14, 9 (1997):

20.

Adizes, I. "Five Myths about Management in the 1990s." *Manage* 48 (July, 1997): 30 32.

Adizes, I. "Looking for Mr./Ms. Perfect: The Search for the Right Professional Manager in a Growing Company. *Progress* 2, 1 (1998): 14–15.

Adizes, I. "Self-Esteem: Who Cares?" *The Adizes Institute Journal of Organizational Transformation* 1, 1 (1998): 7–16.

Working Papers

Adizes, I. Establishing a Program for Arts Administration: Summary of the UCLA Conference and a Report on Implementation. In the *Management in the Arts Research Program Publication Series*, Publication 1. Division of Research, GSM. Los Angeles: UCLA, 1969.

Adizes, I. "The Roles of Art in Post-Industrial Society." Presented at the *Center for the Study of Democratic Institutions.* Santa Barbara, CA: January, 1973.

Adizes, I. "Administering for the Arts: Problems in Practice." *Management in the Arts Program Research Papers*, #15. GSM. Los Angeles: UCLA, October, 1971.

Adizes, I. "A New Framework for Management Theory." Santa Barbara: The Adizes Institute, June, 1987.

Adizes, I. and Haldeman, H.R. "Why Gorbachev Might Fail." Santa Barbara: The Adizes Institute, January, 1988.

Adizes, I. "The Common Principles of Managing Oneself, a Family, a Corporation or a Society." Santa Barbara: The Adizes Institute, September, 1990.

VIDEO

Adizes, I. (1984). *The Adizes Program in Video.* Santa Barbara: The Adizes Institute.

Adizes, I. *Program A: Overview of the Adizes Process of Management.*

Set of 3 videotapes. Santa Barbara: Adizes Institute Publications, 1993

  The Adizes Process of Management. 55 min.

  The Adizes Program. Questions and Answers #1

  The Adizes Program. Questions and Answers # 2

Adizes I. *Program B: The Management Process.* Set of 4 videotapes. Santa Barbara: Adizes Institute Publications, 1993

  The Roles of Management. 28 min.

  Mismanagement Styles. 41 min.

  The Structural Causes of Deadwood. 38 min.

  What is a Good Manager? 41 min.

Adizes I. *Program C: Organizational Lifecycles.* Set of 4 videotapes. Santa Barbara: Adizes Institute Publications, 1993

  The Growth Phases of Organizational Lifecycles. 39 min.

  The Aging Phases of Organizational Lifecycles. 38 min.

  Analysis of Lifecycles. 52 min.

  Treating the Growing and Aging Problems of Organizations. 56 min.

Adizes, I. *Program D: Decision Making and Implementation.* Set of 2 videotapes. Santa Barbara: Adizes Institute Publications, 1993.

  CAPI: Predicting Managerial Effectiveness. 45 min.

  The Adizes Process of Decision Making. 49 min.

Adizes, I. *From Entrepreneurship to Professional Management.* Speech to the Council of Growing Companies. Santa Barbara: Adizes Institute Publications, 1993.

Adizes, I. *The Young Company's Lifecycle: Are You Ready for the Future?* Keynote Address to the Inc. 500 Awards. Santa Barbara: Adizes Institute Publications, 1996.

AUDIO

Adizes, I. *Analysis of Management.* 6 audio cassettes. Santa Barbara: Adizes Institute Publications, 1988.

Adizes, I. *Analysis of Lifecycles*. 6 audio cassettes. Santa Barbara: Adizes Institute Publications, 1989.

CD

Caric, N., Horvat, Z. and Vukic, B. *The Adizes Program: An Interactive Compilation of the Writings of Dr. Ichak Adizes and the Programs of the Adizes Institute*. Santa Barbara: Adizes Institute Publications, 1998.

ABOUT THE ADIZES INSTITUTE

The Adizes Institute provides organizations worldwide with the managerial resources to achieve extraordinary results while developing and nurturing a constructive, cooperative organizational culture.

Since its establishment in 1975, the Adizes Institute has served hundreds of organizations worldwide, from fledging companies to Fortune 100s, not-for-profit organizations, and governments. Through its network of international locations, the Adizes Institute has provided services to organizations in 45 countries.

The Adizes Institute is the research, publishing, licensing, training, and certification arm for the Adizes® methodology. The Adizes® methodology, developed over the past 35 years by Dr. Ichak Adizes, is a highly evolved proprietary, structured, pragmatic system for accelerating organizational change.

The Adizes Institute is closely associated with the Adizes Graduate School that grants master's and doctoral degrees in the study of Leadership and Change.